The Time of Youth

DATE DUE

The Time of Youth

Work, Social Change, and Politics in Africa

ALCINDA HONWANA

Kumarian Press
An Imprint of Stylus Publishing

Published by Stylus Publishing, LLC
22883 Quicksilver Drive
Sterling, Virginia 20166–2102

Bulk Purchases
Quantity discounts are available
for use in workshops and for staff
development.
Call 1–800–232–0223

Library of Congress Cataloging-in-Publication Data

Honwana, Alcinda Manuel.
  The time of youth : work, social change, and politics in Africa / Alcinda M. Honwana.
  — 1st ed.
     p. cm.
  Includes bibliographical references and index.
  ISBN 978–1–56549–471–8 (alk. paper) — ISBN 978–1–56549–472–5 (pbk. : alk. paper) — ISBN 978–1–56549–473–2 (library networkable e-edition) — ISBN 978–1–56549–474–9 (consumer e-edition) 1. Young adults—Africa—Economic conditions—21st century. 2. Young adults—Africa—Social conditions—21st century. 3. Young adults—Employment—Africa. 4. Unemployed youth—Africa. 5. Africa—Economic conditions—21st century. 6. Africa—Social conditions—21st century. I. Title.
√ HQ799.A35H665 2012
  305.242096—dc23
                                                                        2012003535

Printed in the United States of America

∞All first editions printed on acid-free paper that meets the American National Standards Institute Z39-48 Standard.

First Edition, 2012

10   9   8   7   6   5   4   3   2   1

To my daughters, Nyeleti and Nandhi,
for being a constant inspiration in my life

Contents

Acknowledgments

This book was made possible by the many young people who generously allowed me to gain insights into their lives, sharing their time, describing their experiences, and discussing their views with me. To them I owe my biggest debt of gratitude.

I am indebted to all the research assistants who contributed to this project over the years, particularly Sidy Ba, Dorra Chaouachi, Katya Chavel, Charles Chiconela, Ziyad Chonara, Celso Give, Celso Inguane, Dércio Ivan, Yassine Lechiheb, Milton Machel, Sandra Manuel, Noureddine Mhamdi, Nabeelah Mussá, Najmeddine Najlaoui, Tarek Rekik, and Lindsey Reynolds. Their research, interviews, assistance with literature reviews, and guidance in navigating youth spaces were precious.

I am grateful to colleagues who read and commented on the proposal and various drafts chapters: Ibrahim Abdullah, Brigitte Bagnol, Hakim Ben Hammouda, Jean Comaroff, Peter Geschiere, Joe Hanlon, Beatrice Hibou, Hazel Johnson, Raphie Kaplinsky, Ron Kassimir, and Teresa Smart. I am also thankful to Nabil Mâalel, Zohair El Khadi, Sleheddinne Ben Fredj, Rezgui Mondher, Mia Couto, Carlos Nuno Castel-Branco, Paula Monjane, Albertina Mucavele, and Stephanie Urdang for the stimulating conversations.

The Department of Anthropology and Archeology of Eduardo Mondlane University in Maputo, the Institute of Economic and Social Studies in Maputo, Kula Estudos e Pesquisa Aplicada in Maputo, the Department of History at Cheikh Anta Diop University in Dakar, the West Africa Research Centre in Dakar, Codesria and ENDA in Dakar, the Department of Anthropology at Witwatersrand University in Johannesburg, the Ali Belhouane Youth Cultural Club in Tunis, and the UNDP Country Office in Tunisia all made their facilities available to me and provided invaluable support; I particularly thank Adriano Biza, Hélder Nhamaze, Ndiouga Benga, Ousmane Sene, Ebrima Sall, Carlos Cardoso, Fabrizio Terenzio, Sami Essid, Aida Robbana, Francesc Revuelto-Lanao, and Fodé Said Condé.

A special word of thanks goes to Grey Osterud, my editor, for her guidance throughout the writing process.

This research was possible thanks to a grant from the Ford Foundation, which allowed me to conduct fieldwork in Mozambique, Senegal, and South

Africa; I am grateful to Alice Brown and her colleagues for believing in this project. The Conflict Prevention and Policy Forum at the Social Science Research Council in New York supported my research trip to Tunisia; I particularly thank Tatiana Carayannis.

I owe my deepest gratitude to my husband, João, and my daughters, Nyeleti and Nandhi, for their love and unwavering support. They endured my prolonged absences on research trips and the innumerable hours I spent in front of the computer. This book became a family project, as I often discussed these issues with my daughters, who are both over eighteen, and was inspired by their fascinating insights. My husband was often on hand to share ideas and read drafts; his acute political sense and fine editing skills were invaluable. Writing this book would have been a very lonely process without them.

Preface

I have been conducting research on young people in Africa for almost two decades. My work with young men and women affected by armed conflict, which culminated in *Child Soldiers in Africa* (2006), was a logical precursor to this project. As difficult as the social reintegration of former child soldiers was, the situation of youths who were not directly involved in war was not much easier. The trauma that former child soldiers had suffered presented specific psychosocial challenges, but their social and economic transition to adult independence was no different from that of other young people living in conditions of economic scarcity, unemployment, and myriad social ills. This examination of the challenges faced by young people more generally grew directly from that work.

The research for this book began in 2008 in Mozambique and was expanded to South Africa, Senegal, and Tunisia, which I visited during the first half of 2011. In these four countries I met young people from a range of social and economic backgrounds. I conducted individual interviews and focus-group discussions with students, young professionals, musicians and other artists, activists from various fields, and unemployed young men and women carrying out the most diverse activities to try to make ends meet. Young people were eager to tell their stories. In long individual interviews I listened to their life stories and their views about their peers, their elders, the economy, and politics. Focus-group discussions were undertaken with diverse groups of young people. Some were all female, some all male, and some mixed. Others involved people with common interests, such as musicians and performers. I also spoke with groups belonging to particular organizations, such as party youth leagues and civil society associations. Most focus groups considered specific topics, and participants debated and exchanged views among themselves. I also took time to interact with young people in places where they normally hung out, such as youth clubs, restaurants, and bars. Occasionally I was invited for meals at their homes and had the opportunity to meet their parents, siblings, and other relatives. The fact that my research assistants were themselves quite young facilitated my access to their social networks; I met their friends and then the friends of those friends, creating a snowball effect. My research assistants mediated between my young informants and me, as they advised me about the "dos and don'ts" and explained what was considered "cool" and "uncool." They provided useful insights regarding ways of broaching difficult subjects. Although I speak the major languages of all four countries, they also translated and helped interpret some of the discussions conducted with young people in their mother tongues, especially Wolof in Senegal and Arabic in Tunisia.

In addition, I interviewed government officials, religious leaders, scholars, journalists, and public intellectuals who are concerned about youth. These interviews provided information about the ways these societies look at young people, specific policies and programs designed for them, and youths' place in the economy, society, and culture.

Most of the research was conducted in urban settings, although I occasionally visited rural areas. Many young people who grow up in the economically undeveloped countryside seek a solution to their pressing problems in the cities. African cities are teeming with young men and women trying to survive on the margins of formal socioeconomic structures. For many, the city becomes a place to forge new ways of living free from the constraints of rural society. In the countryside, youth have no platform for action not only because resources are limited but also because older people tend to monopolize power; indeed, some call rural communities gerontocracies. The city promises anonymity, a degree of chaos that allows for personal freedom. Here they find possibilities for improvisation, experimentation, and *desenrascar*—literally, to disentangle themselves from a situation, and metaphorically, to improvise a solution from almost nothing at the very last moment.

The young people I interviewed described their daily life struggles as well as their aspirations. They shared amazing stories of resilience and survival under dire circumstances. What do you do when you come from a poor family and at the age of twenty-seven you still have no job? How can you have a steady girlfriend if you cannot afford to take her out for a drink and offer her a cell phone card to call you, or even buy a card to call her yourself? How can you marry? What do you do when you have children and you cannot afford to feed them, much less live in your own household? What kind of a future awaits you when just getting through each day is a struggle? These were some of the difficult questions that some youths would throw back at me; of course, I had no answers. I was amazed by their agency as they actively set out to live as fully as possible despite their circumstances. I was equally struck by their capacity to understand the broader structural forces that shape their everyday lives. I was most impressed by their creativity and the commitment to citizenship that they sustained amid such a chaotic and often improvised existence. Young people are involved in a myriad of associations and activist groups and deeply engaged with the issues that matter to them, often on the margins of formal political structures and ideologies.

Young people were very clear about the ways they wanted me to portray them and the messages they hoped I would deliver on their behalf. They are keenly aware of the disapproving ways parents and elders, governments, and the media generally depict them. In this book I try to bring their own voices to the fore by using as many direct quotations as possible and providing information about who they are in order to allow the reader greater insight into their lives. The book focuses on the stories of many of these youths: men in Maputo who survive by scavenging in the city's garbage dump; Mozambican *mukheristas*, young women who engage in small-scale, cross-border trading without paying import taxes; young South Africans whose only form of livelihood is sporadic overnight shelf-packing in supermarkets; Senegalese street vendors and those desperate enough to try to make the dangerous crossing to Europe in small *pirogues* (boats); Tunisian university graduates working in European-owned call centers; young women and men who get "sugar daddies" and "sugar mamas" to be able to pay high school fees and buy fashionable goods. I also introduce readers to rappers who criticize the status quo, protesters who force governments to reverse unsound policies, and revolutionaries who topple dictatorships. Indeed, young men and women do not merely wait for their lives to change. They are proactive and wake up each day with the goal of making their own lives better despite their depressing circumstances. These stories are those of young people who are surviving and thriving against the odds.

Rather than generalizing or making comparisons among youths' experiences in the four countries, this book explores young Africans' varied situations and their responses to the challenges they face. While it does not cover all aspects of young people's lives, the various case studies presented reflect some of the main activities undertaken and referred to by young people at that time in those places.

Why did I focus on Mozambique, South Africa, Senegal, and Tunisia? Being Mozambican and having done extensive research on Mozambique made that case a natural choice. But I sought to do research that would encompass the experiences of youth beyond any one country, to develop a broader view and understanding of the condition of youth and the coping strategies they are adopting across Africa. I decided to look at South Africa and Senegal because I have lived in both countries and have an extensive network of contacts that could facilitate my research. Following the events that initiated the "Arab Spring" (which, thus far, has been an "African

Spring"), it became obvious that I had to include either Tunisia or Egypt in my research; I focused on Tunisia because that was where the upheaval started. Over the past decade I have been fortunate to develop a wider understanding of the interconnections and specificities of young people's experiences in various African countries and beyond through engagement in multi-country and multi-regional studies and discussions. This book builds on those exchanges, drawing from the rich insights and debates with colleagues working on youth in various national and regional contexts.

The Time of Youth

Chapter 1

Youth

In 1963 Bob Dylan wrote "The Times They Are a-Changin'," a song that prefigured the youth uprisings of 1968 in Europe and the United States.[1] Half a century later, in August 2011, thousands of British youths from the most impoverished boroughs of London and other cities took to the streets to protest the killing of Mark Duggan, a twenty-nine-year-old black British man, in Tottenham, North London. In addition to burning police cars, they took advantage of the chaos to loot and destroy shops. They stole electronics and fashion statements such as Nike sneakers, Hugo Boss clothing, television sets, mobile phones, computers, and iPods—all desirable symbols of a consumer culture from which many young people, especially the unemployed and disadvantaged, felt excluded. As Ken Livingstone, former mayor of London, observed, this is the first generation of youth who expect to be worse off than their parents. Young people in these neighborhoods feel deprived. They feel they have no stake in British society, and they are prepared to do anything because they have nothing to lose.

Though unexpected, the riots in Britain were not isolated incidents. In October 2005 young people in Paris suburbs took to the streets burning buildings and cars. The protests were sparked by the deaths of Bouna Traoré, age fifteen, and Zyed Benna, age seventeen, of Mauritanian and Tunisian descent respectively, whose immigrant fathers worked as dustmen in the streets of Paris. The young men died of electrocution in a power station they entered while fleeing from the police. In the economically marginalized Paris *banlieues* (suburbs) populated by mostly North African immigrant families, the relationship between young people and the police was already very tense. Police brutality was routine, and youths would flee when a police car approached even if they had not committed any offense. Nicolas Sarkozy, then minister of the interior, was quoted as saying publicly that he wanted "to rid the town of hooligans," "to clean the *racaille* [scum] of the suburbs with *Kärcher*" [a brand of high-pressure water washer] (Canet et al. 2009). In such a climate of mistrust, residents were appalled by the government's declaration that the police had done nothing wrong, and the riots took a turn for the worse, spreading to other French cities. Thousands of vehicles were burned, at least one person was killed, and about three thousand protesters were arrested.

In North Africa, a twenty-nine-day youth uprising in Tunisia led to the ouster of President Zine al-Abidine Ben Ali on January 14, 2011. Like the uprisings in London and Paris, the Tunisian revolution was triggered by the death of a young man: the self-immolation of Mohamed Bouazizi, a twenty-six-year-old unemployed street vendor from the inland town of Sidi Bouzid, following the confiscation of his wares by a municipal police officer. Bouazizi's death symbolized the despair of an entire generation of young men and women grappling with unemployment and bleak future prospects. Thousands of youths came out into the streets and cyberspace to demand jobs, better living conditions, and respect for their dignity. The brutal and disproportionate use of force by the authorities radicalized the protests. Youths chanting "Ben Ali Degagé!" (Ben Ali Go!) demanded the president's departure. The Tunisian revolution quickly spread across the Arab world, and a few weeks later young Egyptians took control of Tahrir (Liberation) Square for days of protests that toppled the forty-year reign of Hosni Mubarak in February 2011. Conflicts between youth and the state also erupted in Bahrain, Yemen, and Syria. The youth-led armed rebellion in Libya that began in February overthrew Moamar Gaddafi and culminated in his death in October 2011.

In September 2010 I was in Maputo when thousands of Mozambican youths staged riots against the government to protest the rise in prices of basic staples such as bread, water, and fuel. Angry youths blocked the streets of the capital, burned tires, and confronted the police who tried to disperse the crowds. The police used batons and tear gas and fired bullets at the young protesters, causing numerous injuries and more than ten deaths. In June 2011, shortly after I visited Senegal, hundreds of young people, rallying alongside the Y'en a Marre! (Enough Is Enough!) Movement, clashed with police. They were denouncing the eighty-five-year-old president's push to change the constitution to enable him to win a third term and create the post of vice-president, supposedly for his son. Thousands of protesters gathered outside the National Assembly, where lawmakers were debating the proposed constitutional amendment, protesting government corruption, high unemployment, and other social ills. Clouds of tear gas enveloped the square as police fought the demonstrators with rubber bullets and water cannons. The demonstrations quickly spread from central Dakar into the suburbs and three major towns in the interior. More than a hundred protesters were injured during the two days of rioting.

These events illustrate what is happening around the world: young people, in rich and poor countries alike, share the same concerns and aspirations and are beginning to assert their rights as citizens. They are rising up against unemployment, socioeconomic marginalization, unsound economic policies, corrupt governments, political exclusion, and lack of respect for their rights. These are cries for freedom by a generation yearning to make a place for itself in the world. In the cities of Senegal, Britain, Egypt, Tunisia, France, and Mozambique, frustrated young people strive to receive a good education, find decent jobs, attain adult status, and partake in the fruits and symbols of global capitalist consumption. The idea of a utopia full of freedoms and opportunities is beginning to erode, as is the assumption that the state will uphold the social contract with its citizenry and put in place effective institutions and welfare systems.

Youth are a critical indicator of the state of a nation, of its politics, economy, and social and cultural life. Studying youth involves not only studying the lives of young people themselves, in all their diversity, but also understanding the social, political, economic, and cultural concerns of adults. The two generations are entangled in complex processes of construction and reconstruction, the making and remaking of society (Honwana and De Boeck 2005; Griffin 1993).

This book focuses on young people in Africa, where the marginalization of youth appears to be most serious. But the examples already cited suggest that the issue is global and that the African experience has broader relevance. The book is based primarily on interviews conducted with youths over eighteen years of age in four countries: Mozambique, Senegal, South Africa, and Tunisia. It explores young people's everyday activities and coping strategies in the face of inadequate education, massive unemployment, poverty, and HIV/AIDS.

Youth in Waithood

The majority of African youths are today grappling with a lack of jobs and deficient education. After they leave school with few skills they are unable to obtain work and become independent—to build, buy, or rent a house for themselves, support their relatives, get married, establish families, and gain social recognition as adults. These attributes of adulthood are becoming increasingly unattainable by the majority of young people in Africa. They are forced to live in a liminal, neither-here-nor-there state; they are no longer children who require care, yet they are not yet considered mature social adults.[2] They lead a precarious existence; their efforts are centered on trying to survive each and every day. Young Mozambicans used the Portuguese term *desenrascar a vida* (eke out a living); young Senegalese and Tunisians employed the French term *débrouillage* (making do); and young South Africans spoke about "just getting by." All these expressions vividly convey the extemporaneous nature of these young people's lives.

Waithood, a portmanteau term of "wait" and "-hood," is the best way to describe this period of suspension between childhood and adulthood. It represents a prolonged adolescence or an involuntary delay in reaching adulthood, in which young people are unable to find employment, get married, and establish their own families. I became interested in exploring waithood because many of my young interlocutors in these countries repeatedly expressed the sense of being "on hold" or "stuck" (Sommers 2012) in a situation with bleak future prospects. Mohamed,[3] a twenty-eight-year-old Tunisian man, pointed out, "I finished my studies but can't find a job; I can't help my parents and marry my girlfriend." Twenty-four-year-old Tandu, from South Africa, commented, "I survive on odd jobs to try and make ends meet." These narratives make it clear that, in order to understand the predicament of youth in Africa today, it is fundamental to examine their waithood experience and their struggle to become independent adults.

The notion of waithood was first used by Navtej Dhillon and Tarik Yousef (2007) and Diane Singerman (2007) in their work on youth in the Middle East and North Africa. Waithood suggests the multifaceted nature of the transition, which goes beyond securing a job and extends to other aspects of life, such as access to learning opportunities, household formation, and civic participation. Young people in waithood are increasingly unable to become social adults and full-fledged citizens. While the notion of waithood might give a sense of passively lingering, I want to push this concept further to show that young people in waithood are not really inactively "waiting" for their situation to change. Despite the challenges, youth in waithood are dynamic and using their creativity to invent new forms of being and interacting with society. Waithood accounts for a multiplicity of young people's experiences, ranging from daily survival strategies such as street vending and cross-border trade to involvement in gangs and criminal activities.

Waithood represents the contradictions of modernity, in which young people's opportunities and expectations are simultaneously broadened and constrained. They are enlarged by the new technologies of information and communication that make young people more globally integrated. Youth relate to local social structures and cultural patterns, but they are also connected to global culture via mobile telephones, cyberspace, television, and advertising. At the same time, they are also constrained by lack of access to basic resources due to unsound socioeconomic policies, epidemics, and political repression. There is no doubt that this situation also stems from bad governance and the social and economic policies espoused by international financial institutions that were imposed on Africa and other countries in the global South. The structural adjustment programs (later known as the poverty reduction strategy programs) deeply weakened the state's ability to determine national socioeconomic policies and priorities and to uphold the social contract. As various scholars observed, structural adjustment policies were against state investments in health, education, transport, and telecommunications. They favored the removal of trade barriers that protected local producers, the relaxation of tax regimes as well as the privatization of agriculture, land, and food production and distribution (Manji 1998; Manji et al. 2011). The result was the increase of socioeconomic disparities and the "gradual transformation of citizens into consumers. Power and influence over social policy were increasingly determined by wealth. But those who had no means to participate in consumer society—the pauperised, the landless, the jobless, the never-employed— . . . were left effectively disenfranchised" (Manji 2011).

Indeed, young people grappling with waithood constitute the majority of the jobless disenfranchised population. Meanwhile, neoliberal frameworks encourage them to become ardent globalized consumers; governments try to impress on them patriotism and nationalist ideologies; religious institutions attempt to instill in them the ideal of being a "good Muslim" or "good Christian"; and their parents and relatives talk about the importance of education for employment and social prestige (Singerman 2007). It is in these contradictory situations that young people try to make sense of their lives.

Nevertheless, waithood does not affect every young African man or woman in the same way. Some have become adults too soon, as child soldiers, child laborers, or surrogate parents to younger siblings after their parents died. Others can never attain the economic autonomy that allows them to partake on the social responsibilities of adulthood. At ten, a child soldier is an adult; at thirty, an unemployed and unmarried man is still a youth. But many children who assume adult roles at a tender age are later pushed back into waithood as they grow up and try to attain their independence. Moreover, waithood manifests itself differently among a small group of elite youths who are generally able to afford a good education in private schools and abroad and are often well connected to networks of the powerful that facilitate their access to secure jobs. Some privileged youths may choose to avoid the responsibilities of adulthood, as some may continue to live with and depend on their parents, and hop from job to job. For the vast majority of young Africans, however, waithood is involuntary. Rather than being a short interruption in their transition to adulthood, waithood may last for extended periods, well into their thirties and even their forties. Some never get out of it and remain permanently in the precarious and improvised life that waithood imposes. Prolonged waithood is becoming the rule rather than the exception. For many, being young in Africa today is synonymous with living in involuntary waithood.

Waithood is also a reality in other parts of the world. In the United States and the UK terms such as *twixters, kidults, adultolescents,*[4] and *thresholders* (Apter 2001) have been used to describe youths who are in limbo between childhood and adulthood, stuck in what some scholars called "emerging adulthood" (Arnett 2004). Expressions like the "boomerang" or "yo-yo" generation have been used to describe college graduates who return home and continue to depend on their parents. In Japan *freeters* (furita)[5] and *parasaito shinguru* (parasite singles) refer to the growing number of young people who are having difficulties joining the labor force and forming their own families (Miyamoto 2002, 2004; Kosugi 2006). In Italy, *bamboccioni* (big dummy boys) is a sarcastic term that indicates the growing number of young men in their mid-twenties and thirties who are still unmarried and living with their parents.[6] While the specific reasons for delayed adulthood differ from one context to another, this phenomenon appears to be affecting young people around the globe. It is this global "waithood generation," which is increasingly unable to succeed in the job market, and feels completely marginalized and with no prospects for the future, that is coming out to the streets to say "enough is enough!" They are protesting massive unemployment, corporate greed, and corrupt governments and are demanding jobs, freedom, and better futures.

This book presents five fundamental arguments. First, the majority of young Africans are in waithood; because of its pervasiveness and prolonged duration, waithood is becoming a more permanent state and, arguably, gradually replacing conventional adulthood. Second, waithood is not about geography but essentially about inequality. The experiences of youth transitions to adulthood in the West show that underprivileged and working-class youths in Europe and North America experience conditions very similar to those of poor and marginalized youths in Africa, in the same way that the condition of privileged young Africans corresponds to that of their Western counterparts. The current crisis of the middle class all over the world resulting from the economic downturn is steadily expanding the numbers of those experiencing waithood, as well-educated, middle-class youth everywhere are increasingly unable to find stable employment. Third, the experiences of youth in waithood in the global South, particularly Africa, are crucial to understanding youth in today's world. Not only have they been most acutely affected by the failures of neoliberalism and national politics, but also they embody, in a very sharp way, the contradictions of the modern world. Fourth, waithood is creative; young people have not resigned themselves to the hardships of their situation but are using their agency and creativity to fashion new "youthscapes" (Maira and Soep 2005) or subcultures with alternative forms of livelihood and social relationships in the margins of mainstream society. Fifth, waithood is transformative. The waithood generation possesses a tremendous potential for transformation. Young people today understand that the struggle to overcome their predicament requires radical social change. No longer defined by political parties' ideology yet rejecting being cast as apathetic, they are engaging in civil society organizations and using popular culture as well as new technologies of information, communication, and social networking to confront the status quo. From more or less spontaneous street riots and protests in the streets of Maputo, Dakar, Madrid, London, New York, and Santiago, to revolutions that overthrew dictatorships in Tunisia, Egypt, and Libya the waithood generation is taking it upon itself to redress the wrongs of contemporary society and remake the world.

This book contributes to the growing body of literature that examines youths' experiences and their outlook on life in the context of the global economic downturn. It addresses the richly textured everyday experiences of young Africans in waithood: their vulnerabilities and anxieties, their hopes and dreams, their possibilities and constraints, their resolve and their bubbling creativity. It explores how young people are facing more globally the challenges confronting them by drawing upon and reshaping existing practices and by inventing new ones. They take inspiration from events, experiences, and exchanges that occur both within and beyond their immediate vicinity, both in cyberspace and in the nonvirtual world, creating an interlocking web that links local, national, and global realities (Nayak 2003; Herrera and Bayat 2010).

Exploring the Countries

While there are similarities in the way waithood is manifested in all four countries, each country presents its specificities, which derive from its particular political, economic, social, and cultural histories. This section explores such specificities in each of the countries.

Mozambique has a population of twenty-three million, of which 64 percent are under the age of thirty-five; 38 percent live in urban areas.[7] A former Portuguese colony, Mozambique won its independence in 1975 following a ten-year struggle led by the Mozambique Liberation Front (FRELIMO, in Portuguese), which is now the ruling party. In the 1980s the country was engulfed in a civil war when the Mozambique National Resistance (RENAMO, in Portuguese) challenged FRELIMO's socialist approach. Supported by former Portuguese interests and officials of the apartheid regime in South Africa, RENAMO waged a sixteen-year war that destabilized the country and worsened its already unstable social and economic situation. The war ended with a peace accord in 1992, and the first elections were held in 1994. FRELIMO won the elections and established a democratic government.

At independence Mozambique was considered one of the world's poorest countries, but in the late 1980s the government embarked on a series of macroeconomic reforms that, combined with assistance from international donors, led to a dramatic rise in the country's growth rate. In spite of these gains, Mozambique remains dependent on foreign assistance for more than half of its annual budget, and the majority of the population still lives below the poverty line. Despite 8.3 percent GDP growth in 2010, the gap between rich and poor and the cost of living have increased substantially. In February 2008 and September 2010 ordinary Mozambicans, especially youth, came out into the streets to protest the rising prices of fuel, water, electricity, and bread, forcing the government to lower the prices. Subsistence agriculture continues to employ the vast majority of the country's work force, and agricultural productivity is low.[8] Many young people migrate from rural areas to the cities. The unemployment rate was estimated to be 21 percent in 2004 and is much higher among youth, although exact figures are not available.

Located at the southern end of Africa, South Africa had a population of about forty-nine million in July 2011, and 67 percent are below thirty-five years of age.[9] The majority of the population (62 percent) resides in urban areas. Just half of the people live below the poverty line. Dutch settlers (whose descendants were called Boers) arrived in South Africa in 1652 and established a stopover point on the spice route between the Netherlands and the Far East, founding the city of Cape Town. After the British seized the Cape of Good Hope area in 1806, many of the Dutch settlers trekked north to found their own republics. The discovery of diamonds and gold spurred immigration and intensified the subjugation of the native inhabitants. After the Boers were defeated in the Boer War (1899–1902), the British and the Afrikaners, as the Boers then became known, ruled together beginning in 1910 under the Union of South Africa, which became a republic in 1961 after a whites-only referendum. In 1948 the National Party was voted into power and instituted a policy of apartheid—the "separate development" of the races—that favored the white minority. The African National Congress (ANC) led the opposition to apartheid, and many top ANC leaders, such as Nelson Mandela, spent decades in South Africa's prisons. Internal protests and insurgency, as well as boycotts by some Western nations and institutions, led to the regime's eventual willingness to negotiate a peaceful transition to majority rule.[10]

South Africa emerged from its long history of apartheid with the democratic elections of 1994, in which Nelson Mandela was elected president and the ANC was chosen to lead the government of the new South African Republic. Mandela was succeeded by Thabo Mbeki and then Jacob Zuma, as the ANC continued to win general elections. South Africa is struggling to address the legacy of apartheid, especially inequalities in housing, education, and healthcare. South Africa is not as impoverished as many sub-Saharan nations; it is an emerging market with an abundant supply of natural resources and well-developed financial, legal, communications, energy, and transport systems. Economic growth was robust from 2004 to 2007 as South Africa reaped the benefits of macroeconomic stability and a global commodities boom, but growth began to slow in late 2007 because of the electricity crisis and the impact of the global financial crisis on commodity prices and demand. Unemployment remains high, close to 30 percent in 2010. Racial disparities are marked: youth unemployment reached 53.4 percent for black Africans, in contrast to only 14.5 percent for whites. Daunting economic problems remain from the apartheid era, including widespread poverty, inadequate housing and infrastructure, and a shortage of public transit, reflecting the continuing economic marginality of most black people. The government largely maintains the pro-business policies of the past and is facing growing pressure to deliver basic services to low-income areas and to increase job opportunities. More than a quarter of South Africa's population currently receives social grants to cover their basic needs.[11]

Senegal is located in West Africa, and its capital, Dakar, is at the westernmost point on the continent. In 2011 its population was estimated at 13.7 million; 58 percent live in rural areas. The fifteen to thirty-five age group constituted about 35 percent of the total population in 2006. In terms of religion, the vast majority is Muslim at 94 percent. The French colonies of Senegal and the French Sudan were merged in 1959 and granted their independence as the Mali Federation in 1960. The union broke up after only a few months. The Socialist Party ruled the country for forty years until President Abdoulaye Wade was elected in 2000. Since his reelection in 2007 he has shown an increasingly autocratic governing style, amending the constitution over a dozen times to increase executive power and weaken the opposition.[12] In June 2011, protests by youth and civil society groups led to the overturn of a constitutional amendment aimed at easing the president's victory at the polls and establishing the post of vice-president, which could go to his son.

Dakar is the country's economic center and offers the overwhelming majority of nonagricultural employment. The interior is much less developed, creating serious regional economic imbalances. Senegal relies heavily on donor assistance. The country's key export-oriented industries are phosphate mining, fertilizer production, and commercial fishing; it is also working on iron ore and oil exploration projects. In 1994 the government undertook an ambitious economic reform program with the support of the international donor community, which resulted in GDP growth averaging over 5 percent annually during the period from 1995 to 2007. But unemployment soared to 48 percent in 2007,[13] with youth unemployment reaching 30 percent in 2009.[14] The rate of job creation has long been inadequate to absorb young people and continues to prompt illegal migrants to leave Senegal in search of work in Europe.[15]

Tunisia is located in North Africa between Algeria and Libya. It has a population of ten million; 53 percent of the population is under the age of thirty. Most people (87 percent) are Muslim; a few are Christian or Jewish. Two-thirds of its population lives in urban areas.[16] The French invaded Tunisia in 1881 and established it as a protectorate. The country gained its independence in 1956, and Habib Bourguiba, its first president, established a one-party state. He ruled the country for thirty-one years, repressing Islamic fundamentalism and establishing rights for women unmatched by any other Arab nation.[17] Zine El-Abidine Ben Ali, a former minister of the interior and prime minister, led a bloodless coup against Bourguiba and became president in 1987. Until January 2011, Ben Ali and his Constitutional Democratic Rally (RCD) party exerted near-total control over parliament, state and local governments, and most political activity, and the family of Ben Ali and his wife controlled most entrepreneurial activities. On January 14, 2011, Ben Ali fled the country for Saudi Arabia following weeks of mounting antigovernment protests. His departure was greeted by widespread euphoria. Since then, however, disputes over reform priorities, political instability, economic crisis, labor unrest, tensions between the privileged coastal region and relatively impoverished interior, and lingering insecurity continue, while the flow of refugees from Libya creates pressing humanitarian needs.

Tunisia has a diverse economy, with important mining, tourism, and manufacturing sectors. Governmental control of economic affairs, while still heavy, has gradually lessened over the past decade with increasing privatization. Tunisia cultivated strong ties with the European Union, its largest trading partner, as well as the United States. Unemployment rates have increased substantially in the last decade, reaching 14 percent in 2010; youth unemployment, including among university graduates, was 30 percent by March 2011. Despite many political and economic characteristics shared across the region, Tunisia exhibits a number of unique attributes; it has a relatively small territory and a sizable and highly educated middle class. Migration to Europe, especially France and Italy, has been steady for many years, although in the last few years migration flows decreased substantially.

Defining Youth

Youth is commonly defined as the period between childhood and adulthood, taking into account both chronological age and the biological process of maturation. But, as many authors have pointed out, age categories are not natural; they constitute cultural systems with particular sets of meanings and values. Age categories are embedded in personal relationships, institutional structures, social practices, politics, laws, and public policies (Mintz 2008; Sukarieh and Tannock 2008). The relationship between social position and age is not only complex but also contested, because age divisions involve power relations. In fact, age classifications produce a particular social order to which each individual is bound. Pierre Bourdieu argues that "youth and age are not self-evident data but are socially constructed, in the struggle between the young and the old" and explains that age is "socially manipulated and manipulable. . . . Talking about 'the young' as a social unit, a constituted group, with common interests, relating these interests to a biologically defined age is, in itself, an obvious manipulation" (1993, 95). Youth is also a time of growth, of searching for meanings and belonging; a stage of molding characters, interests, and goals; a process of constructing and reconfiguring identities; a creative period with both risks and possibilities.

Far from constituting a universal category, youth is the historical offspring of modernity. According to Jean and John Comaroff, "modernity . . . casts 'youth' as both the essential precondition and the indefinite postponement of maturity" (2005, 20). In modern capitalist society, youth has been a site of self-conscious social and cultural reproduction through education—the space in which society seeks to attain its potential, in which it invests in its human capital, and in which, says Michel Foucault, society "hides its dreams" (1976, 81). Youth is generally an intense period marked by great energy, enthusiasm, and creativity—thence the expression "you're as young as you feel," which is popular among older adults (Fussell 2007).

In the industrialized world, age thresholds have standardized the life course into three main phases: education, representing childhood and dependence; work, marking adulthood and independence; and rest, cor-responding to retirement and old age (France 2007). Implicit in this model are social and cultural assumptions about physical development, maturity, responsibility, and independence (Mintz 2008). In this view, youth is simply a transitional phase from education to work, from immaturity to maturity, or from childhood to adulthood. These assumptions, however, are subjected to alterations due to socioeconomic, political, and cultural conditions. In many European countries and in North America, for example, old age is undergoing redefinition as adults' life expectancy rises and policymakers, worried about burdensome pension obligations, consider raising the age of retirement. In 2010 changes to extend the retirement age proposed by the French government were met with riots; the protests came not only from older workers but also from youth, who feared that if the older generation did not retire they would be less able to secure decent jobs.

Age categories have shifted profoundly from one historical period to an-other. Youth acquires distinct meanings in different places and times (Nayak 2003; Bayat and Herrera 2010) and must be understood as a situated and mutable social category. The boundaries between what constitutes youth and what constitutes adulthood are continuously being redefined. Gender and class also play pivotal roles in differentiating youth. In Sierra Leone a young person who is educated and employed is often perceived as a social adult (Wai 2008), and *youth* is often used as a derogatory term applied to uneducated, unemployed young people, who are sometimes labeled *lumpen* (Abdullah 1998). The West African expression *youthman* illustrates the gen-dered character of youth. Youthman has no feminine form but subsumes young, unmarried women, indicating women's peripheral status. Gender has a profound influence on the length of youth; girls are often married young, assuming adult roles as wives and mothers (Okwany 2008), while men can remain youths up to and beyond the age of thirty (Whyte 2006). These class and gendered dimensions of youth become central to the spaces that they create for socioeconomic, cultural, and political action (Wai 2008). Moreover, definitions based on age ranges do not account for situations in which AIDS orphans are forced to head households and become caregivers at a tender age (Poku 2006; Campbell et al. 2009).

In 1985 the United Nations established the International Year of the Youth and defined youth as all those between the ages of fifteen and twenty-five (United Nations 2007). The World Bank's definition of youth includes those between the ages of fifteen and twenty-four (World Bank 2007). The African Union defines youth as those aged fifteen to thirty-five (African Union 2006, 3). In many countries in the global South the age bracket defining youth is much broader than it is in the global North, starting well below fifteen and extending to thirty-five years of age. The fluidity of the age categories defining youth reflects its social and cultural nature, which is context-specific (Tyyskä 2005). The strict age definitions adopted by international bodies are not helpful to understand youth as a socially constructed category. Social scientists working in Africa have tended to define youth not as a particular age range but as a social category characterized by particular cultural views about roles, rights, and responsibilities (Durham 2000; De Boeck and Honwana 2005). Some scholars have suggested that age stratification approaches should be replaced by an analysis that focuses on social processes and how an individual's life may evolve through time (Johnson-Hanks 2002; Cole and Durham 2008). Youth is understood to be a process, a social shifter (Durham 2000). It is not only a transitional phase, but it also constitutes a here-and-now moment with particular experiences, practices, and concerns. This book understands youth as defined by social expectations and responsibilities and considers all those who have not yet been able to attain social adulthood, despite their age, as youth.

Demographically, Africa is a youthful continent. In 2006, about 44 percent of the population in sub-Saharan Africa was under fifteen years of age, making it the youngest region of the world. Although the AIDS epidemic has ravaged families and communities across the continent, it has not had a major effect on overall population size and its age structure because of extremely high fertility rates (Ashford 2007). Between 2010 and 2015 the number of youth living in sub-Saharan Africa is expected to increase by 19.4 million (Taiwo and Moyo 2011). Demographers estimate that fertility rates will begin to decline in the coming decades and that this will be the largest youth cohort in the continent's history (Barker 2005). We are, indeed, living in the age of youth.

Young Africans' lives are amazingly varied, reflecting the cultural diversity and uneven economic development that characterize the continent. Their differing socioeconomic conditions and cultural backgrounds affect their life chances and outlooks. On average, today's youth are better educated than their parents. While many still fall far below global averages, some have qualifications that compare favorably with those of their counterparts in the global North. They are better connected with the rest of the world than earlier generations of Africans, navigating the "communications highway" and gradually overcoming social and cultural factors that once limited their access to information and the world beyond their locality. E-mail, text messaging, YouTube, Twitter, Facebook, and mobile telecommunications are their privileged modes of communication, as they are of youth worldwide (Bayat and Herrera 2010). As a result, African youth are more determined to find ways to close the gap between the limited opportunities before them and what they now perceive to be possible in the global arena. They seek to create better and more meaningful lives for themselves, not merely to live out their days within the constraints of the situations they now inhabit.

Studies of African Youth

Studies of youth in Africa are relatively recent. While in the 1940s and 1950s anthropologists such as Edward Evans-Pritchard (1940), Meyer Fortes (1945), and Audrey Richards (1956) studied youth initiations, they examined the subject from the perspective of how the elder generation transmitted culture to the younger generation. In the 1960s, and building on Van Gennep's (1960) work on rites of passage, Victor Turner (1969) developed the concept of liminality—a condition in the midst of the initiation process in which the young person is no longer who he or she was but not yet who he or she will become. The notion of liminality allowed researchers to focus on youth themselves and remains relevant to understanding the social positions of young people today. However, earlier anthropological studies downplayed intergenerational tensions in "traditional" societies, and it was only in the 1970s and 1980s that scholars such as Pierre-Philippe Rey (1973), Jean La Fontaine (1977), and Claude Meillassoux (1981) began to expose the tensions over power and knowledge between the young and the elders.

In the late 1980s, youth started to become a major topic of scholarly concern in Africa. Some scholars focused on the notion of generation as "key to understanding the construction of social knowledge and power relations" (Aguilar 1998, 6; see also Burgess 2005). Publications such as *The Politics of Age and Gerontocracy in Africa* (Aguilar 1998); a 2005 special issue of *Africa Today* focusing on youth and citizenship in East Africa edited by Tony Burgess; *Rethinking Age in Africa* (Aguilar 2007); and *Generations in Africa: Connections and Conflicts*, edited by Erdmute Alber et al. (2008), used the notion of generations to analyze the difficult predicaments of youth (Cole 2004; Vigh 2006) and to address the relationship of youth with globalization (Cole and Durham 2007). The notion of generational change became instrumental for examining young people as citizens who both conform to and challenge the standards imposed on them by traditional hierarchies, national politics, and global forces (Burgess 2005; Abbink and van Kessel 2005; Honwana and De Boeck 2005; Christiansen et al. 2006).

Postcolonial studies of youth also focused on activism and social movements, highlighting young people's politics and resistance against colonialism, apartheid, and other forms of domination (Mbembe 1985; Last 1991; Bayart et al. 1992; Kakwenzire 1996; Diouf 1996; Momoh 2000;

Marks 2001; Obadare 2010; see also Toulabor 1995; Bundy 1987; Seekings and Everatt 1993; Toungara 1995; Kurimoto and Simonse 1998; Argenti 1998, 2007; Collignon and Diouf 2001; Reynolds 2008). They also addressed young people's involvement in religious movements and popular culture (Meyer 1995; Ssewakiryanga 1999; Gondola 1999; MacGaffey and Bazenguissa-Ganga 2000; Saavedra-Casco 2006; Suriano 2006; Ntarangwi 2009; Weiss 2009; Guadeloupe and Geschiere 2008; van Dijk 2008). Others looked at young people's cultural production in art, music, theater, and fashion, as well as everyday practices in which young people act as cultural agents in their own right.

The tribulations of young Africans at this difficult juncture in the continent's history have taken center stage in many studies highlighting "youth at risk" or "youth in trouble." As Jon Abbink (2005) asserted, to be young in contemporary Africa has come to mean being disadvantaged, vulnerable, and marginal, both economically and politically. Young Africans are severely affected by violent conflicts, prompting social scientists to examine the complex issues surrounding youth participation in wars and other forms of violence as child soldiers, protection racketeers, and criminal gangs (La Hausse 1990; Richards 1996; Bazenguissa-Ganga 1996; Abdullah and Bangura 1997; Abdullah 1998; Utas 2003; Shepler 2005; Honwana 1999, 2006; Shaw 2007; Coulter 2009). Rather than seeing young people caught up in violence as passive victims, these studies portray them as active, though not autonomous, social agents. Another important theme is the exclusion of youth from labor markets and the formal economy. Some studies focused on young people's education and training, involvement in urbanization, and quest for jobs and livelihoods, as well as their engagement in the informal economy (Ly 1988; El Kenz 1996; Okojie 2003; Chigunta 2007; Chimanikire 2009; Agbu 2009; Ndjio 2008; Jenkins 2008; Kinyanjui 2008). This set of studies on youth violence and socioeconomic marginalization underlines key debates about structure versus agency, greed and grievance, old wars and new wars. At the same time, they raise new issues about the social and economic consequences of neoliberal structural adjustment policies in Africa.

The spread of HIV/AIDS, STDs, and other epidemics represents a significant risk to young Africans (Poku and Whiteside 2004; Poku 2006; Campbell et al. 2009; Mwiturubani et al. 2009). While epidemiological and biomedical approaches were initially central to the analysis, anthropological and sociological approaches gained traction as the focus was broadened to encompass the social and cultural contexts in which individuals are exposed to and affected by disease. Gender relations, sexuality, intimacy, and marital relations also became important domains of social inquiry (Biaya 2001;

Nyamnjoh 2005; Nyanzi et al. 2005; Manuel 2008; Thomas and Cole 2009; Masvawure 2010; Groes-Green 2011; Hunter 2007, 2010).

Some researchers have examined the impact of globalization on young people's lives, emphasizing the way globalization processes are mediated by age and generation (Cole and Durham 2007; see also Weiss 2009). Globalization has also been examined in the context of young people's lives in time and space. Cole and Durham (2008) underline the importance of temporality in young people's lives by elucidating the ways in which they perceive the future. In *Makers and Breakers* Filip De Boeck and I stressed young people's active and creative roles in fashioning novel practices in their societies and not merely imitating Western cultural practices (De Boeck and Honwana 2005). Rather than living in the shadow of globalization, young people in Africa draw from global and local realities to articulate and manage their "'local' lives" (Pilkington 2004; Kjeldgaard and Askegaard 2006). Concepts of hybridity and creolization have not helped to understand young Africans' relationship with the global world. Brad Weiss points out very clearly that the consumption practices of young men in Arusha's barbershops are not a mixture of global and local but fully grounded in Tanzanian realities (Weiss 2009). As Henrietta Moore reminds us, "The plural, unpredictable nature of processes of change and transformation means that analytical frameworks can no longer depend on binaries: local/global, inside/outside, micro/macro" (Moore 2011, 3). The critical issue is the way relations of power influence and structure social interactions. Indeed, many young people feel marginalized in relation to dominant power structures and hegemonic ideologies. While they comprehend their position on the margins of mainstream society, they do not define it as their permanent condition; that is why they engage in social change.

Current studies on African youth recognize the diversity of experience as well as the agency and creativity of young people as they try to overcome serious everyday challenges. In societies undergoing globalization and modernization, young people are under increasing pressure to cope with and to adapt to change in all aspects of life (Bendit and Hahn-Bleibtreu 2008). These challenges are forcing researchers to rethink their conceptual frameworks and devise new approaches to explore the lived experiences of young people today. The present situation of African youth in waithood poses fundamental challenges to existing understandings of youth transitions to adulthood and their engagement in social change more globally. By focusing on young people's experiences of waithood, this book aims at opening new avenues for understanding and conceptualizing youth in the context of failed neoliberal policies and global socioeconomic and political crisis.

The book comprises eight chapters. This introductory chapter is followed by Chapter 2, an in-depth examination of waithood, a twilight zone in which young people are expected to be mature but are not yet socially recognized as full adults. While focusing on the diversity of young people's pathways toward adulthood in Africa, Chapter 2 examines waithood as both a challenging and a creative stage in young people's lives. The chapter also discusses youth transitions to adulthood in the developed world and identifies some similarities in young people's transitional experiences more globally. It recognizes the changing nature of adulthood as a destination of youth transitions and suggests that waithood is critical to understanding the predicament of this generation.

Chapter 3 analyzes young people's aspirations and the challenges they face in waithood. It examines the structural conditions that affect their lives and analyzes problems in the education systems and the labor markets that make it difficult for young people to find employment and sustainable livelihoods. The chapter is critical of the neoliberal economic policies espoused by international financial institutions, especially structural adjustment reforms in Africa, that have not generated much-needed employment or reduced poverty.

Chapter 4 examines the coping mechanisms and survival strategies adopted by young men and women in waithood. It focuses on some of the particular activities they undertake, exploring some of the constraints they are confronted with and the successes they achieve. Examples include the cross-border trading activities of young Mozambicans and Tunisians, the temporary shelf-packing and merchandising jobs held by young South Africans, and the dangerous journeys undertaken by Senegalese and Tunisian youths who attempt to migrate to Europe. Through these case studies and stories of lived experience, we discover that young Africans are active agents in reshaping their lives and their societies.

Chapter 5 explores issues of intimacy, looking at sexuality, courtship, and marriage. Sexual relationships among young people in waithood take new forms that reflect their particular circumstances. Sexuality and courtship constitute important sites of identity formation and the negotiation of notions of manhood and womanhood, and formerly unquestioned gender norms and identities are altered to fit young people's unprecedented social positions. These new emerging patterns of sexuality, courtship, and marriage are challenging dominant notions of masculinity and femininity in these societies.

Chapter 6 examines young people's rejection of old-fashioned party politics. But young people in waithood are not apathetic; they are politically engaged mainly in civil society associations outside mainstream structures, using music and popular culture as well as the new cyber-social networks as ways of contesting the status quo. This rejection of "old-style" politics is also apparent in the West and other world regions where young people face the same crisis of joblessness leading to restricted futures. Globally, the younger generation is responding to the crisis by coming out to the streets to voice their protests in new forms of civic and political participation. It appears that the "waithood generation" is asserting itself and creating new geographies of political intervention and citizenship.

Chapter 7 looks at young people's engagement in social change that significantly alters the course of history and enacts profound social and political transformations. In the 1960s and the 1970s in Mozambique young people led the struggle for independence from Portuguese colonialism, and the youth uprisings in Soweto contributed to the demise of apartheid in South Africa. Recently a youth-led revolution in Tunisia ended twenty-three years of dictatorship and inspired youth uprisings across North Africa and the Middle East. This chapter examines in detail the Tunisian revolution from the factors that triggered the protests to its actors. It also considers the challenges facing youth during the post–Ben Ali transition to democracy. Theories about generations and social change are examined to understand the role being played today by this waithood generation.

The concluding chapter looks at global waithood and interrogates still-unfolding worldwide developments in which the waithood generation appears to be playing a critical role. This generation is reshaping and reinterpreting itself politically and is engaged in a range of collective protests against unemployment, corrupt politics, and corporate greediness. Where these developments will lead is anyone's guess, but it appears that the waithood generation may have an impact comparable to that of the generation of 1968 (Berman 1996) that carried out the youth uprisings in Europe and North America.

Chapter 2

Waithood

A young woman I interviewed in Tunisia occupies an ambiguous position between childhood, which she has left behind, and adulthood, which she has not yet attained. Twenty-eight-year-old Zahira has been unable to find steady employment after finishing her studies in social communication at the University of Tunis. She comes from a working-class family in the central region of Sidi Bouzid and is eager to work and support herself and her relatives. "I have had several temporary jobs as a shop assistant and a dispatcher at a call center. . . . The jobs had nothing to do with my training and were not stable enough for me to plan my future," Zahira told me. A young man in Sierra Leone is in a similar situation.

> My name is Ahmed. I am 32 years of age. I am not married but I have three children, two boys and a girl. . . . I attended secondary school in Makeni. . . . Currently, I do not have a regular job where I can make consistent income. . . . I am what they call a "youthman.". . . I was in the army for almost fourteen years and my pension cannot support me. I survive on friends and petty sponsorship [small remittances] from my brother, who is overseas. (Quoted in Olonisakin and Ismail 2008, 5)

His position as a "youthman" is full of contradictions: he is in his thirties and a father of three, but he remains unmarried, unemployed, and dependent on others. Zahira and Ahmed are both experiencing *waithood*, a prolonged and uncertain stage between childhood and adulthood that is characterized by their inability to enter the labor market and attain the social markers of adulthood.

Almost everywhere in the world the transition to adulthood can no longer be taken for granted as an orderly process by which young people attain personal autonomy and social recognition. Today the passage to adulthood seems much more difficult than before. Young people cannot take their futures for granted. They see no prospects for steady employment and cannot be sure that their efforts to get an education will be rewarded. As they embark on intimate relationships, they are uncertain whether they will ever be in a position to marry. Neoliberal economic reforms, rapid social change, and political transformations have disrupted the ways previous generations negotiated the transition to adult life (Pollock 2002).

This chapter makes three key arguments. First, the majority of young Africans today live in waithood, a twilight zone between childhood and adulthood. Waithood is a neither-here-nor-there position in which young people are expected to be independent from their parents but are not yet recognized as social adults. No longer just a brief transitional stage in the life course, waithood is becoming a permanent condition, as many young people remain stuck in this in-between situation. Indeed, waithood is becoming a new but socially attenuated form of adulthood.

Second, waithood does not represent pathology or a "failed" transition on the part of a "lost generation." Transitional processes are not universal, linear, or uniform; they vary individually as well as from one time and place to another. The life course is shaped by socioeconomic and cultural factors and reshaped by history. Transitions should be understood within the specific conditions experienced by young people. In Africa, waithood appears to be the only possibility open to the majority of young people, and they are creatively harnessing all the means at their disposal to manage their lives.

Third, although their situation and particular conditions are different, some young people in the West are facing similar predicaments as their movement toward adulthood stalls. Those who come from middle-class backgrounds and hold college degrees lament their inability to find jobs that pay enough to allow them to live independently, while their parents worry about the "boomerang generation" that returns home after graduation. In the inner-city neighborhoods of London, Birmingham, and Manchester, New York, Chicago, and Los Angeles, working-class young people, especially those of color, are increasingly unable to find any jobs at all. Despite living in the most economically developed nations of the world, these impoverished and marginalized young people have something in common with working-class youth such as Ahmed and with well-educated young people such as Zahira.

Most of the academic analyses of this problem have been conducted within life-course and transition studies. Next I outline the main premises of these theoretical approaches and show their limitations for our understanding of the specific realities experienced by young Africans in waithood.

Life Course and Transition Studies

Life course studies deal with patterns of human development that occur across the life span and are shaped by culture, society, and history. Glen Elder (1974) first articulated the notion that people's lives develop over time in patterned ways that are influenced by their social and historical circumstances. The concept of age cohorts, similar to that of generations, is understood as "an aggregate of individuals . . . who experience the same events within the same time interval" (Ryder 1965, 845) and is at the core of this theoretical tradition. Situating young people in birth cohorts—for example, as the "children of the Great Depression" whose lives Elder analyzed—permits us to trace their movement through age-graded life patterns embedded in institutions. The notion of age cohorts allows for an analytical framework that relates age-grades to social structures over the life span (Ryder 1965; Riley et al. 1988).

Another important tenet of life-course studies is the concept of normative time tables (Neugarten and Datan 1973)—the expectation that individuals will move from one stage to the next in a timely fashion. This concept was crucial to the emergence of transition studies in sociology and social psychology. The term *transition* is closely associated with the psychological idea of development that lies at the core of life-course studies. It assumes a linear progression from one identifiable status to another, and in both frameworks youth appears to be simply a developmental stage (Wyn and Woodman 2006, 497). The assumption that youth consists primarily of a process of transition from psychological immaturity to maturity was uncritically incorporated into much of the youth research carried out in the 1960s and 1970s (Cohen and Ainley 2000).

French sociologist Olivier Galland (1991) analyzed three dimensions of youth transitions: professional transitions from school to work; residential transitions from the parental home to a home of one's own; and relationship transitions from being single to getting married and forming a family. When these three transitions take place in a sequential or synchronized manner—for example, when a person completes his or her education, secures a job, finds a place to live, and then marries and has children—entering adulthood follows a standardized path and is seen as unproblematic.

This model is inapplicable to many young people, especially those who are disadvantaged by gender, race, or social class. Women and impoverished youths may make some of these transitions much earlier (Molgat 2007) or much later, if at all. Indeed, these transitions are now subject to considerable fragmentation, interruptions, and reversals (Bradley and Devadason

2008; Dwyer and Wyn 2001; Holdsworth and Morgan 2005; Pilcher et al. 2003; Pollock 2008; Walther 2006). They rarely follow the neat unidirectional pattern projected in Galland's model. Wide variations in access to opportunities for education and professional and occupational training, employment, and social support mean that the timing and order of these transitions depend on young people's specific situations. Social, economic, and political conditions both constrain and enable youths to carve out particular pathways into adulthood.

Gender, race, and class are important determinants in these transitions. Young children's gender-specific experiences may lead them to negotiate the transitions to adulthood differently (Maccoby 1998). For example, young women are less likely than young men of similar social status to achieve success in highly competitive, male-dominated occupations. But in the United States, young women of color growing up in poverty are more likely to finish school and find work than their male counterparts. Inner-city men are more likely to engage in risky behaviors, be pronounced delinquent, and end up in prison or dead. The stigma of incarceration and a criminal record further diminishes their ability to find legal employment (Kmec and Furstenberg 2002).

Similarly, racial segregation and inequality expose young people of color to a higher level of material deprivation. Studies on transitions to adulthood in urban South Africa show that under apartheid black youths had the least access to societal resources and the greatest restrictions on work and migration (Lam and Seekings 2005). White youths had advantages in a wide range of areas, including better-funded schools, privileged access to the labor market, unrestricted residential mobility, and greater access to social services (Fiske and Ladd 2004). These factors strongly affected the ways members of these groups made the transition to adulthood.

During my fieldwork I came across many young men and women who were experiencing great difficulties in attaining social adulthood. While gender, social class, race, and socioeconomic conditions influence their lives, the current global economic crisis and contraction in employment opportunities, as well as the social disruptions caused by conflict, violence, and HIV/AIDS, are having a devastating effect on the future prospects of the next generation.

Waithood

In African countries the socialization of young people into adult life was traditionally marked by a series of symbolic and educational steps and was the responsibility of the entire community. In many societies, initiation rituals generally conferred on young men the right to be accepted among adults, receive land, leave the parental home, and marry; they offered young women the means to become good wives and mothers. For both men and women, marriage was a crucial step in a ritualized journey to adulthood. This traditional path to adulthood has gradually been eroded by urbanization, modernization, and globalization, as youths increasingly migrate to urban centers for schooling or employment. Formal education became one of the principal agents for socializing and training the next generation. Wage labor provides youth with newfound independence from parents and kinship groups (Calvès et al. 2007).

Today, young Africans are forced to grow up quickly, yet they find it very difficult to achieve social and economic autonomy. The existing markers of adulthood—getting a job or some form of livelihood; leaving their parents' house and building their own home; getting married; having children; and providing for the family—are no longer readily attainable under the socioeconomic and political conditions that prevail in most countries.

African societies are struggling with economic decline and decaying infrastructure, strained healthcare and educational systems, high unemployment rates, and insecure livelihoods, all of which seriously weaken the social fabric. So extreme is the situation, particularly with the current global economic crisis, that most governments are unable to provide their citizens with basic social and economic resources. The decline of opportunities in rural areas has led young men and women to migrate to the cities, where their chances of finding employment remain very slim. Young people increasingly are forced to survive in an oversaturated informal economy.

All these factors create serious constraints on youths' ability to attain adult independence. Adulthood eludes them as they are deprived of its main building blocks: skills, jobs, housing, and marriage. The difficulties they experience in one area spill over into other areas and have a debilitating effect on their entire lives (Dhillon and Yousef 2007). Youths find themselves in waithood—perpetually waiting to enter adulthood (Dhillon and Yousef 2007; Singerman 2007). They are consigned to a liminal space in which they are neither dependent children nor autonomous adults. In West Africa the term *youthman* is commonly used to refer to people who have not attained social adulthood despite their biological adulthood (Abdullah 1998). Even men over forty continue to be seen as youths because of their inability to gain a stable livelihood, live independently, and marry. The very existence of this expression, as Ibrahim Abdullah observes, stands as a metaphor for Africa's poverty and attests to the pervasiveness of waithood across the continent. The lyrics of a popular song from Sierra Leone lament the conditions of a youthman's life.

> I feel sorry for the youthman today
> The system is bad for the youthman today
> Every day and every night they suffer
> The youthman want to sleep but no place
> The youthman want to eat but no food
> The youthman want good dress but no good dress
> The youthman want to buy but no money
> The youthman want to work
> If no work, how do you expect him to eat?[1]

In South Africa, similarly, Mark Hunter has found the Xizulu term *umnqolo* used to describe a grown but unmarried man who lives with his parents, capturing the idea of men who are not progressing in life. This masculine word has a feminine counterpart. The Xizulu term *uzendazamshiya* indicates an unmarried woman of marriageable age who is still living in her parents' home, indicating that she has been left behind (Hunter 2010, 155). Young men and women experience waithood in very different ways. For men, waithood entails facing the pressures of finding a steady job; securing the resources to purchase, build, or rent a home; and covering the costs of marriage and family formation. Although women are increasingly being educated and have always engaged in productive labor alongside household chores, marriage and motherhood are still the most important markers of adulthood. Yet their ability to attain this social status depends on men's moving beyond waithood (Singerman 2007; Calvès et al. 2007).

Waithood involves a long process of negotiating personal identity and financial independence in circumstances of deep socioeconomic crisis. Narratives from a young woman in Mali and young men in South Africa and Nigeria point to the impact of structural conditions on their lives and highlight their inescapable socioeconomic vulnerability. Nyele, a young Malian woman, describes how she was led into a way of life that offers no real future:

> I come from a poor family and was kicked out of high school because I was unable to make steady progress. I was unable to pay for an additional school year . . . but I had to survive. Like my other girl friends, I was hired as a waitress in a restaurant. . . . Men who frequented the restaurant started to give me tips and relations developed between some of them and me. Sometimes I went out with some of them and started to enjoy the easy money. Now it is hard for me to abandon this life of secret prostitution. Despite all the adverse consequences such as AIDS and other STDs and the social stigma, it is hard for me to

just stay there and do nothing, and to keep asking for help from my
relatives. (Quoted in Olonisakin and Ismail 2008, 10)

Bongani, a thirty-year-old man from Soweto in South Africa, completed
a high school diploma (*matric*) in 2000.

After finishing matric I tried to get a job but it was hard to get a good
job. . . . In my first job I worked as a cleaner for a big company for
about two years. Then I found another job [where] I had to go door
to door selling vacuum cleaners. I didn't stay long because the owner
of the company was racist; he didn't treat the black employees well.
. . . I have not been able to get any proper jobs since then. . . . I look
for temporary jobs in merchandizing and shelf-packing in retail stores
and supermarkets like ShopRite. . . . I am not married but I have a
child. . . . Without a job it is difficult to organize my life properly.

Bongani recognizes that his life is not in order. He has become a father but
not a husband, and economic constraints prevent him from assuming the
position of a fully adult man.

Akinde, a young Nigerian male, migrated in search of work and, like
the waitress who also earned money as a prostitute, slipped into an illegal
but more lucrative hustle.

I came to Lagos from a neighboring state as a teenager. I left secondary school midway . . . and proceeded to learn auto-mechanic work.
. . . Poor patronization made me . . . [an] escort for smuggled vehicles
from Cotonou. Escorts with auto-mechanic skills are usually required
to help repair vehicles if they break down on the road. After a year of
being an escort I began smuggling vehicles across the border myself.
I feel smuggling is extremely more profitable because I earn a lot of
money and I have become highly connected to important people in
society who require their cars to be smuggled across the border in
order to dodge official taxes. . . . I was driven to smuggling vehicles
because there is a demand for it [and] it brings me sufficient income.
. . . Nigeria is a country where everyone has to fend for himself, the
government cares for no one, and those in power are only using their
positions to enrich themselves. (Quoted in Olonisakin and Ismail
2008, 17)

Marc Sommers highlights the difficulties faced by young Rwandans trying to achieve financial independence and partake in adult obligations. A

twenty-four-year-old Rwandan man said, "All the guys here can't afford to marry a woman because they can't build a house. Male and female youth are failing to get married" (Sommers 2012, 115). A forty-five-year-old man agreed that "there are no youth able to marry in my *umudugudu* (a village, the smallest political administrative unit), even if they are old enough to do so" (Sommers 2012, 115). Limited access to land and lack of employment opportunities in the countryside drive many to the capital, Kigali, in search of work. But, as a twenty-three-year-old woman pointed out, "male youth in town [Kigali] can end up as thieves and the female youth end up as prostitutes. They can get HIV/AIDS or become pregnant" (Sommers 2012, 137). Sommers concludes that the widespread inability of young men and women to attain full adulthood creates a vast array of social problems, including crime, prostitution, and the spread of HIV/AIDS. These concerns are shared across the continent.

Although none of these young people feel completely helpless, they all recognize the external factors that limit their actions and their ability to thrive and succeed. But they continue to fight and use their agency and creativity to find solutions for everyday life challenges.

The experiences of young Africans indicate that transitions between stages in the life course are complex and do not always follow predetermined trajectories. If we assume that transitions should follow a prescribed linear path, the condition of young men and women in waithood would be considered anomalous or even deviant. Indeed, insistence on normative, sequential transitions neglects social change and "pathologizes" transitions outside that norm (Jones 2009, 86). The theoretical models postulated by life-course studies fail to capture the multiplicity of young people's positions and oversimplify the various processes that affect people's lives (Wyn and White 1997). As Gary Pollock points out, "The start and end-points [of transitions] and the unidirectional link between [these points] are . . . inappropriate to represent contemporary experiences" (2002, 63). Instead, we must consider the complexities and diversity of young lives (Jones 2009; Kassimir and Flanagan 2009). The notion of "failed transitions" should be abandoned because it places the blame on young people themselves rather than on the system that is failing them. Many authors have moved away from linear conceptions of the transition to adulthood to embrace more fluid, multilevel, and contextual approaches that accommodate societal developments and varied personal trajectories (Chisholm 1999). These approaches provide space for both personal agency and structural factors in shaping life transitions (Beck 1992; Beck et al. 1994) and allow youth to be seen as actively navigating their way toward adult life (Woolley 2004).

Although waithood could be understood simply as a transitional phase between childhood and adulthood, I argue that, given its pervasiveness and the large numbers of young people who experience it for long periods, or even for their entire lives, waithood is gaining a more permanent status and becoming a new form of adulthood. In the section that follows I discuss the changing nature of adulthood and the ways waithood is replacing the traditional ideal of adulthood.

Problematizing Adulthood

Adulthood, the presumed destination of youth transitions, is not a stable category. Changes in what it means to be a grownup pose significant problems for the conceptualization of transitions. In post–World War II Europe and North America, adulthood was strongly associated with stability and became synonymous with the classic combination of gainful employment, residential independence, marriage, and parenthood (Lee 2001; Blatterer 2007, 2009). These attributes, which were mainly based on the experiences of males, became critical expressions of what it meant to be a mature person and paved the way for an institutionalized life course with adulthood at its center (Kohli 1986; Blatterer 2010). These ideas were developed in societies with relatively stable economies and expanding labor markets, as well as conformity with regard to family formation and gender relations (Beck 2000; Harvey 1989; Hobsbawm 1995; Lee 2001; Marwick 1999; Blatterer 2010).

Changes in gender dynamics, employment patterns, and consumption have refashioned accepted wisdom about adulthood in the West. Notions of male and female adulthood have been altered with the rise in married women's paid employment and the diminishing role of men as family breadwinners (Brannen and Nilsen 2002). Similarly, the labor market has begun to favor a more flexible and mobile work force, limiting adults' job stability and leaning toward more flexible young and unattached workers (Bauman 2001; Beck 2000; Bourdieu 1998; Capelli 2003; Gouliquer 2000; Sennett 1998). Consumption patterns have blurred the boundaries between adult and youthful fashions in clothing, hairstyles, and other "lifestyle" products, showing a decline in age-specific notions of appropriate attire and appearance. All these shifts have contributed to transformations of what adulthood means in contemporary Western societies.

Although the normative ideal of adulthood is now subject to redefinition, it continues to be equated with full personhood (Fraser 2000, 113). According to sociologist Harry Blatterer (2010), this linkage provides adulthood with political value and mediates individuals' interactions in the domestic domain, as well as with public institutions such as schools, employers, and the state. In many societies, too, the traditional ideal of adulthood remains robust despite the fact that the socioeconomic conditions that would enable people to attain it have severely eroded.[2]

In Africa, notions of adulthood have shifted and been called into question by pervasive and often fundamental socioeconomic transformations. Traditional ideals depicted male adulthood as synonymous with being a provider and a person of some authority: a worker, a husband, a father, and a contributing member of the community. Female adulthood was attached to marriage, motherhood, and caregiving. However, structural adjustment policies have greatly contributed to the acceleration of impoverishment across the continent. Men encountered difficulties in securing regular employment and became increasingly unable to fulfill their role as providers. Marital breakdown and family instability ensued, and the proportion of households headed by women with children growing up without the support of their fathers rose sharply. The social instability created by significant increases in criminal activity, interpersonal violence, and alcohol abuse, especially by men, became a widespread problem (Silberschmidt 2005). As men struggled to be able to marry and provide for their families and women were forced to support their children by themselves, traditional ideals of masculinity and femininity gradually eroded. For young people growing up in these circumstances, the old notions of adulthood appear to be incompatible with new socioeconomic realities.

In South Africa the vast majority of participants in the focus groups I held with young people in the townships of Soweto and Alexandra had grown up without a father. Many were raised by their grandmothers, which suggests family fragmentation among the impoverished black community. In *Fractured Families: A Crisis for South Africa* (2011) Gail Eddy and Lucy Holborn conclude that stable families are the privilege of a minority of children. The prevalence of HIV/AIDS, poverty, and unemployment contribute to the breakdown of family bonds. The divorce rate has reached unprecedented levels, and HIV/AIDS has left many children without both parents. Grandparents and extended family members often step into the breach. About one in twelve South African children lives in a "skip-generation" household with grandparents or great-aunts and great-uncles (Eddy and Holborn 2011). The nuclear family has never been the norm in South Africa; under apartheid the labor system commonly split families, sending the men to the mines or the cities to work while the women and children eked out their existence in the rural areas. But today family breakdown has reached unprecedented levels: more than nine million children, nearly half of all children, are growing up with absent, though living, fathers (Eddy and Holborn 2011).

For many youths the traditional model of adulthood, although still valued as an ideal by their elders, has long been absent from their lives. Young people are forced to invent their own model of what it means to be a mature person in their concrete circumstances. As waithood has become an indefinite state in which young people are forced to survive by improvising new forms of livelihood and social relationships, it is becoming the only sort of adulthood that the vast majority of young Africans can attain. They have high aspirations, and each and every day they struggle to improve their lives through every means available to them.

The Unimagined Future

One of the classic questions frequently posed to children and young people is, what would you like to be when you grow up? The ways in which young people think about, envision, and plan for the future reflect their relationship with time, their age and stage of development, and their social environment, all of which are shaped by societal pressures.

People conceptualize and experience the relationship between the present and the future in a variety of ways. At the heart of this discussion is Helga Nowotny's concept of the "extended present," a prolonged here-and-now moment that "helps diminish the uncertainties for the future by recalling cyclicality and seeking to combine it with linearity. It stresses the necessity of structuring but also the possibilities of restructuring" (Nowotny 1994, 58). The extended present is not merely a straight line leading to the future but involves recurring experiences as well as what might be seen as progress. Most important, it allows people to make significant changes in direction as their circumstances and desires shift. Understood in these terms, the present experiences of young people have a tremendous influence on how they perceive their future.

Rapid social changes provoked by social, economic, and political upheavals may alter the line of progress, and the future may seem never to arrive or to arrive before its time (Nowotny 1994). In effect, people cease to think about the long term, and the future is absorbed into the extended present. As Julia Brannen and Ann Nilsen suggest, lived experiences become imprisoned in an all-pervasive "here and now" (2002, 517). When the possibilities for long-term self-projections are foreclosed, young people have few expectations beyond the present and tend to acquire a practical attitude that is focused on their day-to-day lives (Blatterer 2010). This foreshortened time horizon is widespread among impoverished youths and is largely responsible for their behaving in ways that may not serve their future well.

In Africa young people in waithood live mainly in the present. The distant future is difficult to envision in the face of daily social and economic hardships. Adulthood as a destination in which they will settle into a secure job, a house, and a family appears remote and unachievable. Their everyday present becomes their life, and they focus on the here and now. For many young people in waithood, daily life is a struggle. Their future appears foreclosed because they live with AIDS or are HIV-positive, because of wars and conflicts, and because of the absence of decent jobs and the precarious nature of possible livelihoods. In such situations young Africans cannot afford the luxury of dreaming about what they would like to be when they grow up; rather, the issue is whether they will go to bed hungry. For them, the future is today, and the next day, and the next, taking one day at a time.

The experience and outlook of a group of young men I met in Maputo who make a living by scavenging on the city's garbage dump vividly exemplify this situation. Jonasse, who is twenty-seven years old, picks over the garbage dump in Hulene for things to eat, use, or sell. He dropped out of primary school in grade six when his father died, and he, his mother, and his four siblings struggled to survive on their own. So he decided to leave home and fend for himself. Unable to find work, he ended up joining a friend who had been eking out a living on the dump. Jonasse has been living off the dump for about ten years. Every morning he gets up very early to wait for the garbage trucks to arrive. If he is late, then he will miss the chance to make money from unloading the trucks and the opportunity to collect the best items. The scavengers look through the trash for plastic, glass, and metal they can sell to recycling companies. They also search for treasures such as car tires, computer parts, appliances, and other electronics that may be repaired and sold in the nearby market of Xiquelene.

Jonasse admits that life on the garbage dump is extremely hard. There is a lot of competition and backstabbing among the scavengers; "you have to rely on yourself and your close friends, and you have to watch out because this is like a jungle." His goal is to get a single meal every day. Indeed, his life is so tough that all his energies are focused on his daily survival. When I asked how he saw the future, Jonasse responded: "The future? My life is about today and [to] make sure I don't miss a good truck, one that might come with something to eat or something I may be able to sell in the market to be able to eat."

Both within and beyond the African continent young people are living their lives differently than previous generations, in part because they face entirely new conditions and in part because they are responding to novel situations in new ways. In the process they are creating new meanings for both youth and adulthood. The circumstances that enabled the previous generations to achieve normative adulthood no longer exist, and this generation is negotiating new experiences on the basis of the social, economic, political, and cultural resources and repertoires available to them. Youth identities and subjectivities are central to understanding the interplay between structure and agency in their lives as well as their capacity to act and make choices within a constrained existence (Pollock 2002; France 2007).

Marc Molgat argues that "the challenge for youth studies is to not discard research on transitions too quickly but to better identify them and understand their significance from the perspective of young people living in ever-changing socio-economic structures" (2007, 513). However, Mary Bucholtz (2002) contends that youth cannot be seen simply as a transition because it involves its own distinctive identities, experiences, and practices, which are neither a rehearsal for an adult life nor necessarily oriented toward a future adulthood. Youth is not just about becoming an adult; it is also about being in the present. In this sense waithood is not a passing transition for many young Africans but the undeviating reality in their lives.

Prolonged Transitions to Adulthood in Developed Societies

In economically developed societies the transition to adulthood has also become prolonged (Arnett 1998; Shanahan 2000). Young people now stay in school longer and obtain their first paid jobs at older ages; it takes them longer to establish stable occupations and work careers. They also marry later and have their first child later than their counterparts in the mid-twentieth century (Arnett and Taber 1994). Life-course events that were once normatively defined and institutionally structured are increasingly left to individuals to decide on their own; young people must take on new responsibilities for living with the consequences of their actions and decisions (Bauman 2001; Beck 1992). Transitions to adulthood have become more individualized, and specific identities shape youths' particular trajectories and biographies (Schwartz et al. 2005).

According to social psychologist Jeffrey Arnett, there has been a dramatic change in the transition to adulthood in the Western world. In the past, young people grew up quickly and made enduring life choices at a relatively early age. "As recently as 1970 the typical 21-year-old was married or about to be married, caring for a newborn child or expecting one soon, done with education or about to be done, and settled into a long-term job or the role of full-time mother" (Arnett 2004, 3). Today, however, twenty-one-year-olds are studying for postgraduate degrees or professional credentials; those who are working change jobs frequently in search of better pay or prospects of greater personal fulfillment. On average, both marriage and parenthood have been put off for more than five years. As Arnett points out, while the freedom to explore different options may be exciting and elicit high hopes, it can also provoke uncertainty and anxiety because people's lives are unsettled, and many have no idea where their explorations will lead.[3] Because of its specificities and historical uniqueness, Arnett calls this period "emerging adulthood," a new phase in the life course characterized by self-focused identity explorations, relative instability, and open possibilities (2004, 8).

In 2002 and 2005 *Newsweek* and *Time* magazines published feature articles about delayed transitions to adulthood among youth in the United States and Great Britain.[4] They examined cases of "full-grown men and women still living with their parents . . . hopping from job to job and date to date, having fun but seemingly going nowhere" (Grossman 2005, 3). The expressions "boomerang generation" and "yo-yo generation" are used to depict young men and women who return home and continue to depend on their parents after graduating from college (Jones 2009). From age eighteen to thirty, or even beyond, they delay the assumption of adult responsibilities. These articles called them "twixters"—stuck between adolescence and adulthood—or "adultolescents"—adults who are still adolescent.

Japanese scholars have long pointed to changes in youth transitions following the onset of the economic recession in the early 1990s and the sharp decline in the number of company positions available for prospective high school and university graduates. *Freeters* and the *parasaito shinguru* (parasite singles) are expressions that refer to this growing number of young Japanese who are unable to participate in the labor market and form their own families (Miyamoto 2002, 2004; Kosugi 2002, 2006). Freeters are seen as deviations from the traditional transition model in Japanese society, in which students become full-time tenured employees upon graduation and are trained in companies to become full-fledged workers. In Italy, *bamboccioni* (big dummy boys) is a sarcastic expression that describes the growing number of young men in their mid-twenties and thirties who are still unmarried and living with their parents. Young Italians and Japanese are unable to obtain the job security because

> traditional employees enjoy cast-iron protections, so companies are reluctant to create such positions. So, only temporary or part-time work is available for most newcomers to the workplace. Young Japanese and Italians pursue increasingly cautious lifestyles. Nearly 80 percent of unmarried Japanese between the ages of eighteen and thirty-five live with their parents. The ratio is nearly as high in Italy.[5]

Researchers in developed countries believe that the emergence of "adulto-lescents" or "thresholders" (Apter 2001) is tied to the declining effectiveness of socioeconomic and cultural processes that had previously helped young people make the transition to adulthood. Society is increasingly unable to provide youth with the necessary conditions for them to take their places in the adult world (Arnett 2000; Schwartz et al. 2005).

Jeffrey Arnett's concept of emerging adulthood has been criticized for over-emphasizing young people's agency and neglecting the structural and institu-tional constraints that affect their life decisions. Thus, it becomes a middle-class phenomenon in which adultolescents are able to rely on family support; not all young people can afford to indulge in exploring their self-identity. Most seriously, some claim, Arnett's model fails to acknowledge mechanisms of social exclusion in developed societies (Bynner 2005; Jones 2009).

Disadvantaged Youths in the United States and Britain

Young people from poor, working-class, and immigrant families in the developed world cannot afford the luxury of stalling for a few years. Many have no prospects for regular employment and secure livelihoods and are forced to grow up fast to take care of themselves and their families. An impoverished twenty-year-old single mother cannot afford to engage in the self-focused exploration characteristic of emerging adulthood. In the United States she has to scramble to make ends meet through a combination of food stamps and low-paying jobs (Arnett 2004, 22).

Racial-ethnic and class disadvantages compound one another. African American and Latino youths in the United States are much less likely to graduate high school and go on to college than their white and Asian Ameri-can counterparts. They have much greater difficulty finding employment than white youth with similar levels of education. As the *Time* magazine article pointed out, between 1975 and 2002 the average wage for male work-ers aged twenty-five to twenty-nine with a high school diploma declined by 11 percent and the differential between their earnings and those of young men with some college or a degree widened significantly (Grossman 2005). These gaps have a particularly strong effect on inner-city youths of color, who have much higher rates of unemployment than their white counterparts.

In recent decades the United States has incarcerated an unprecedented num-ber of young African American and Latino males. While rates of employment and marriage have been falling, incarceration rates for males have been rising (Furstenberg et al. 1999; Ellwood and Jencks 2004; Fussell and Furstenberg 2005; Wilson 1996). This disheartening trend prompted Becky Pettit and Bruce Western (2004) to suggest that spending time in prison should be considered a "new stage in the life course." Indeed, incarceration has become a normal or expected event in the lives of young inner-city men (Bonczar and Beck 1997; Freeman 1996; Garland 2001). After release, these youths suffer a loss in social status and are shut out of job opportunities. Some criminologists worry that imprisonment delays transitions to adulthood as young men miss out on experiences through which they learn to be responsible for themselves.

Single parenthood and high school dropout rates are highest among African American and Latino youths living in urban environments (Ellwood and Jencks 2004). As Stacey Bosick and Angela Gover point out, these facts show that the conventional markers for the transition to adulthood do not adequately capture the experiences of males coming of age in the inner city (2010, 94). Here youths are trapped in a social environment of systemic failure. Although a few who enjoy unusual family supports and connections with mainstream society manage to break away, the majority remains trapped within the system. In isolated neighborhoods few young men know any adult man who holds a regular job, and few young women know any adult woman who has a stable domestic partnership with the father of her children (Bosick and Gover 2010).

Conditions in Britain are depressingly similar. Here, many of the children and grandchildren of immigrants from the former colonies in Asia, the Caribbean, and Africa are relegated to poverty and confined in densely populated urban or suburban neighborhoods devoid of jobs. As Robert MacDonald and others argue, "Opportunities in youth and final destinations in adulthood are still strongly influenced by an individual's original location in the class structure" (MacDonald et al. 2005, 874). Their study of youths from poor neighborhoods in Britain reveals the pervasive unemployment and underemployment to which many working-class people are now consigned. Few are able to secure long-term employment, and most never move far from their condition of deprivation and hardship (Toynbee 2003; MacDonald and Marsh 2005).

The riots in London and other cities in August 2011 highlighted the socioeconomic disparities within British society. Rioters were not identified by the color of their skin but by their socioeconomic position. These were poor, working-class youths—white, black, and South Asian; Muslim and Christian; children of immigrants and of British-born parents—united in their anger against the establishment symbolized by the police and the affluence that surrounded them. They burned police cars and looted expensive shops. Following the riots, the public has been grappling with these events and trying to understand their underlying causes. Some have blamed widening social inequalities and declining public services, while others have condemned the rioters as antisocial criminals and selfish opportunists.

Theresa May, the Conservative Home Secretary, spoke for many privileged Britons, saying: "There is no excuse for violence. There is no excuse for looters. There is no excuse for thuggery on our streets."

Those who observed the riots from the inside offer another perspective. Chavez Campbell is an eighteen-year-old black man from Wood Green in North London. A promising amateur boxer, he grew up in a single-parent family and has twelve half-brothers and sisters. He was lucky to have found boxing after he dropped out of school at the age of eleven for being involved in a fight. He commented on the August riots in his neighborhood:

> I did see the riots coming and the government should have seen it coming, too. Jobs are hard to get and, when they do become available, youths don't get the jobs. There is nothing to do; they are closing youth clubs so the streets are just crazy. They are full of people who have no ambitions, or have ambitions but can't fulfill them. . . . It doesn't justify it, but they think: "I ain't got no money for this, I ain't got no money for that, I can't get a job but I need it." The only way they are going to get it is stealing. They are going to be ruthless and do anything they can to get it.[6]

Campbell believes that the government must take responsibility for addressing poverty and providing services for youth.

Jay Kast, a recording artist and youth worker living in Newham, East London, sympathized with the rioters' anger, saying that many young people have few prospects and nothing to lose: "Duggan's death was the last straw, but these riots are based on years of tension. . . . I was brought up on the streets of east London. . . . I feel the same anger as these rioters do. A few years ago, I would have been out there rioting with them. It's their pain speaking." Kast explained that in the past he had worked in government-subsidized arts programs to help young people write lyrics, make their own music, and organize musical events. But in the last year the government cut the funding, and all the programs had been shut down. "That was a slap in the face to all the youth. So they just went back out onto the streets, went back to having no hope."[7]

A comment submitted to France 24's *Observers* blog voiced opinions that are common among Britons:

> The core problem is a mix of both white and ethnic races, and they both carry the same set of what I would call genetic failures. They come from homes where there is unemployment and income is based on social benefits. These adolescents are poorly educated, lack

acceptable social skills, have little skills for employment and have effectively been swept under the carpet by successive governments of all political colours. The problem basically is embarrassing, not been robustly addressed. . . . For a wealthy country [like] the UK, this is self-serving greed, short sightedness and unwillingness to accept the problem. Once we accept responsibility, as a country, for the problem then and only then can we start to correct it.[8]

While this commentator went on to criticize the system that favored corporations and financial speculators over the people's welfare and pointed to the pervasive lack of social justice, others blamed the rioters, calling them "spoilt," undisciplined, and self-indulgent. A commentator who took issue with the former educator's social and political analysis contended: "Youth seem to think they have the right to take whatever they want, hurting their own economy, and then they blame the government for not providing enough for them. Many such people have obviously never learned that they must take responsibility for their own actions and life, and part of that is the risk that they will not be able to have all they ever dreamed of."[9]

Theories of youth subcultures would lend insight into the motivations and life experiences of the young people who participated in the riots, as well as the resulting moral panic about youths' rebellious behavior. Unlike the British skinheads, mods, and rockers whose subcultures were studied in the 1960s, all of whom were white and native-born with native-born parents, the underclass youths who took part in the recent riots came from a variety of cultural, ethnic, and racial backgrounds. Yet they shared a common experience of exclusion and alienation from mainstream society. Critics of the subculture approach suggest that subcultures should be seen as loose, flexible, even fluid associations. That seems to have been the case with the young people who participated in the August riots. These actions were undertaken not by gangs or groups with stable, long-term affiliations but by more spontaneous and flexible gatherings.

Young British rioters, like inner-city youths in the United States, stand in stark contrast to the upper-middle-class British and American youths Arnett studied, who are able to rely on parental support while they enjoy a prolonged adolescence. In this case youth in transition to adulthood appear to be suspended in a liminal state (van Gennep 1960; Turner 1969). The lack of social support during this period of indefinite duration leaves young people hanging, enjoying neither the protection of childhood nor the autonomy of adulthood (Barry 2005).

Working-class youths and young people of color in these affluent societies may well have more in common with struggling African youths than they do with middle-class white young people in their own countries. Like those on the periphery, they have no clear prospects for the future and feel they have no stake in society.

The majority of young Africans find themselves in waithood with bleak prospects for the future. Very few can afford a smooth passage into an independent adulthood. Waithood must be better understood in order to design effective support strategies for youth. But young people in contemporary Africa are not waiting for their elders to do something—for educators to offer job-training programs; for parents or relatives to make a place for them in a family enterprise; for public officials to offer them micro-loans to start their own businesses; or for social workers to address their difficulties in forming families and raising children. Instead, young people are working out their own lives and livelihoods on the basis of the resources available to them. In this sense waithood is not a failed transition, a form of deviance, or a pathology from which young people suffer. Rather, it is a new and difficult phase that young people are actively and creatively engaging with in order to find solutions for their everyday problems.

Amid the global economic downturn and deepening poverty and in the context of corruption and bad governance, young Africans today face enormous challenges. The next chapter discusses youth aspirations and explores the structural problems in education and the labor markets that result from unsound economic policies and that have consigned so many youths to waithood.

Chapter 3

Aspirations

Liggey, which means "work" in Wolof, the national language of Senegal, is one of the most notable virtues in Senegalese culture. Liggey is celebrated as an important marker of adulthood because the ability to work and provide defines a person's self-worth and position in the family. This idea prevails in all four countries I studied. Yet, the majority of young men and women are unable to find work and attain a socially valued status as responsible men and women, as well as the sense of dignity embedded in the notion of liggey.

Young people's main aspirations center on obtaining a good education and acquiring skills that can guarantee them long-term employment and stable livelihoods so they can become financially independent and support themselves and others. They have a clear view of the structural conditions that hinder their ability to achieve these goals, particularly the shortcomings of the education system, the high levels of unemployment, and the difficulties in securing stable livelihoods.

The educational and employment opportunities available in Africa today are insufficient to enable young people to fulfill their basic aspirations, particularly in an economic environment marked by rapid technological innovation and globalization, as well as structural adjustment policies that failed to stimulate economic growth and employment and exacerbated poverty. Education systems are unable to provide youth with the tools they need to compete in, or even enter, a labor market that requires high levels of specialized technical skills. While the mismatch between the education system and the needs of the labor market contributes to youth unemployment, the heart of the problem is the unavailability of jobs. Neoliberal economic policies have not been able to revamp African economies and generate much-needed employment. Entrepreneurship is often presented as an alternative to getting a job, particularly in view of the contraction in the labor market. However, young people are not being adequately prepared to become successful entrepreneurs, and very few policies and programs promote and support those who attempt to start their own businesses.

Young Africans today, in contrast to previous generations, are well informed about developments in the rest of the world. New technologies of information and communication facilitate their global reach and make them aware of possibilities beyond their localities, raising their aspirations and creating new expectations. Conversations with young people in wait-hood reveal that they are aware of their predicament. They find themselves caught within the contractions in their societies; their lives are enlarged by the possibilities generated by modernity but simultaneously restricted by the limitations they experience every day.

Young people I interviewed in Mozambique, Senegal, South Africa, and Tunisia were troubled by the daunting difficulties they faced in fulfilling their aspirations. They shared concerns about the limited educational and employment opportunities available to them. In the focus-group discussions I conducted with youths in these four countries, education was one of their main concerns.

Education

African governments have made significant progress in increasing access to primary schools, in part through the United Nations' Millennium Development Goals. While basic education has expanded, its quality has not improved. As Niko, a thirty-eight-year-old South African man, put it, "It is not enough to get children into schools; it is necessary to teach them something useful while they are there." In many countries students spend years in school without learning core competencies that are increasingly necessary in the workplace. In most countries, despite improved enrollment and completion rates, few students are acquiring the skills that would enable them to succeed in the economy.

Globalization has created serious dislocations in labor markets. The development and diffusion of new technologies have accelerated changes in employment patterns that favor skilled over unskilled labor and formal educational preparation over on-the-job training (UNCTAD 2001). Employers demand workers who are capable of critical thinking and problem solving rather than merely following a fixed routine (Fasih 2008). As young people pointed out, these new labor market demands are not being matched by the education system. Curricula and teaching methods have remained largely unchanged rather than keeping pace with transformations in the workplace. Schools have failed to adjust to new technologies and to develop students' technological skills (Al-Samarrai and Bennell 2007).

While young people's aspirations are still focused on obtaining an education that provides them with the skills needed to secure stable employment, they are also grappling with the fact that today some of those who succeed are not well educated; they managed to acquire wealth and power through illicit means. However, many young people I spoke with still believe that their ability to become respected social adults depends primarily on being educated and having stable employment. When considering their educational experiences and outcomes of their training (or lack of training), the young participants in this research highlighted three main areas of concern: (1) the low quality of teaching and learning, (2) the absence of skills-oriented curricula, and (3) social disparities in access to education.

The Low Quality of Teaching and Learning

Low levels of academic attainment are related to the poor quality of teaching, particularly teachers' inadequate knowledge, limited pedagogical ability, and low productivity. Young men and women in Senegal said that many teachers enter the profession by default because no other employment opportunities are available. The profession is undervalued, and its standing is marred by low entrance requirements and poor training. In South Africa, black youths complained about the inadequacy of teachers in township and rural schools. "There are very few experienced and well-trained teachers in township schools, especially in math and science," said Sipho, a twenty-five-year-old in Soweto.

Young Mozambicans believe that the quality of education has decreased in the past decade or so. Maria, a nineteen-year-old who lives in Maputo, stated that "most teachers, especially outside the big cities, are not as well trained scientifically as before. . . . Some teachers do not set as good an example to students because of their behavior. Some sell good grades to students. . . . Those who can afford to pay the teacher will get good grades on their essays." Teachers' low salaries may contribute to their accepting gifts from students whose parents can afford them. Teachers are often forced to supplement their income with private tutorials and encourage their pupils to join the tutorials for a fee. The fact that teachers are underpaid damages their morale and motivation to excel. Teachers' strikes for higher salaries and better working conditions have taken place in many countries. Mamadou, a twenty-six-year-old Senegalese man, explained: "At my university we didn't have lectures for about two months while the professors were on strike. They were demanding better salaries and better housing conditions. The government made many promises to them but did not deliver." Indeed, the demand for quality instruction needs to be linked to the improvement of teachers' wages and working conditions. As several young people pointed out, it is the system that needs to be corrected because teachers, like students, are victims of the system.

UNESCO has acknowledged the challenge of reversing the acute shortage of qualified teachers in Africa. A special report on educational capacity building in Africa acknowledges that "with the teacher crisis, quality has often been a hostage of quantity. The trend is to recruit as many teachers [as possible], even if they do not have the necessary qualifications, in order to respond to expanding enrolment" (UNESCO 2005, 6). Apart from the need to enhance the quality of existing teachers through in-service training, refresher courses, and professional development programs, additional well-qualified teachers will be needed. UNESCO recognizes that teacher education is intrinsically linked to the renewal of school curricula, the improvement of learning outcomes, and the establishment of a positive school environment.

The quality of schools' physical space and amenities also matters. Young people decried the decay of the educational infrastructure. In Alexandra and Soweto in South Africa, youths were very critical of the condition of school buildings in their areas. "We need better schools. In some township schools the walls are falling down. . . . There aren't enough tables and chairs for students; many are broken and do not get repaired," said twenty-five-year-old Kenny from Alexandra. Similarly, in Senegal, schools lacked the basic conditions required to enable teachers and pupils to work properly. "I come from Kaolack, and there are primary schools that do not have enough classrooms, and classrooms are ill equipped," said twenty-four-year-old Ibrahima. In all four countries youths described overcrowded classrooms and crumbling buildings, which are not conducive to teaching and learning. The UK Department for International Development (DFID) estimated in 2009 that about US$30 billion would be necessary to address the shortfall in provision of suitable and safe learning environments in most African countries (Leaths et al. 2009).

Absence of Skills-Oriented Curricula

Curricula do not focus on developing skills that meet current labor market demands. In a situation where educational prerequisites and skill requirements are rising sharply, many graduates are unprepared for the few available jobs. This issue has been the focus of contentious debates among educators, especially at the intermediate and higher levels, about "ability-based" curricula and students' "employability" as employers claim that graduates lack the "transferable skills" required in the workplace. Jonathan, a twenty-four-year-old South African, attested that "many high school courses focus on theory alone and many students are not good in theory. . . . Lack of skills training is a problem because jobs require practical knowledge." In the same vein a thirty-two-year-old Senegalese man, Babacar, commented on how their lack of practical knowledge and experience affects graduates in search of employment: "Our curriculum follows the French tradition and it is very theoretical. . . . It doesn't prepare us adequately for the job market. . . . The first thing employers ask [for] when we look for jobs is practical skills and experience, and we don't have any."

Susana, a twenty-five-year-old Mozambican woman, thinks that students' lack of skills has to do with their schools' lack of resources "to do things properly; education is carried out on the cheap." She elaborated: "We don't have adequate teaching material; books and exercise books are not available for everyone. . . . Students have to copy down or take notes on what the teacher says. There are very few functioning laboratories for science, physics, and computers to help students gain hands-on experience." Domi, a twenty-three-year-old South African man, concurred: "In my school the physics and biology labs were very old and full of dust. . . . Students didn't use them because the chemicals were not up to date and were dangerous. Computer labs were only available for math and business students from grade 10 onwards." These youths were also concerned about the unavailability of internships with businesses.

Technical and vocational training in Africa suffers from a lack of resources and has been unable to provide young people with the skills that businesses demand. In addition, it became too expensive in the context of structural adjustment programs and public spending cuts. Only 2 to 6 percent of education budgets are devoted to this type of education.[1] Skills-development strategies often fall outside donors' priorities. Inadequate investment in vocational education aggravates the mismatch between school curricula and job-market needs. In Mozambique and South Africa the result has been a shift away from technical training, and secondary and vocational schools are struggling to absorb youngsters from primary school (Wegner 2008).

In higher education, attempts to develop a skills-based curriculum and to define and develop transferable skills have failed to yield acceptable and generalizable pedagogical practices (Holmes 2002). The emphasis on the employability of graduates is seen as problematic by those who espouse liberal-humanist values. For example, Jon Gubbay (1994) provides a cogent critique of the employment-related justification for transferable skills. As Len Holmes (2002) points out, however, the divide between vocationalism and liberal humanism has dogged higher education for decades and stands as an obstacle to much-needed curriculum reforms.

This issue is particularly pressing in countries like Tunisia, where the number of graduates has soared. Fully 57 percent of Tunisians entering the labor market today are university educated, and there are many more graduates than the job market has been able to absorb. Tunisian economists Nabil Mâalel and Zouhair El Kadhi believe that this situation is the result of neoliberal policies promoted by the International Monetary Fund and the World Bank. As El Kadhi explains, "The Tunisian government was often more preoccupied with pleasing the international institutions rather than looking at what was good and effective for the country, and the education policy was one such instance. We suddenly started producing an excess of graduates. There were graduate schools everywhere, some of the fields of study were quite unusual, and there are no links between the educational system's outputs and the needs of the labor market."[2]

Social Disparities in Access to Education

Young Mozambicans from poor families often cannot afford to finish their primary education. Some, especially orphans, feel compelled to leave their homes and villages to seek some form of livelihood in the cities. When the intergenerational transfer of resources fails to sustain young people and offer them a path toward the future, they have no choice but to fend for themselves. Their lack of education and skills excludes them from most forms of stable and remunerative work. Uneducated and unemployed, they have no realistic possibility of achieving social adulthood. Andre, a twenty-five-year-old man from Marracuene, near Maputo, explained: "My parents could not afford to keep me in school. It is not my fault that I did not study. I wanted to study but I had no means to remain in school. . . . I needed money to pay for the uniform, school books and stationery." Another young man asserted, "I decided to leave school and try to find work, but it is very hard. I can only survive by doing *biscatos* [odd jobs]."

When incomplete schooling inhibits a youth's entry into the labor force, the result can be chronic joblessness. Unemployment early in a person's working life may permanently impair his or her productivity and employment opportunities (O'Higgins 1997, 2001). Youthful unemployment sets a precedent for exclusion from the workforce that can become a devastating lifelong pattern. Many uneducated young men and women in both urban and rural settings who try to make ends meet by doing precarious and often unsafe jobs are caught in this predicament.

Rural youths who migrate to the cities find themselves on the margins with no secure livelihood. Bettina Holzhausen asserts that it is almost impossible for young men and women to find wage labor in the countryside. The only demand for workers comes from agriculture, which is seasonal; construction, with short-term contracts; and occasional development projects.

Most young people hang around without work from the day they drop out of school. They often wind up engaging in dangerous and dodgy activities such as smuggling, prostitution, and theft in order to earn urgently needed cash.[3] Poverty pushes them out of school to enter a job market that has very little to offer. In this vicious circle, income disparities lead to disparities in educational attainment, which in turn perpetuate and exacerbate income inequalities.

Upward social mobility and better life prospects are among the most important aspirations young people express. They see access to higher levels of education and to secure, long-term employment as the major path toward realizing their dreams. Students from disadvantaged areas and poor social backgrounds have difficulty getting a foothold on the first rungs of this ladder. Although many university graduates also struggle to find jobs, higher education still holds a mystique; it appears to be a precondition for achievement. This issue was hotly debated in focus groups with young black South Africans. Students from the townships have very limited access to good postsecondary education because of their lower matric (high school degree) average. A focus-group member in Alexandra explained: "There is still discrimination based on geography, and somehow based on race. . . . Because of the weak education we get in the township schools, we are unable to have the required grades to enroll in university. The children of people from the northern suburbs [more affluent areas of Johannesburg] who go to good schools are the ones who will become doctors and engineers." Twenty-five-year-old Sipho of Soweto concurred: "White and black and colored middle-class students can more easily have access to university."

A matric endorsement with a minimum of three subjects passed at the higher, rather than standard, grade is required to enroll in a university, and some institutions impose additional requirements. Many high school graduates from township and rural schools are unable to meet those prerequisites. Many township students finish with a standard or lower grade, which can only provide them access to technical schools and diploma programs. In this parallel track students need to be enrolled for nine years to get a qualification equivalent to a master's degree from a university. Many township youths cannot afford the luxury of studying full time for so long because they need to provide for themselves, and often for their families as well. Distance-learning programs, which offer more flexible entry requirements, are an option for some.

Twenty-six-year-old Lindiwe from Soweto finished high school with matric levels that were too low to allow her to enter a regular university. She chose to enroll in a distance-learning university that offers open admission. In 2008 she began a four-year psychology course at the University of

South Africa (UNISA), but due to financial constraints she is only able to take one or two subjects a year. Subjects cost R860 (about US$120) each, and students can take them at their own pace. Over three years Lindiwe has been able to complete only six subjects, but she has not lost hope and expects to finish her course eventually. Her applications for state grants were unsuccessful. Some grants are available, but the competition is stiff. "I know of people who got exemptions to enter the university, but the fees were very high and they didn't manage to get bursaries; there aren't enough bursaries or loan schemes available for students. Black students are not accessing universities as they would desire," said thirty-five-year-old Robert of Troyeville. Lindiwe tries to finance her course by saving the money she makes from short-term shelf-packing jobs in supermarkets and retail stores. Sometimes her grandmother and father provide a bit of support, but she is struggling to keep up with her payment schedule. Lindiwe says, "My financial situation affects the quality of my learning as I cannot keep going with the regularity the course requires; sometimes I have to interrupt for lack of resources."

With the problems in their schools compounded by imbalances in the educational system, it is no wonder that black students coming out of township high schools are unable to reach performance levels comparable to those of students in the best public (Model C[4]) or private schools. In September 2010 the Congress of South Africa Trade Unions (COSATU) suggested a wide range of reforms to make the education system more equitable, including the elimination of the three-tiered structure of secondary education that distinguishes among private institutions, Model C public schools, and ordinary public schools. It called for the redistribution of resources toward ordinary public schools in working-class and poor communities in the townships.[5]

Youth Unemployment

In Africa, rates of unemployment and underemployment are extremely high among youth. Although the gross domestic product grew significantly in many countries in the early 2000s and the continent enjoyed an average annual growth rate of 6 percent in 2006, economic expansion did not translate into significant job creation and opportunities for young people. Reliable youth unemployment statistics for Africa are not available, and the figures that do exist offer little insight into the impact of unemployment on young people in waithood. Major international and country-based censuses and surveys apply the definitions of youth used by the United Nations and the World Bank—men and women aged between fifteen and twenty-four—and focus predominantly on those searching for jobs in the formal economy. This definition is problematic because in many African countries the category "youth" may include individuals up to the age of thirty-five. For the sake of comparability with international statistics, the data leave out a significant number of young people. Moreover, people over thirty-five increasingly have also been unable to attain the conventional markers of adulthood; with no jobs, they are unable to marry and raise a family. Finally, beyond the scope of official employment statistics, many young men and women fend for themselves on the margins of the formal economy. Even some youths within the fifteen-to-twenty-four age bracket escape official statistics because they search for work in the informal sector. Women in particular are more likely to work in casual labor and petty trading, as the flexibility of the informal economy allows them to combine wage work with their household duties (UNECA 2005).

Waithood is an important concept for understanding the position of contemporary African youth, whose problems are not primarily located within chronological age categories but rather in the reality of their lived experiences. If what defines an adult is his or her ability to be independent and care for others, then many young Africans today are unable to become adults at all. Because so many youths are in this situation for extended periods, waithood is not the exception but is quickly becoming the norm, however uncomfortable it is. It is imperative that both the international community and national governments recognize young people in waithood and move away from statistics that distort reality. In doing so, they will be in a better position to address the problems faced by contemporary youth.

In many African countries the majority of young people is engaged in the informal economy, while only a very small proportion holds jobs in the formal economy, some as informal workers in formal businesses. Young men and women are found along the streets of major cities selling fruit, prepaid telephone cards, small electronic gadgets, and a variety of other goods. According to the International Labour Organization (ILO), rates of labor-force participation differ significantly by gender, as young women have more difficulty getting jobs than young men (Okojie 2003; ILO 2007, 2010). Young women work predominantly in the informal sector, as hairdressers, dressmakers, traders, domestic workers, and the like. For lack of better opportunities, some engage in prostitution, while others migrate or are trafficked abroad.

In discussing the challenges of youth employment, young people underscored three key contributing factors: (1) unsound economic policies,

(2) university graduates' unemployment and underemployment, and (3) inadequate support for youth entrepreneurship.

Unsound Economic Policies

"Jobless growth isn't just bad social policy, it is bad economics," stated Juan Somavia, director-general of the ILO, in a 2006 meeting.[6] Many analysts believe that the current economic situation in Africa results from the neoliberal economic policies promoted by the World Bank and the International Monetary Fund (Rogerson 1997; Potts 2000). Structural adjustment meant shifting policies to favor the market and the private sector, as well as removing trade barriers favoring local producers. These economic reforms exacerbated job losses in the private sector as well as the public sector, and more people had to resort to the informal economy. Christian Rogerson (1997) has demonstrated that the escalation of unemployment across urban Africa is directly associated with the implementation of structural adjustment policies in the 1990s. In 1997 the ILO painted a very gloomy picture of the employment situation:

> The development of productive employment has not kept pace with increased labour supply. In Africa, we find a rapidly increasing labour force . . . together with declining or stagnating levels of wage employment, decreasing real wages and deteriorating working and living conditions. . . . Unemployment and underemployment rates are increasing rapidly, with average urban unemployment rates on the continent having almost doubled over the past 15 years. . . . Youth unemployment remains critical with a majority of school leavers unable to find productive employment. (ILO 1997, 2)

Christina Gladwin (1991) contends that structural adjustment reforms led by the World Bank and International Monetary Fund in Africa failed to stimulate economic growth. Their excessive macroeconomic focus emphasized national and international approaches and paid little attention to the microeconomic realities at the district and village levels. Trade liberalization policies encouraged the wider circulation of goods and services and led to the replacement of domestically produced goods by cheaper imports, seriously affecting local production. In the same vein Firoze Manji (2011) observed that structural adjustment programs barred African states from investing in social infrastructure and in sectors such as education and healthcare. They also forced the privatization of public goods, which became controlled by oligopolies (Manji 2011).

In 2001 the Youth Employment Network was formed as a global alliance of the World Bank, the United Nations, and the ILO to focus on job creation, employability, entrepreneurship, and equal opportunities for youth. One of the key recommendations of this network is that governments diversify their economies in order to promote sectors that help enlarge the productive base and improve young people's access to the labor market. In countries like Mozambique, however, the economy still relies on primary commodities and has not branched out into processing those commodities or engaging in manufacturing that would employ more workers.

Following the creation of the Youth Employment Network, the three main organizations issued reports declaring youth employment a top development priority.[7] The World Bank's *World Development Report: Development and the Next Generation* (2007) generated considerable media and public policy attention. Adopting a human capital approach that defined the main objective as ensuring that youth become productive citizens who contribute to economic development, the report analyzed five transitions—learning, going to work, staying healthy, forming families, and exercising citizenship—to assess how effectively societies are developing young people's potential. "If made well, decisions about these transitions will develop, safe-guard, and properly deploy human capital. If made badly, the consequences will be very costly to correct because dropping out of school, prolonged periods of unemployment, or risky health behaviors can leave permanent scars" (World Bank 2007, 5). Health and education are narrowly defined without reference to broader social and economic policies that affect youth.

Critics of this human capital approach emphasize that neoliberal reforms have imposed tremendous constraints on young people's choices that such programs do not address. Sangeeta Kamat pointed out that after two decades of advocating divestment from public education and health services in developing countries, writing a report "that advocates for health and education needs of young people . . . is . . . a slogan with no mandate" (2007, 1216). The report identifies access to information to make reasonable choices as the main area of intervention and does not discuss the provision of services. This approach is consistent with the "neoliberal framework that emphasizes personal responsibility over public provision" and favors private initiative over state-organized programs (Kamat 2007, 1216). Similarly, Mayssoun Sukarieh and Stuart Tannock (2008) criticize the new focus on youth as a marketing tool to promote neoliberal interests. They argue that "youth employment moves front and centre. . . . Get youth a job, the argument goes, any job really, and we are on our way to resolving all other social and political conflicts and problems. A parallel is constructed between the health of youth and the greater prosperity of business. . . . Youth, finally, are remade as complete neoliberal subjects; indeed, the standard bearers of a brave new market society" (Sukarieh and Tannock 2008, 306–7).

Most African governments embraced structural adjustment policies uncritically and failed to promote policies that increased economic growth and protected the most vulnerable sectors of the population. Recent economic policies have proved unable to lower unemployment and improve youths' employment prospects. Mozambican economist Carlos Nuno Castel-Branco, director of the Institute for Social and Economic Studies in Maputo, has stated that government efforts to address record-high unemployment are falling short. The economic development plan being implemented by the Mozambican government is built around mega-projects focused on commodities and mineral resources that "do not contribute to widening the productive base and have little or no impact on job creation and poverty reduction."[8] This development model facilitates the rapid consolidation of a national elite rather than meeting the needs of the Mozambican people (Castel-Branco 2010). The popular uprisings against rises in the prices of fuel, food, and transport that that took place in Maputo in February 2008 and September 2010 demonstrated young people's discontent with these unsound economic approaches.[9]

The situation is similar in Tunisia, where the fruits of economic growth have not been evenly distributed (Ben Romdhane 2011; Ben Hammouda 2012). Neoliberal economic policies adopted by the old regime of Ben Ali led to a pattern of uneven development that marginalized the central, western, and southern regions of the country and concentrated wealth in the northern and eastern coastal regions. These policies resulted in lower wages and job insecurity and failed to generate enough jobs to employ young people entering the work force. According to Tunisian economist Hakim Ben Hammouda, the World Bank and the International Monetary Fund praised Tunisia's development model because it encouraged foreign investment, created a flexible workforce, and lowered taxes on businesses (2012).

In Senegal youth represent more than half of all job seekers, most of them concentrated in Dakar. Almost everywhere in the continent, struggling rural youths migrate to the cities even though youth unemployment is generally higher in urban than in rural areas (Sarr 2000, 2004).[10] Economist Mamadou Ndione describes the labor force as a pyramid missing its middle: "At the top of the pyramid is a small group of highly qualified people and at the bottom we have a mass of people with few or no qualifications. In the middle, there is a big gap."[11] Ndione thinks that policies aimed at addressing this problem would need to prioritize professional and technical training and create stronger synergies with the labor market in order to fill this gap.

The 2011 South African National Treasury discussion paper *Confronting Youth Unemployment* recognizes the magnitude of the challenge: "South Africa has an acute problem of youth unemployment. . . . Young people are not acquiring the skills or experience needed to drive the economy forward. This inhibits the country's economic development and imposes a larger burden on the state to provide social assistance."[12] The government's program for 2011–12 includes measures to increase job creation and improve young people's education and skills to make them more employable. Recognizing that "these interventions will take time," the report recommends offering employers a subsidy to reduce the financial costs and potential risks of young workers' low productivity, making "the training of young workers more affordable." It also suggests modest direct assistance to job-seekers (South Africa National Treasury 2011, 7, 33). The effectiveness of these new policies in addressing the severe employment problems experienced by young South Africans remains to be seen.

Given the magnitude of the problem, some observers believe that "creating opportunities for the burgeoning number of youth is a challenge that cannot be solved only at the country level. Regional integration policies that expand the opportunity space by increasing the size of economies and markets will be critical" (Kararach, Hanson, and Léautier 2011, 1). While young people will need different kinds of training to become entrepreneurs, job creation is fundamental. Indeed, some analysts believe that, given the current youth bulge in Africa, job creation is the key to resolving youth unemployment and underemployment. More jobs are needed in the areas young people have already been trained for, such as social services and industry. Moreover, the increase of jobs in sectors such as agriculture, trade, and small-scale manufacturing will support the self-creation of more stable livelihoods by young people (Hanlon and Smart 2008). Bringing about this sort of job growth demands more appropriate economic policies by national governments and international institutions.

University Graduates' Unemployment and Underemployment

Recently the face of unemployment in Africa has changed, affecting well-educated as well as undereducated young people. Youths who graduate from secondary schools and universities no longer have an advantage in securing employment; their chances of finding jobs are hampered by the poor quality and academic orientation of their education as well as by the limitations of the labor market. Rates of unemployment and underemployment among university graduates have risen exponentially across the continent over the past decade. The increasing unemployment of well-educated youths, especially university graduates, signals the breakdown of the system. Many young people echo the comment of Tarik, a twenty-seven-year-old Tunisian man: "Before, all you needed to do to be somebody was to go to school, study and then get a job." Now, a degree no longer guarantees access to employment. As twenty-year-old Sagar from Senegal observed: "Today the diploma does not have the same importance it had before. Before, people with university degrees were well regarded socially because of the positions they occupied in society, which came from the jobs they could hold. Today that is gone; a university graduate and someone with no education are in the same boat."

Focusing solely on joblessness does not adequately depict the problems youth face in the labor market because many are underemployed (Cling et al. 2007; Fares et al. 2006). A significant proportion of employed youth hold jobs that do not utilize their level of education; they work part time, are paid very little, and have few opportunities for advancement. Indeed, the recent economic crisis has been strongly felt by those who have kept their jobs but are working shorter hours at reduced wages. Tebogo, a thirty-year-old South African, holds a high school degree and is currently working as a customer-service agent at a major retail store. He has been at his job for four years, but he only works four days a week. Tebogo believes that he has been "discriminated [against] because my manager brings in new people and asks me to train them . . . and then they are promoted and earn more than I do."

In Tunisia, unemployment and underemployment among university graduates skyrocketed during the last decade. Indeed, the situation was so dire that unemployed graduates were at the forefront of the revolution that toppled the regime. Tunisian economist Nabil Mâalel pointed out that the problem is aggravated by the absence of foreign investment in the private sector, which would have helped absorb a trained work force. The state remains the main employer, and the public sector has been the only avenue for secure work. Official estimates put the overall unemployment rate at 14 percent in 2008, but 19 percent among those aged twenty to twenty-four and 30 percent among recent graduates (World Bank 2008b). Young female graduates have more trouble finding jobs than their male counterparts. Following the Tunisian revolution, new data revealed a recent dramatic rise in youth unemployment to 45 percent in 2009 (Paciello 2011). Yet even these figures may underestimate the extent of youth unemployment, as they do not include many of those who, after failing to find work, entered the informal economy or migrated to Europe.

The African Development Bank sees the upward trend in unemployment among university graduates as the consequence of the youth bulge, the rapid expansion of universities, and the mismatch between the demand for and supply of skilled workers (AfDB 2011). But I would add to that list the incapacity of the global economy to generate more jobs. The reality is that even graduates who specialized in technical fields have been unable to find positions. In Senegal, graduates from technical institutes should have fewer difficulties in the job market, but there simply are not enough jobs. Technical institutes focus on business and telecommunications, and the demand for skilled workers in these areas remains quite limited. "That exacerbates the graduate employment problem," said Walid, a twenty-seven-year-old Senegalese man. Moreover, university graduates lack the skills required for lower-level jobs.

Unemployment and underemployment also constitute a serious problem for graduates in Mozambique. Those who finished high school and university degrees hoping to improve their lives have been disappointed, because their education did not lead to careers. "Shoe-shining in Maputo's luxurious Rovuma Hotel is not a job Miguel Munguambe ever imagined doing when he left college with a journalism diploma," writes Maura Quatorze. Munguambe was employed for a while as a reporter at a state-owned magazine but was laid off when it was privatized. He was unable to earn a living from freelancing, so when all else failed, he took up shoe shining. "As he polishes his Swedish client's smart leather shoes, Munguambe discusses the Mozambican economy and the recent depreciation of the country's currency. He sees his current job as a temporary opportunity to earn money and meet new people; and as a chance to discuss current affairs and come up with ideas for stories." He needs to shine up to ten pairs of shoes every morning to earn about the equivalent of US$210 a month, but he continues to freelance for newspapers whenever he can in order to supplement his monthly income and support his family.[13]

A critical concern regarding unemployment among educated youths is the issue of professional experience. Employers tend to regard young graduates as inexperienced and unskilled job-seekers who are a risky investment. Employers consider entry-level wages too high relative to the risk of hiring inexperienced workers. The situation turns into a vicious circle. Nolwazi, a thirty-year-old South African woman, complained: "Getting jobs is very difficult because most industries and companies require years of experience, and where can we get experience? We have to start somewhere. . . . Because we are not given the opportunity to enter the job market properly, we will always have this problem with experience and never get proper employment."

After repeatedly failing to find a job, significant numbers of young people become discouraged and stop looking for work, dropping out of the formal labor force. A survey by the UNECA reveals that 39 percent of unemployed young people have given up actively searching for a job. Nearly half of them said there were no opportunities in their localities, and a quarter said they could not afford transportation to other places (UNECA 2005). Thirty-one-year-old Ntembisa of Soweto explained:

> It is a major challenge to search for a job. You need money to travel everyday into the city to see what is available. . . . A ride from Soweto to Jo'burg is about R20 [US$2.50], and depending where you are in Soweto the ride could cost more than that. . . . You also need money to put together the documents, like CV, criminal records, etc. . . . Then you have to print and photocopy all documents and post or deliver them.

After going through this process several times the potential worker can still end up with no job. Those whom economists call "discouraged workers," who have been unemployed for so long that they have stopped actively looking for work, are generally excluded from official unemployment statistics (Downes 1998).

Many young people feel that jobs are awarded not on the basis of applicants' qualifications but through nepotism and corruption. When only a few openings exist, personal connections matter at least as much as credentials and skills. Young people concurred that this situation was unfair. Malik, a twenty-two-year-old Senegalese man, protested indignantly that "there are privileged youths who manage to get good jobs because their father knows someone important who opens doors. . . . There is a lot of nepotism in Senegal. We don't put the right person in the right place." Niko, a young South African man, had similar views: "Nowadays you need to know the right people to be able to get a job. There is a lot of favoritism and nepotism. There is also corruption, bribery and some people pay money to be put ahead of others for a job." In Mozambique, twenty-seven-year-old Carlos said: "People in human resources of companies that advertise good jobs make a lot of money from young job-seekers desperate to find work. . . . Depending on the type of position advertised, just to make the short list you may have to pay up to 50,000MT [about US$1,700]. And after doing so you have no guarantees that you will get an interview."

Political affiliations matter as well. Some young South Africans mentioned that being a member of the ANC Youth League and knowing party leaders helps, because patrimonial politics still plays an important role. Brandon, a twenty-five-year-old colored[14] man, described his predicament: "I finished a BA at Wits [Witwatersrand University] last year. I have been looking for a job since then, but I cannot find anything. . . . I am not a member of the ANC Youth League and I don't have any important connections so my chances are very low." Fiona, a twenty-one-year-old white female student at Witwatersrand University, saw the problem quite differently: "Jobs are for black and colored people [who were] disadvantaged during apartheid; that's what we, white people, are told when we look for jobs. I am surprised that they [black and colored youths] too can't get jobs. . . . Young whites, especially males, have less job opportunities, which is unfair because we did not experience apartheid nor contribute to it, [so] why are we being penalized? We should all be in the same position and the person's qualifications should be the main criterion" for hiring. The bitter legacy of apartheid is still visible and affects the ways people from different backgrounds think and interact.

Inadequate Support for Youth Entrepreneurship

Unemployed youths could benefit from training in entrepreneurial skills and from public support, especially credit schemes to promote their business ventures. All four countries have some governmental programs to support youth entrepreneurship. While the availability and effectiveness of these schemes vary, young people were critical of the way they are run as well as of their failure to produce results.

During the Ben Ali regime in Tunisia, young entrepreneurs could receive credits from the Tunisian Solidarity Bank (BTS). According to French sociologist Beatrice Hibou (2006), who has analyzed the political economy of repression in Tunisia, the government established the BTS in the mid-1990s to facilitate the development of small enterprises and expand employment. The scheme quickly became an instrument for political control, however, with credit lines being offered to members of the ruling party, the Constitutional Democratic Rally (RCD), often without any expectation of an adequate return. In 2000 the National Employment Fund was established to reduce graduate unemployment (Kallander 2011). After finishing their university degrees, young people wanting to start small businesses were encouraged to apply for microcredit from the BTS at very competitive interest rates (Hibou 2006). According to some young people I interviewed, this scheme was subject to corruption. Nassir, a thirty-one-year-old man from Tozeur, pointed out, "This could have been a good thing, but these BTS funds had strings attached . . . because you had to be from the RCD, or be willing to sign up to the RCD, in order to benefit." Beatrice Hibou concludes, "Young people are reluctant to join the party . . . which suggests that, more than disaffection, there is a real rejection of that framework, which they feel is heavy and outdated and ineffective for obtaining full employment" (Hibou 2006, 233). The Tunisian Solidarity Bank became an instrument of the state used for political control and clientelism. Access to funding and to public and private sector jobs became tightly controlled by those connected to the regime (Goldstone 2011; Kallander 2011; Paciello 2011).

In 1996 the Senegalese government established the National Agency for Youth Employment (ANEJ in French) to promote better links between young people looking for jobs and employers, but the agency has had no impact on the situation of young unemployed people. Babou Faye, the deputy director, said that although its mission is clear, the agency lacks the resources to perform its functions effectively.[15] The government also established the National Fund for the Promotion of Youth (FNPJ in French) to foster young entrepreneurs through microcredits. The young people I met in Senegal affirmed that the fund has not been successful. "It appears to be a political instrument to entice young people into politics," said twenty-year-old Mussa from Liberté. Sadikh, a twenty-seven-year-old man from Thiés, added: "In my opinion, the director of the FNPJ doesn't have the qualifications to run that agency. . . . He has done nothing to help youth. . . . I heard of many people who submitted micro-projects to the agency and never got any response, let alone a positive response. . . . I have never seen or heard of any projects funded by the FNPJ among us [poor people]. . . . It is all for them, those in power . . . and their friends."

Many people I spoke with in Mozambique mentioned that the government has been advocating self-employment and entrepreneurship for youth. But, twenty-eight-year-old Joel stated, "There are no clear policies, and there are no strategies to train and prepare young people to become good and successful entrepreneurs." After the youth-led riots of September 2010, the Mozambican government decided to extend its decentralization grant of 7 million MT (about US$250,000) previously allocated to rural districts to urban districts (Hanlon and Smart 2008).[16] Although the grants were not specifically directed toward youth, the crisis faced by youth in the cities and their potential as a destabilizing force in the country prompted this shift. Young people from the advocacy groups I met in Maputo criticized the lack of transparency in the allocation of the "7 million" funding. In the capital, despite intense lobbying by civil society organizations including the National Youth Council, the Youth Observatory, and the Youth Parliament and support from the Frelimo Youth League (OJM), only a tiny fraction of the grants were allocated to promote youth entrepreneurship. Many youths doubted that such a small amount would make a real difference.

In South Africa affirmative action policies aimed at redressing the imbalances created by apartheid remain controversial. The Black Economic Empowerment (BEE) program was launched by the government in 2003 to provide previously disadvantaged groups—black Africans, coloreds, and

Indians—with economic opportunities from which they had been excluded. The program was aimed at fostering employment equity, skills development, business ownership and management, and preferential procurement. To implement these policies, the government passed the Broad Based Black Economic Empowerment (BBBEE) Act, which also included white women and disabled people among the disadvantaged. The young people I spoke with in South Africa were very disappointed with these policies because they do not see any new opportunities being opened for them. They believe they have benefited only a few black and colored people and Indians, some of whom quickly became millionaires; the benefits have not trickled down to the masses.

Robert, a thirty-five-year-old black man living in Troyeville, contended that "black economic empowerment policies have only benefited a small group in the political elite. . . . There has been an alliance between BEE and the old white South African capital. . . . After the end of apartheid the black political elite started to get access to capital, to a share of the resources previously held exclusively by white people. . . . This process, however, was not extended to the majority." Lindiwe, a young woman from Soweto, shared this opinion: "Black economic empowerment is not working for the majority of South Africans that need it. You need to know someone well placed to have the opportunity to be upgraded by BEE policies. There is nepotism, because they favor their brothers and sisters, their children and friends rather than opening the tenders fairly to everyone who deserves to be promoted. I don't know of anyone in my area who benefited from BEE."

Critics point out that affirmative-action policies, while necessary, have not been implemented to the benefit of the black majority. Many whites think that the government should prioritize equality of qualification and emphasize secondary and higher education for previously disadvantaged youth, which would allow businesses to hire those with the best qualifications and most experience. This debate is still ongoing in a society that is struggling to rid itself of racial discrimination and the legacy of apartheid.

Surviving in the Informal Economy

Young Africans in waithood are striving to become financially independent and improve their lives. The traditional markers of what it means to be an adult no longer hold, and the societal systems that were in place in the past to mediate youth transitions have disappeared. As Joel, a twenty-eight-year-old resident of Maputo, explained: "At the age of eighteen our fathers would go to South Africa as labor migrants to work in the mines . . . [and] come home with enough money to pay *lobolo* [bridewealth] for a girl. They would then go back for another contract and return with more money to build a house and pay for the wedding and other family expenses." Becoming a labor migrant was a rite of passage into adulthood, as work in the mines provided the resources the young men from southern Mozambique needed to become workers, husbands, fathers, and providers for their families, as well as taxpayers and contributors to the wider society.

Today, however, society no longer endows young men and women with the social, economic, cultural, and moral resources they need to follow robust pathways to adulthood. The structural adjustment policies promoted by the World Bank and the International Monetary Fund in Africa failed to promote economic growth and job creation; on the contrary, they exacerbated poverty and unemployment. While it is true that the quality of the educational systems needs to be strengthened and should complement labor-market needs, the key issue is the lack of enough jobs. While society continues to encourage young people to excel at school, their efforts are not being matched with access to employment. Lindiwe, the South African young woman who is struggling to cover the costs of the psychology course at UNISA, has no guarantees that at the end of her studies she will be able to get a job; most likely, she will become another unemployed graduate. The solution to youth unemployment depends on job creation. Without more jobs, even well-trained graduates will remain unemployed.

Because of its pervasiveness and long duration, waithood is not a mere transition to another stage of life but is gradually becoming a major stage in people's lives. Unable to rely on their elders or their governments, they must develop coping strategies for themselves. In view of the impossibility of obtaining work in the formal economy or support for entrepreneurial ventures, young people see themselves being pushed to the margins. Eking out a livelihood in the informal economy becomes their only option.

The informal sector of the economy includes a wide range of small-scale economic activities carried out by individuals and families that aim at their immediate survival. It differs from large-scale development activities sponsored by the state or by private corporations (Cross 2000). Keith Hart argued that these activities, denigrated marginal or black market, should be seen as entrepreneurial and are a potential source of development (Hart 1970). The ILO defined the informal sector primarily in terms of its small size and low capitalization (Sethuraman 1981). The informal economy comprises all forms of employment without social protection, including self-employment in small unregistered enterprises and wage employment in unprotected jobs (Chen 2006).

The dichotomy between the formal and informal economy has been at the core of modern political economy and is one of the tenets of neoliberalism.

As many authors have shown, however, it constitutes a false dichotomy because of the many and diverse interconnections that exist between the two. Analysts agree that a more nuanced approach to the relationship between formal and informal economic activities is needed, especially in light of the policy failures brought about by structural adjustment programs that characterized the informal as "disorganized" and chaotic (Cross 2000; Guha-Khasnobis et al. 2006; Chen 2006).

Debates about the informal economy have crystallized into three dominant schools of thought: dualism, structuralism, and legalism. Dualist scholars argue that informal units and activities operate independently and have few links with the formal economy, so they constitute a distinct and separate sector in which workers are disadvantaged (Sethuraman 1976; Tokman 1978). Structuralism, by contrast, recognizes that the informal and formal economies are intrinsically linked. Firms in the formal economy can reduce their costs through informal production and employment relationships with subordinated economic units and workers from the informal sector; the informal economy provides capitalism with cheap labor, goods, and services (Moser 1978; Portes et al. 1989). The legalist approach focuses on the relationship between informal entrepreneurs and enterprises and the formal regulatory environment and acknowledges that capitalist interests collude with government to set the "rules of the game" (De Soto 1989). Given the heterogeneity of the informal economy, there is some truth in each of these perspectives (Chen 2006). In analyzing the activities that young people carry out in the informal economy, the structuralist approach helps us to understand their linkages with the formal economy, even though they are located on its margins.

Amid the myriad difficulties that they confront every day, young Africans find opportunities for creativity as they fend for themselves. They are not sitting at home and crying over their sorrows; they are struggling to survive and even succeed as best they can. Neglected by the state and rejected by the formal sector of the economy, they carve out new spaces and improvise survival strategies in subcultures outside hegemonic structures. The next chapter explores the everyday actions that young men and women undertake to cope with waithood.

Chapter 4

Getting By

Young Africans adopt a range of survival strategies to cope with waithood. They identify, explore, and try to maximize whatever opportunities they can find in a constant effort to improve their daily lives. Their responses to their predicament vary considerably and are linked to their particular structural positions, which affect the resources they can leverage to lift themselves out of the situations they inhabit. By improvising diverse income-generating activities, some young people manage to sustain themselves and even improve their living conditions, while others continue to flounder as they pursue one *biscato* (odd job) after another.

Keeping in mind the linkages between the formal and informal sectors of the economy, I examine a wide range of survival strategies adopted by young Africans in waithood, from cross-border trading by Mozambicans and Tunisians and the shelf-packing and merchandising jobs of South Africans to dangerous attempts by Senegalese and Tunisians to reach European shores. Most of these activities are entirely located in the informal sector, while some take place on the periphery of the formal sector. The activities and stories presented in this chapter are those of the particular groups of the young men and women I encountered in the field, and they represent only a cross-section of the myriad economic activities in which young people are engaged as they pursue livelihoods.

Despite inadequate educational preparation and a chronic lack of employment, most African youths have not given up their aspirations. Rather than succumbing to passivity, they are constantly on the alert for opportunities, consciously plan possible scenarios, and resourcefully take action in pursuit of a livelihood. Despite their vulnerable and precarious position, these youths seek—and often find—ways of earning money without necessarily being drawn into illegal activities.

The words they use to describe their strategies emphasize the element of improvisation involved in coping with the limitations they face.

Mozambicans use the Portuguese expression *desenrascar a vida* (eke out a living) to characterize their way of life. Tunisians and Senegalese evoke the French term *débrouillage* (making do). South Africans speak of "just getting by" or "trying to get by" to express the same idea. The sense of making it up as they go and of relying on their own wits underlies this terminology.

The majority of young people in waithood are pushed out of the system and forced to survive on the margins of society. Rejected by the state and the formal sector of the economy, they create new spaces and mechanisms for survival and operate in subcultures outside hegemonic structures. Their relationship with the state and the formal sector is marked by tension and mutual distrust. The state enforces laws that delimit and control the space of legitimate activity and mark them as outsiders. Police and municipal officers harass and chase vendors off the streets. Employers often refuse to sign contracts, making young people into informal workers in the formal sector who are subject to their superiors' whims and who fear instant dismissal. Educated youths find themselves without jobs or relegated to the low end of the professional scale. Other expedients are seen as dangerous or outside the law.

We know surprisingly little about the complex subcultures that emerge among people in waithood. They are often located in the interstices of legal and illegal activities in which petty crime, tax evasion, bribery, and swindling flourish and the boundaries between cleverness and crime become blurred. Some people violate the law by engaging in cross-border smuggling. But as those who have analyzed the informal economy have pointed out, we must distinguish between criminal activities and what in the United States is known as "hustling," which often mimics the socially valued and amply rewarded activities of Wall Street bankers. While production and employment arrangements in the informal economy are often semi-legal or extra-legal, most informal workers produce and distribute legal goods and services. Part of the informal economy, however, operates illegally and deals in forbidden goods and services (Cross 2000; Chen et al. 2004).

Cross-Border Trading and Smuggling

Young people carry on cross-border trading in many African countries. This self-employment strategy requires an initial investment to make the trip and purchase the goods as well as a network of wholesalers in the foreign country. These ventures are risky because goods may be confiscated at the border when traders try to evade customs duties on imports. Traders must establish ties with reliable partners, especially customs officials, who will facilitate the safe transit of goods in exchange for money or other gifts.

This section discusses two cases of cross-border trading. In Mozambique young women travel to neighboring South Africa and Swaziland to buy products for resale in local markets. This activity is known as *mukhero*, a term that refers to the low-level tax evasion practiced by small and middling traders. Young Tunisian men carry on similar trading activities by going to Algeria and Libya and smuggling goods back into the country.

Mukhero: Young Women's Survival Strategies in Maputo

In Mozambique, *mukhero* commonly involves clothing, shoes, beauty products, foodstuffs, and alcoholic drinks. With the end of the war in Mozambique in 1992, many people ventured across the border to the small kingdom of Swaziland, just a couple of hours away from Maputo, to bring back goods for sale. With the end of apartheid South Africa became the most important market for Mozambicans. Recently the trade has been extended to such distant places as Brazil, Thailand, India, and China.

Mukhero is predominantly carried on by women who buy merchandise abroad at relatively low cost to resell to local traders or in market stalls, beauty salons, or their homes. The figure of the *mukherista*, a woman who engages in *mukhero*, is well known in southern Mozambique, especially in urban areas. The business appears to be lucrative, because Maputo does not have enough retail stores offering medium- and high-quality clothing. Middle-income people who are unable to travel abroad to shop appreciate the convenience of buying foreign goods locally. Several young women in Mozambique see *mukhero* as a strategy for making a living amid massive unemployment and economic uncertainty. As Mena, a twenty-nine-year-old who lives in Maputo, put it to me, "If you ask girls from the suburbs [poor neighborhoods] of Maputo, many will tell you that they would like to become *mukheristas*." Many are able to thrive or at least sustain themselves and provide for their families through this business.

At the age of thirty-two, Maria has been a *mukherista* for more than seven years. She is a single mother of two children and lives in Maputo. She first worked for a television company and then in the administrative offices of the government district located slightly less than forty miles outside Maputo. She decided to give up that job because of the long commute and low pay. She makes more money through *mukhero* selling the clothes she buys at wholesale stores in South Africa and Swaziland. "Initially I would just buy any clothes and hope that people would like them. But then I started getting a better sense of what people needed or liked most. . . . Now I only purchase by order." Maria also sells Tupperware for a Swazi company. When the business is good, her profits from customers are augmented by monetary gifts from the company. Maria offers credit, and most customers make their payments on time. The biggest problem she faces is at the border, where customs officers often demand bribes. She explains, "I use the border a lot, and I have to keep things running smoothly and, you know, being a woman doing business is not easy." She attempts to avoid import duties: "I take off all the tags, and I separate the clothes into various bags so that only one small bag has tagged clothes that I pay for." Two years ago Maria enrolled in night school on a three-year degree program in public administration, and she pays her school fees with the money from her business.

The story of Anita, a thirty-three-year-old mother of two who lives on the outskirts of Maputo, illustrates the advantages of *mukhero*. She dropped out of high school when she became pregnant; she had never been taught about birth control. After the birth of her child, she was unable to find employment and ended up illegally crossing the border to South Africa, where she got a series of odd jobs, the last one in a night club. She left her son with her parents and sent money home for him, but after three years she returned to Mozambique and opened a hair salon in her neighborhood. Then she decided to start a *mukhero* business selling clothes and shoes bought in South Africa. She preferred to travel by train, because passengers were not thoroughly searched by customs officials at the border. Anita managed to bring in large suitcases without paying import taxes. She made substantial profits; in just two trips she doubled her initial investment. Today, with the new highway between Maputo and the South African city of Witbank, most people travel by car or bus, and it is more difficult to enter the country with big loads without paying import duties. Anita found the process of crossing the border with the merchandise very stressful, so she hired people to make the trip for her. With the money she saved, Anita opened a small bar in her neighborhood and now spends her time managing the beauty salon, the bar, and the *mukhero* business. Despite the illegal nature of her cross-border trading, she exemplifies the successful entrepreneur.

Alda, a twenty-eight-year-old mother of two, travels three times a month to the South African city of Durban, where she buys clothes to sell to clients in Maputo. She began trading in 2004 after seeking work in vain. "Life was difficult. I had to feed my children," she explained. "The journey to Durban is very long, about eight hours. We buy bread and juice on the road or prepare a little *mangungo* [a meal packed at home]." Alda prefers to shop in Durban because she finds the nearby city of Nelspruit crowded with Mozambicans doing the same business. Normally she travels all day and arrives in Durban in the late afternoon or early evening. "Those who have enough money can sleep in hotels, but those of us who don't sleep in the stalls within the market, or at the bus station. When we wake in the morning, we purchase the goods and then take the mini bus back to Maputo." Alda says that this business is profitable, but it has its problems. Both the South African Rand and the Metical are unstable currencies, making it difficult to make a profit. Sometimes she has to reduce prices drastically to get rid of her merchandise. At the customs office at the border, she says, "we have to pay very high taxes and that forces us to evade taxes, which is a risk we have to face every time we cross the border. . . . Sometimes it works, sometimes it doesn't."

Luisa, a twenty-nine-year-old who lives in Marracuene, a small town north of Maputo, is using her profits as a *mukherista* to continue her education. She has a nine-year-old child but never married his father, although they lived together for a couple of years. Luisa says the relationship did not work because her partner did not want her to continue with her studies; she could not accept that and decided to leave. She and her child moved back to her parents' home so she could return to school, where she is now in her final year (12th grade). In order to pay for her education and care for her child, Luisa started doing *mukhero* in 2005. Two Fridays a month she misses school to make the trip to Nelspruit and returns on Saturday night. She often travels with her forty-year-old aunt, who is also in the business. Like Maria, Anita, and Alda, she specializes in clothing. She finds *mukhero* a difficult business, because "you never know if you will get there alive as the *chapas* (minibus taxis) drive so recklessly. Also, at the border some customs officers may sometimes take away our merchandise even if the paperwork is in order. . . . Some women go to *curandeiros* [traditional healers and diviners] to protect themselves and 'open the way' on the road and at the border." Luisa intends to continue doing *mukhero* after she enters the university. She thinks that the government should provide more support to women who are trying to make a living for themselves and their families. She explained emphatically: "When I needed a job, they didn't give me one. Now I just want them to let us work and do our business without imposing heavy taxes on us. . . . If the taxes were affordable we would all pay them and still make a profit, and everyone would be happy. We are not crooks; we are mothers who want to feed our children."

Smuggling in Tunisia

Khaled, a twenty-seven-year-old graduate student in Tunis, expects to finish his degree in 2012, but he has no hope of finding work in his field of study. He comes from Kasserine in west-central Tunisia, just a few miles from the Algerian border. Kasserine is one of the most impoverished regions of the country, with very little state investment and extremely high unemployment rates.[1] Youth unemployment is a major problem, and many young people engage in cross-border trading.

I was invited to lunch at Khaled's parents' home in Kasserine. We ate a delicious meal that included lamb *meshwi*, a regional specialty, couscous, and salads prepared by his mother and sister. I spent about three hours talking with Khaled, his parents, and his sister. Their mother raised Khaled and his siblings alone while their father spent fourteen years in France working in the car manufacturing industry. He sent remittances home and visited the family every year. Khaled's mother began the cross-border business to help support the children. Three or four times a month, she crosses the border to the nearest town in Algeria to buy carpets, textiles, and women's fashions, which she sells to small retailers and in the local market. Over the years she has built up her own clientele, and now customers come to purchase goods from a stall in the back of her house. Merchandise "is much cheaper in Algeria" because, according to Khaled, the Algerian government subsidizes the costs of foodstuffs, clothing, and other products. "Everything is much cheaper in Algeria. . . . We survive because of Algeria."

After completing his secondary education in Kasserine, Khaled enrolled in a program in cultural studies and youth programming in Tunis. He got a small grant from the Ministry of Education, but it does not cover all his costs. During his summer vacations, Khaled travels to Algeria to buy goods to resell in Kasserine. With his mother's assistance he found his niche buying and selling young men's clothing. An investment of 300TND (about US$200) yields a net profit of about 150TND (US$100), which he uses to subsidize his studies. He finds traveling across the border difficult and risky. "Customs officers can confiscate your merchandise, or people can rob you before you have a chance to sell your products. It is harder for young people doing small business because they prefer to work with traders doing big business . . . but they are also more respectful to older women, like my mother, so I often try to travel with her." Khaled thinks that "it doesn't look like I will have a full-time job when I finish my course next year. . . . That's why I have to continue doing this trade during my vacations, so that I will have something going in case I am unable to get a job."

Cross-border smuggling is a common activity for young people in the western and southern regions, especially on the Ben Garden border with Libya and the Kasserine border with Algeria. Many young Tunisians trade in clothing, electronics, foodstuffs, and cars. A few smuggle drugs, but Nourddine, a twenty-eight-year-old man who lives in Sidi Bouzid, explained that most people think drug smuggling and other highly profitable ventures were "controlled by people close to the former president's family and to the government" in Tunis. Good connections open doors and offer protection at the higher echelons of the customs and security apparatus. Young people involved in smuggling networks face greater risks than those who trade to make ends meet. Nourddine and Khaled differentiated these forms of trade, characterizing smuggling as a large-scale illegal activity and their cross-border trade in clothing as petty and "not so illegal."

Mohamed, who helped his father smuggle cars from Libya into Tunisia, saw the business as a survival strategy and a way of improving his family's economic situation. Now twenty-three, he comes from the southern town of Ben Garden. I met him in Tunis, where he is enrolled in a university course in film and media studies. Mohamed is the eldest of three children; his mother is a housewife, and his father worked for many years as a nurse before taking up the car business. His father and his associates would bring luxury cars from Libya into Tunisia without paying all the necessary customs taxes; their network included customs officials who would facilitate their illegal entry. Mohamed enjoyed going with his father to Libya, and his friends thought this business was "cool." The profits enabled the family to enjoy a better standard of living. "Before I left Ben Garden to come and study here, my father bought me a house there so that I would have a place to go back to after my studies." Mohamed hopes that eventually he won't have to smuggle cars. "I don't want to join my father's business. . . . I want to make movies and write scripts. I know life is very difficult, so I cannot say I will never do it. I have to see how my life turns out after my university studies."

The stories of young Mozambicans and Tunisians involved in cross-border trade highlight three issues. First, the profitability of the business depends greatly on traders' ability to evade import duties. Anita was so successful at tax evasion that she was able to hire people to work for her rather than making the trips herself. Moreover, she invested her profits in more legitimate businesses. Many *mukheristas* have great difficulty bringing their merchandise across the border; some bribe customs agents, while others resort to diviners for help in "clearing the way." In Tunisia, too, traders contend with customs officials who demand more money than they can afford and threaten to confiscate their merchandise. They realize that alliances with large-scale traders and smugglers bring better returns.

Second, most *mukheristas* are unmarried women raising children by themselves. Their image as independent businesswomen who can make it without men in their lives, the allure of traveling abroad and dealing with fashion and beauty products, and the financial success that some achieve make this business especially attractive to girls.

Third, cross-border trading is risky. Dramatic fluctuations in exchange rates can destabilize the business. Travelers ride in recklessly driven minibuses and are exposed to robbery. Smuggling promises higher returns but entails serious dangers ranging from imprisonment to death. Nevertheless, young people who feel that their lives are already at risk carry on with these activities because those who succeed are able to achieve a more comfortable existence.

Making a Living in the Streets

In major cities and capitals across the continent it is common to see young people selling a variety of products in the streets, washing cars, helping to park and guard cars, scavenging trash cans and garbage dumps, or sitting on a corner waiting for any opportunity to make a little money. This section examines the stories of a group of young men who scavenge in the garbage dump in Maputo and explores the predicament of young street vendors in Dakar.

Scavenging in a Garbage Dump

Jonasse, the twenty-seven-year-old man who makes a living from the garbage dump in Hulene, a neighborhood on the outskirts of Maputo, is part of a group of fifteen men between the ages of eighteen and thirty-two whom I met there in February 2011. Few had much schooling; some had attended school through grade 7, but the majority did not go beyond primary school, and three had never been to school and could neither read nor write. Most were born on the outskirts of Maputo or in nearby rural districts and, like Jonasse, were pushed out of their homes at a tender age by poverty and family breakdown. Then they had to fend for themselves. Most have nowhere else to call home and sleep in dumpsters. Outsiders associate them with criminal activities, violence, drug use, and heavy drinking, and those who live in nearby neighborhoods fear the youths who live on the dump.

These young men's main activity is picking out goods from garbage to sell to recycle depots and in the market. They do not repair the objects they gather from the trash but sell them to small craftsmen. Sometimes people come to the dump to buy things from them. Chico explained: "I collect metal from the garbage dump, and I already have my customers. Every week I take the metal to them, and they weigh it and pay me back. For one kilogram of metal I can get 5MT. The person I sell to is an intermediary and I suspect that he makes a lot more than me."

Julio elaborated: "We collect a lot of tires, and tires are a good business as many people come looking for them. . . . We also collect plastic bottles, glass, electronic appliances, computer parts, and other stuff." On a good day Jonasse said he makes between 150MT and 200MT (about US$5–7). But he has as many bad days as good ones.

The young men also make money doing odd jobs. People ask them to pick up garbage from their property or to clean sewers and drains. Antonio, who is twenty-three, recounted: "Yesterday we went to do a job for a man who needed to clean the sewage pipes in his back yard. . . . We do all these dirty, smelly jobs." Eighteen-year-old Chico sometimes cleans the garden of a lady who lives in the Polana neighborhood. "I spend three or four hours tending her garden and that helps me make some extra cash, but it is not a lot."

Apart from looking after themselves, some of the young men try to support their relatives. Simão, who is twenty-eight, provides some scavenged goods to his father: "My father repairs shoes at home and whenever I come across rejects of leather here in the garbage dump I save them for him. My father also uses tires to make flip-flops, and I also help him with those materials."

Some of these young men have family responsibilities. Three live with partners and have children, though they are not formally married; four have children but have not taken responsibility for them; and two have regular girlfriends. Orlando described his situation: "I have no money to marry her. She is the mother of my two children: one is a four-month-old baby, and the other is two years old. I don't want my children to be like me; I want them to study and go to university to become doctors and engineers. . . . I struggle everyday to try and provide for them, but it is very hard." Andre, who is twenty-five, explained why he is not involved in a romantic relationship: "I have no [financial resources] to have a girlfriend, let alone to get married. I just go out with girls sometimes but I have no attachments. . . . Girlfriends want money; they want to buy *mechas* [hair extensions], and they want *giro* [prepaid mobile phone cards], and I don't have money."

Most of the young men I met in the garbage dump do not have a national identification card (BI). It costs 180MT (about US$6) to apply for a BI, which they cannot afford. Without formal identification cards these young men operate on the margins of society and are unable to access any public services and institutions, including education, training, or healthcare. They are left out of government statistics and appear to be nonentities.

The government had plans to close the dump at Hulene and open another one at Mahlanpswene, about fifteen miles outside the city. The young men were very angry about this decision, for they were not prepared to move out of the city and feared losing the source of their livelihood. They criticized the government for failing to create jobs and provide opportunities for decent livelihoods for youth. As twenty-five-year-old Julio warned, "If the government closes the garbage dump, we will have to rob and do bad stuff to survive . . . and we might end up in jail." Thirty-year-old David concurred with this bleak assessment of the consequences: "If the government moves the garbage dump to Mahlanpswene, we will not have a way of living, and we will have to find illegal means to survive. Then they will say that we are bandits, but they are the ones who make us bandits. . . . We only want to *desenrascar a vida* [to survive each day]."

Stories of aggression, robbery, and violence perpetrated by young men from the garbage dump are complemented by tales of their binge drinking and drug use. I was warned not to wear any jewelry and to leave my purse, watch, mobile phone, and camera behind before meeting them. People in the area were quite surprised to see me talking with a group of fifteen young men under a tree on the edge of the dump. Some would come close enough to listen in on the conversation until they were fiercely chased away by the young men, who had a bad reputation in the neighborhood. Tomas, a nineteen-year-old student whom I interviewed afterward, stated that "they [the young men who live on the dump] are very aggressive; we fear them here because they always create trouble. . . . They use drugs and drink a lot, and you don't want to be closer to them or upset them. . . . We stay away from them."

Initially the youths in this group were very suspicious of my intentions, but soon the conversation became more open and relaxed. Simão told me that if I were a journalist, they wouldn't allow me to be there, let alone speak to me. He explained: "Journalists lie. . . . Some months ago journalists from a television station came to talk to us. . . . We spoke freely with them and then they went on TV and said that we were criminals, that we were involved in the assassinations that happened in Matola. . . . They made us responsible for all the bad stuff that happens around here, which is not true. It was all lies. . . . We don't want journalists here!" These youths justify their aggressive behavior by pointing out the conditions they have to endure. Chico, at eighteen the youngest of the group, said that "this is not a good or nice place to be. Living in a garbage dump is not something we choose to do . . . but we have no other way of surviving. This life is hard and it makes us tough. . . . That's what some people do not understand."

Others believe that because of their precarious means of sustenance these young men are prone to carry out robberies. There were strong allegations of their involvement in violence and looting during the Maputo riots in February 2008 and September 2010. But they vehemently deny any involvement in violence, looting, and unlawful activities. Twenty-seven-year-old Orlando protested: "People say we are thieves, that we kill people, that we wear masks and go out to rob other people, that we are bandits. . . . That is all false; those are pure lies." Instead, they present themselves as victims of poverty and insist that they are only trying to *desenrascar a vida*.

When asked what they would need to be able to turn their lives around, they mentioned having a *txova* (push cart stall) in the market or 3,000MT (about US$1,000). Their strategies for attaining a better life were built around buying and selling goods at a small but steady profit. Chico declared: "I would like to go out and buy products to sell in the market. . . . I could buy iron bars to sell in Xiquelene, [but] without a *txova* it is impossible to do that." Orlando concurred: "To be successful I would need a good stall in the market and some money to buy products to sell. I would like to sell groceries, sweets, biscuits, sodas, and the like." Jonasse had a similar dream: "I too would be happy with a stall to sell to people in the street, especially those traveling along the national highway. I could have drinks and food for them to buy on the road. That would be a good business."

Tabliers and Ambulants in Dakar

In Africa street vendors are an integral component of urban economies. It is very common to see young people in the streets hawking new and used clothing, beauty products, groceries, electronic gadgets, and the like. Although street trading has deep historical roots in Africa, the lack of jobs that followed failed economic reforms and the downsizing of the public and private sectors in the past decades have forced many young people into street selling (Bhowmik 2004). Some young Senegalese work in small street kiosks, and others carry their wares on their heads or in backpacks and sell to people walking by or in cars caught in traffic jams.[2] In Dakar there is a clear distinction between those with fixed stalls inside the market; those who operate from semi-fixed stalls, known as *tabliers*, and use folding tables or wheeled pushcarts inside or outside the market; and *ambulants*, those who hawk their wares in the streets.[3] Street vending has few barriers to entry and enables people with no other recourse to earn a living. The majority of young vendors in Dakar are *tabliers* or *ambulants*, rather than vendors who operate in officially sanctioned off-street markets.

Young vendors may work on a casual basis, when an opportunity arises or they need money, while others rely on this occupation and work long hours. Some are hired by traders to sell merchandise in the streets. A few are independent and buy and resell goods on their own, but that requires an initial capital investment that many cannot muster. They operate mainly in the streets, sidewalks, and alleyways, and near markets. Young women work mainly as *tabliers,* selling fruits and vegetables. Others are employed in market stalls selling beauty products, women's clothing, and foodstuffs.

The authorities often harass vendors for conducting their business on the streets. Police and municipal officers frequently chase them away, confiscate their merchandise, or demand bribes. In November 2007 the Senegalese government banned street selling and ordered the police to tear down roadside stands. In response, thousands of young vendors staged protest riots for two days in the streets of Dakar. They threw stones, burned tires, ransacked government buildings, and completely disrupted life in the city center. Police used tear gas to disperse them and arrested at least two hundred people. Then the government retracted its new policy, lifting the ban until the late December Muslim holiday of Eid al-Adha, known locally as Tabaski, and announced its intention to provide specific areas for street vendors.[4] But vendors prefer to move freely, which allows them greater access to customers.

It is difficult for young people to obtain the financing necessary to start and develop their businesses. As Moustapha pointed out, "Even if you want to be a street vendor, you need some money to start the business. The government is not helping young people at all. . . . They build huge and expensive highways and monuments rather than using the money to create opportunities for young people."

BIRIMA is one of the few organizations working to address this problem and support young entrepreneurs. Founded in 2007 by the world-famous Senegalese musician and antipoverty activist Youssou N'Dour, BIRIMA provides small loans to young people with good business ideas. N'Dour came up with the idea when a young man borrowed CFA 60,000 (about US$120) from him to buy and sell shoes. After the young man returned the money, N'Dour realized he could help young people with access to micro-credit.[5] He set up a partnership between BIRIMA and the Italian clothing company Benetton to conduct an international campaign to promote and support entrepreneurship among young Africans.[6] By 2010, BIRIMA had loaned about CFA 200M (US$400,000) to 1,182 young people.[7]

Young Senegalese worry about the fact that Dakar has so many migrants from neighboring countries such as Guinea, Mauritania, and Mali. The migrants, who struggle to get by because they lack family support and local connections, do all kinds of work, and many sell in the streets. "Guineans here do anything because they want to survive and be able to send money home. There are many street vendors from Guinea," affirmed Bemba, a twenty-five-year-old man who lives in Colobane, a neighborhood in Dakar. He added that Senegalese who come from the interior regions of Touba, Kolba, Kaolack, and Tambacounda also drive taxis and sell goods in the streets. "The Dakarois [natives of Dakar] need to stop being picky and choosy about what they can or cannot do. Any job is a job, and it is better that we take what is available rather than sit at home. If we don't want to be a street vendor or a taxi driver, the foreigners and those from other regions will do these jobs," he declared. In the same vein, twenty-year-old Makhtar, who also lives in Colobane, commented that "some young people have attitudes and don't want to work in construction or sell stuff in the street. They want office jobs. They just want to wear a tie and a suit and impress the girls."

Twenty-six-year-old Ndiaye, who lives in Parcelles Assenies, sells goods on the street but does not consider this activity a real job. He explained: "What I do is not a proper job. I am just trying to survive. . . . I see this as a temporary thing to help me move forward and get a better situation." Ndiaye is also student and hopes one day to find a "proper" job.

A substantial number of students sell products in the market and in the street to subsidize their studies and help their families. Makhtar mentioned: "I know of graduates and people studying at the university who have to do small jobs on the side, and some sell in the streets. . . . They try to find proper jobs but nothing is available." It is disappointing for those who finish their degrees to have to resort to street vending alongside their less-educated counterparts, and such poor prospects discourage other young people from pursuing their studies.

Young people who eke out a living by street selling share special problems. Poverty and deprivation compel them to spend their days hawking goods for very little gain. While many have very little education, even some better-educated youths must resort to this expedient. Young people surviving by working on the streets are constantly harassed by the authorities, who try to control public space. Young street vendors are vulnerable to violence. Not only are those scavenging on the Maputo rubbish dump believed to be involved in criminal activities, but when pushed into a corner, young Senegalese peddlers became violent in their protest of the government ban. Moreover, most of these young men have no effective citizenship rights. They have no ID cards, no residential address or place of work that can be registered in national censuses and surveys, and no access to public social services. They are everywhere, but in official terms they do not exist.

Informal Workers in Formal Work

As a result of the crisis in employment, young people are also taking jobs in the formal sector that offer no security or prospects for advancement. Educated youths are forced to accept low-wage, dead-end, and temporary jobs with no contracts or benefits. While they are well aware that they are underemployed and exploited, they have very little margin to maneuver. They realize that complaints or even attempts at negotiation may result in dismissal, since there is a long queue of other young people at the door waiting to grab the opportunity. The experiences of young men and women working as casual laborers in the private sector illustrate the challenges they encounter as they try to survive waithood.

Young Women Workers in European Call Centers in Tunisia

During my visit to Tunisia I spoke with several unemployed university graduates, mainly women, who worked for European telemarketing call centers. In the past decade or so several major companies have located call centers in Tunisia, in part because the country guarantees the availability of communications networks at low cost. It also has a qualified, multilingual, and competent work force that meets all the requirements of customer-relationship management in the European market. Labor costs are much lower than European standards for workers with the same levels of skill and training.

Aicha is a vibrant and outspoken twenty-six-year-old woman whom I met in Nabeul, a tourist-oriented coastal town in northeastern Tunisia. She has been living there for more than a year and works as an administrative assistant at a cultural center. Aicha grew up in Korba, where she and her brother, now eighteen, had a very comfortable childhood. Her father was an accountant in the local hospital, and her mother was a nurse. When she was ten, however, her father died, and the family struggled to get by on her mother's salary. After finishing high school in Korba, Aicha went to Tunis to pursue a university course in cultural studies. She received a loan of 1,500TND a year (about US$1,000), which she has been paying back with interest since getting a job a year after she graduated.

"I was still in college when I noticed that the prospects for the future were not good for me," she recalled. She continued:

> It was at university that I became aware of the situation in the country. I remember taking part in a student strike in 2006, which was orga-nized to protest the lack of employment for graduates. The output of my institute was four hundred graduates a year and the government was only absorbing thirty graduates a year. We were demanding the creation of more posts or alternatively that the government should stop producing more graduates without jobs.

At that time student protests were unavailing and the same policies continued.

As she expected, after graduating Aicha was unable to find full-time employment, so she took a couple of temporary jobs at telemarketing call centers. She worked for three months for a French company calling clients in France to persuade them to buy new products. This job paid her a monthly salary of 400TND (about US$325). She did not seek work at other call centers because she disliked the work and hoped she could find a job in her field of education. After months of unsuccessful job searches in Tunis, Aicha decided to go back home to Korba and try her luck there.

In Korba the job market was even worse, and Aicha resigned herself to taking a temporary position at a telemarketing center in Korba. She soon realized that the sales scheme defrauded customers. "We had to call older people, mainly senior citizens in Europe, and tell them that they had won special gifts and ask them to give credit-card details and home addresses in order for them to obtain the gifts. . . . I did not stay long there as I soon realized it involved fraud. . . . Unfortunately, some call centers for foreign companies operating here are quite shady."

Working in call centers has enabled young graduates with a good command of French and other international languages to find work selling products to customers in Europe. Telemarketing centers have proliferated in the last decade, especially in the northern part of the country. Most centers operate for French companies, but some serve Italian and German enterprises. They prefer to hire women because, as Aicha pointed out, "they believe that women are more patient, more polite, and more persuasive than men." Many young people I spoke with complained that call centers exploit young people who have few alternatives. Workers have no contracts and are employed for short periods on a temporary basis; monthly renewals are dependent on the supervisor. They generally work ten- to twelve-hour shifts with a one-hour break for lunch and one or two fifteen-minute breaks to use the restroom. They are under constant surveillance to ensure they take no unauthorized breaks, make calls continuously, and interact with customers in a polite and persuasive manner. They are expected to be persistent and encourage clients to purchase whatever they are selling. Moreover, they are forbidden to let the customers know that they are not in France. The activity is based on deceit.

Zeinab, a twenty-four-year-old from Tunis, is the youngest of three sisters. She grew up in a middle-class suburb of Tunis; her father is a civil servant and her mother a housewife. Her two older sisters are married and have their own families. Zeinab finished a degree in economics in 2010. While trying to find stable employment, she decided to take a temporary job in a call center to avoid depending completely on her parents. "We were given a script and a supervisor was always controlling us so we did not move away from the script. I was paid 350TND (about US$240) each month, but they did not pay me for the first month as the supervisor said it was a month for training and probation. I was furious! They took advantage of me because they know we need jobs."

Faiza also shared her experiences of work at a telemarketing call center. She is twenty-seven years old and lives in the northern town of Metline. She finished a degree in linguistics, specializing in Arabic, in 2010. She comes from a family of modest means and has two brothers and two sisters. Faiza had many difficulties finding employment after finishing at the university. Initially she thought that it was because she wears the *hijab* (veil). She explained: "Before the revolution women were not allowed to wear the *hijab* at school and other public institutions; it was forbidden by law. . . . I could only wear it on the street and at home." But then Faiza realized that it was not the *hijab* that made her unable to find a job, since so many other young people had the same problem. In the past year she has been working in call centers in the area surrounding Metline to contribute to the family budget. She asserted that "most call centers are not well organized and the conditions of work are not good. The staff is obliged to sit for hours in uncomfortable chairs. . . . Many do not offer contracts, and they do not declare their revenue to the state."

Shelf-Packing and Merchandising Jobs in South Africa

Ntembisa, a thirty-one-year-old man who lives in Soweto, has a high school degree (matric). He could not continue on to the university because of his lower matric average and had to start working. Ntembisa was able to find a job at a retail store. He worked there for two years but was laid off during a retrenchment in 2005. Since then, despite endless job searches, he has been unable to find permanent employment. He survives on small and irregular earnings from occasional shelf-packing and merchandising jobs in retail stores. Ntembisa learned to bake while doing a short-term job at a bakery, and he now bakes biscuits at home and sells them in the market. A two-liter bucket of biscuits brings him about R250 (about $US36), and he has been able to bake two to three buckets three times a month.

I spent an entire day with Lindiwe, a twenty-six-year-old woman who also lives in Soweto. I visited her home and met her grandmother and brother. She finished her high school degree in 2006, but her grades were too low for admission to the university. So Lindiwe wanted to get a job to help support her relatives. Her mother died many years ago, and she lives with her grandmother, her father, and one brother in a two-room house. She had difficulty finding employment and held a number of temporary jobs in retail stores as a cashier, shelf-packer, and merchandiser. Currently she is registered with a couple of temporary employment agencies and waits for a call. Lindiwe said that an overnight or weekend job in a local supermarket or retail store might earn her between R100 and R150 (US$14–20) per night.

Tsego, a twenty-three-year-old woman who finished her high school degree in 2007, lives with her mother in Rooderport, a town near Johannesburg.

She has a nine-month-old baby but did not marry the child's father; they are not together anymore, and he offers no child support. Tsego had a job in a retail shop in Rooderport for eight months before being laid off. While looking for work, she relies on occasional shelf-packing and merchandising jobs. These overnight or weekend jobs are very irregular, and she cannot plan ahead because she is never sure when the employment agency will call. Her mother, who is a nurse, provides some support for her and the child.

Linky, a twenty-eight-year-old woman, was born and raised in Alexandra Township, where she did her primary and early secondary education. She was an excellent student and in grade 10 was offered a bursary to study at St. Mary's school in Johannesburg, a Model C school with a fine reputation.[8] She finished matric with flying colors and wanted to study medicine. After the sponsor of her bursary died, however, Linky was unable to get funds to continue her academic career. Back in Alexandra, she volunteered to teach English to primary school children and to serve as a librarian for a local nonprofit organization. In the meantime she made money working as a merchandiser in retail stores and supermarkets. Like Ntembisa, Linky baked and cooked food for sale to supplement her income. Winning a cooking competition at the Hilton hotel in Johannesburg paid her tuition for a six-month course in cooking and hospitality. She landed temporary positions in hotels and restaurants as a chef's assistant and kitchen supervisor until she saved enough to start her own business. Her company, based in Alexandra, caters weddings and special events. She recognizes that she was fortunate to get a break through the cooking competition; many of her friends still have to rely on temporary jobs in retail stores.

Most merchandizing and shelf-packing jobs are obtained through temporary employment agencies that contact workers when they are needed. Most jobs are short term, lasting overnight or over a weekend. Ntembisa, Lindiwe, Tsego, and Linky had no direct contact with the companies they worked for, as all contacts were mediated by the recruiting agencies; the companies pay the agencies, which, in turn, pay the workers. The young people I interviewed believe that these agencies get a big cut of their pay. Ndomingozi, a twenty-nine-year-old woman from Kwazulu Natal who lives in Johannesburg Park, stated that "employers work together with the agencies, which operate as labor brokers. . . . We, the labor force, get the worst end of the bargain. The employers get the work done, and the agencies take huge cuts from workers' salaries as commission. . . . And we cannot complain, because someone else will do the job." Similarly, Ntembisa stated, "I just get what they give me and do not object or argue because they will always get someone else."

Most of the young men and women I spoke with in South Africa who had high school diplomas were forced to rely on odd jobs in wholesale and retail stores. They are relegated to short-term, dead-end jobs that do not offer decent wages or financial stability, let alone possibilities for careers.

Young Men in the Chapa-Cem Taxi Industry in Maputo

Chapa-cem, the privately owned and operated minibus taxis that provide much of Maputo's public transportation,[9] employ many young people as drivers and fare collectors. The industry is estimated to include about five thousand vehicles, mostly fifteen-seat and twenty-five-seat reconditioned minibuses operated by about one thousand private, family-run enterprises in Maputo and Matola, a neighboring city approximately nine miles away. They operate on routes designated by the municipality with fares stipulated by the government. However, they have no access to direct government subsidies and credits (USAID 2006). There is a large demand for *chapas* (as they are commonly known) because the public transportation system is extremely limited. Middle-class entrepreneurs often invest in the *chapa* industry, which appears quite profitable. The workers, however, feel exploited. Each *chapa* is operated by a driver and a fare collector and runs on the same route all day. Crews work very long hours, starting at about 5 a.m. and ending at about 8 p.m. with just an hour off for lunch. The taxis operate without schedules and depart whenever they are full. They stop anywhere passengers ask to board or disembark and tend to carry more than their designated capacity, with passengers standing through their entire journey.

Pedro, a twenty-five-year-old man from Matola, is a fare collector for a *chapa*. He and his brothers live with their mother. After his father's death Pedro dropped out of school because his mother could not afford to pay for fees and school supplies. His elder brother, who is now twenty-eight, managed to get a job as a *chapa* driver and convinced his boss to hire Pedro to collect fares on his *chapa*. Pedro has been working with his brother for three years, but he is dissatisfied because of the long hours they have to put in for the little money they make. Jobs are insecure and depend entirely on the *chapa* owner. He explained: "I am happy because I have something, but we spend the entire day in the *chapa* and in the end we don't make much money. . . . Most of the money goes to the boss who owns the taxi. We don't have contracts or fixed salaries. Some days are better than others depending on the number of passengers we get."

Joel, a thirty-two-year-old *chapa* driver in Maputo, previously worked for a private manufacturing company but was laid off. He would prefer a more secure job with a proper contract and benefits, but this was the only job he could get. Joel explained that *chapa* drivers get a reputation for bad driving because their incomes depend on how many passengers they carry. "People say we drive too fast, yes, I cannot deny that some drivers drive recklessly, but . . . that is the nature of our job. In order to get more clients we need to get to them before the other *chapas*. Every day I have to make a certain amount for my boss, so if I go faster and do more trips, I can make more money."

Other drivers in Maputo and Matola become infuriated with *chapas* that halt traffic and cause accidents by abruptly stopping to pick up or drop off passengers. They try to beat red lights and perform dangerous maneuvers to overtake cars. Pedro felt that *chapa* drivers are unfairly blamed: "When something goes wrong on the roads it is always our fault. . . . They say *chapas* do not follow the driving rules and do not respect passengers and other drivers. But that is not true. . . . Sure, there are problems and accidents, but when you work on the road there are always risks." *Chapa* drivers see their risky road behavior not as the result of bad manners or ignorance of the driving rules, but as a strategy for survival in a competitive industry.

Municipal officials and traffic police frequently stop the *chapas* to check their registration and driving permits. *Chapeiros* (*chapa* workers) feel they are frequently harassed; even when their papers are in order, the authorities mistreat them. Joel explained that this attitude is related to *chapeiros'* bad reputation. David, a thirty-year-old driver, pointed out that their ignorance of the law makes them vulnerable to police abuse. "We run around all day in the *chapa,* and we don't have the time to get to know our rights. Sometimes municipal officers create complications for us. Because our bosses don't want to hear about trouble, we have to pay them bribes, and move on." Young men in the *chapa* industry emphasized the precariousness of their job situation. Without the protections that contractual agreements could provide, their vulnerability is compounded by lack of insurance. In the event of illness they are not paid and may even be dismissed. In case of an accident, they are responsible for all personal damages because most owners insure only the vehicle. Marcos, a twenty-seven-year-old driver, recounted: "Two years ago, a bike rider cut me off suddenly. I didn't see him in time to stop the vehicle, and I hit him. . . . I took him to the hospital for medical care and I had to pay for his treatment myself. My boss didn't care about the problem and even penalized me for the time I took off work to provide assistance to the cyclist." Marcos, who attended high school until grade 10, thought he would drive a *chapa* temporarily until he found a more secure job in a state or private company. But four years have passed and he is still a *chapa* driver.

Most of the *chapeiros* interviewed agree that working on the *chapa* is not an ideal job. Pedro declared that his work as a fare collector "is not a proper job. I see it as a *biscato* . . . because this job is not stable." Similarly, Joel said, "Of course I would prefer to have a safe and more secure job, but I have no *padrinho* [godfather or patron]. . . . And I am stuck with this job. At least I have something." Marcos and Pedro concurred that despite the difficult working conditions they consider themselves lucky to be working. "There are many people suffering because they cannot find work and put food on the table . . . so we cannot complain too much," concluded Pedro.

Jobs in Tunisian call centers and in the Mozambican taxi industry are negotiated directly with employers, but workers have no bargaining power given current levels of unemployment. In South Africa temporary employment agencies function as intermediaries between workers and companies and take a percentage of workers' earnings to cover their services. While there are variations in the duration of their employment, all are faced with uncertainty as they depend on others' mercy. Despite the fact that they work in the formal sector, these young workers subsist in conditions of extreme vulnerability. They have no contracts, are not protected under labor laws or collective bargaining agreements, and have no social protections; they are informally employed at the lowest levels of the formal sector. Global competition has led many firms to adopt more flexible labor policies and engage in informal employment relationships to reduce costs. Companies set up informal employment relationships in order to avoid their obligations as employers. Workers have no choice but to accept the terms they dictate. As Martha Chen (2006) points out, this pattern requires us to reexamine the notion that informal employment is voluntary. The young men and women I interviewed would prefer more secure jobs with contracts and social protections. Their informal employment is not a matter of free choice.

The Plight of Young Migrants Crossing to Europe

North and West Africans have a long history of labor migration to Europe. In the early 1960s Senegalese and Tunisian men left to work in France, filling that country's demand for labor (Patterson 2010; Poeze 2010; Flahaux 2010). Their families stayed at home; the men would send remittances and visit regularly. These initial migratory movements were organized between states, and migrants were legally documented. In the 1970s, following French President Giscard d'Estaing's policies of *regroupement familiale* (family re-unification),[10] African migrants to France were able to bring their wives and children with them. The migration flow decreased slightly in 1977 when the French government decided to halt family reunifications following a rise in unemployment (Poeze 2010). The tightening of borders in France in the

1980s prompted many Senegalese and Tunisians to favor Italy (Riccio 2004, 2005; Patterson 2010). As unemployment has risen, irregular or illegal migration to Europe by Tunisians and Senegalese youths has sharply increased.

As far as Tunisia was concerned, irregular migration to Europe was never a major issue because the government's tight controls at sea discouraged many people from attempting to cross as unemployment soared (Boubakri 2004; Samy 2008; Sika 2009).[11] Tunisia enacted a law in 2004 providing for the surveillance of all vessels leaving its ports. According to the Tunisian Ministry of Foreign Affairs, the rate of irregular migration decreased from 0.7 percent in 2000 to 0.5 percent in 2005 (Fargues 2005; Sika 2009). Data from the Tunisian National Institute for Statistics (INS) show that in 2009 there were about one million Tunisian migrants living abroad, the vast majority in Europe. Indeed, Tunisian migrants formed approximately 10 percent of the total population. Most of these labor migrants are youths.

Crossing to the Mediterranean Island of Lampedusa

Metline is a beautiful coastal town in the northern part of Tunisia facing the Italian island of Lampedusa. Just 125 miles away, Lampedusa symbolizes the dreams of many young unemployed Tunisians longing for a better life in Europe. Hundreds of young men risk their lives in small fishing boats, hiding from the maritime patrols and trying to make it across the rough and treacherous sea. Once in Italy, they seek asylum or acquire local papers through dubious networks. Many end up being caught and sent back to Tunisia. Immigration of youths to Europe, known among Tunisians as *harraga* or *brûlé* (burn—that is, burn your papers so that they cannot know where you come from), is a response to the high rates of youth unemployment.[12]

Sami is a twenty-seven-year-old man who grew up in Metline. He has two sisters and a younger brother. His older sister is married and has two children, but he and his other siblings still live with their parents. Sami earned his degree at the university and then went to Mahdia, a town near the city of Sousse on the east coast, to study information technology and management. Since finishing his bachelor's degree, Sami has been unable to secure full-time employment. While waiting to find a job, he earns some money as a day laborer in construction and agriculture. He had a serious girlfriend for four years, but last year she left him because he could not afford to marry her. Sami confessed that he often becomes desperate about his situation, and he dreams about migrating to Europe as some of his friends have done. But, he said, "you need money to do that. You must pay the people who take you across. . . . It costs a lot of money, and for now I cannot afford it."

Thousands of young people from Metline, Bizerte, and nearby coastal towns have embarked clandestinely for Lampedusa. Between January and March 2011, more than five thousand young Tunisians landed in Lampedusa and sought political asylum in Italy. The massive exodus resulted from the political unrest in the country and the disruption of the coastal police after the fall of Ben Ali's regime. According to a report in the UK *Daily Mail*, the number of immigrants in Lampedusa doubled the island's population. How was Europe going to deal with this massive wave of migration? Issuing them residence permits in the European Union might encourage more North Africans to cross the Mediterranean, but sending them back to their unstable homeland would also be questionable. After much consideration, Italian authorities decided to issue more than twenty thousand temporary visas for a three-month period to allow the migrants to travel within Europe before settling on a final destination. This policy was met by a wave of protest, especially in France, where about three-fourths of the migrants planned to go because they spoke the language and already had relatives living there. Outraged, France called for a temporary suspension of the Schengen Agreement, which precipitated a diplomatic incident with Italy and threatened the unity of the EU.[13] Some of the migrants who sought political asylum during this period were unskilled workers and escaped convicts, and a number of them were repatriated.

In the southern and central regions young Tunisians try to escape unemployment by migrating to Libya, the neighboring, oil-rich country (Boubakri 2004). Khalifi, a twenty-one-year-old from Regueb, a small town in the region of Sidi Bouzid, comes from an impoverished working-class family. His father abandoned the family for another woman when Khalifi and his twin brother were only ten years old. Khalifi left school after grade 8 because he didn't like to study. He was unable to find a job in his hometown. At the age of nineteen, Khalifi decided to immigrate to Libya to try to earn a living and send some money to the family. He made the four-hour road trip to the border and ended up in Sirte, where he and his brother worked for two years, mainly as casual laborers in construction. Khalifi was quite happy because he was able to earn a lot more money, the equivalent to 35TND (about US$24) a day, while in Tunisia the same type of work would pay only 10TND (about US$6) a day.[14] With the outbreak of civil war in Libya, Khalifi, his brother, and their friends had to return home. They hope to go back when the war is over, but they worry about the negative impact that the upheaval in Libya will have on young Tunisians whose livelihoods are tied to their ability to work in that country.

Senegalese Youths' Journey to Europe

Senegalese youths try to reach Spain by traversing the desert and taking small fishing boats across the Mediterranean Sea. An average of 350 pirogues filled with migrants are intercepted at the Spanish coast every week (Carling 2007). Between 2005 and 2007 an estimated fifty thousand Senegalese migrated illegally to Europe. Many perished during this long, dangerous journey, and others were apprehended and repatriated (Bassene 2010; Lessault and Beauchemin 2009). In 2008 Caritas International studied a group of fifty young migrants who had been repatriated to Senegal. The majority were males aged twenty to twenty-nine (Bassene 2010). Data from the International Programme on Migration (ILO 2006) indicates that half of all migrants come from Dakar and Saint Louis; other important departure points are Kayar in Thiés and Ziguinchor in Casamance (Bassene 2010).

One unsuccessful migrant tells a vivid story of his attempt to reach Europe. Abdoulaye, a twenty-four-year-old *ambulant*, sells clothes and shoes in the streets of Dakar and around the well-known Sandaga market. He was born in Dakar, but his parents are originally from Thiés. His family was very poor, and he dropped out of secondary school when he was in grade 7. Abdoulaye started selling goods in the street many years ago and regrets that he must still do so in order to survive. He is a devoted Muslim from the Mouride Brotherhood.[15]

Tired of being unable to change his life for the better, in 2007 Abdoulaye decided to follow some of his friends who were leaving for Morocco to make the crossing to Europe. He saved the money, contacted the intermediaries who control the trade, and called his parents and his *marabout* (spiritual leader) to say good-bye and ask for their blessing.[16] On a very hot Dakar afternoon, sitting in a small café in the Medina neighborhood, I listened attentively as Abdoulaye described his adventurous boat trip toward Spain:

> The departure point was at Mbour [a small town on the coast] and I joined a group of other young people there. The organizer of the trip came to collect the money from all of us. . . . We paid 300,000 francs CFA [about US$600]. My group had about one hundred people, mostly young men and a few young women. There was also a handful of adults. . . . Late at night, we boarded various small boats, which took us to the large pirogue at sea. We did all this after midnight to avoid being caught by the coast guard. . . . In case of trouble, the boat had a huge canvas to hide everybody. We arrived at the coast of Mauritania in the evening, but we had to wait at sea until late at night to dock. Each person had to take food and water for the trip.

We spent the day in Mauritania in a few houses arranged by the fishermen in the Quartier Cinquieme. . . . At midnight we boarded the pirogue for Morocco, but with a new crew member, a Mauritanian who would be our navigator. . . . We had to abort the trip because the sea was particularly violent. The pirogue was tossed in all directions, and it looked like we were going to capsize. . . . People started praying, using their *gris-gris* [protection amulets], and the women, as well as some men, started crying. . . . It was really bad. The problem was that we were too many for that pirogue. There wasn't much space; we were on top of one another.

When we finally got back to shore, about fifteen people decided to abandon the trip altogether. I believe most of the women gave up, as did some men. . . . I was not sure if I should continue with the trip, so I decided to call my *marabout* for advice, and he told me not to give up. The trip to Morocco took about two days, but this time we did not make it to shore; we stayed at sea waiting for it to be dark to proceed toward the [Spanish] Canary Islands. . . . The fishermen said that the coast guard in Morocco would catch us if we went closer to shore. . . . We waited for many, many hours at sea. . . . It was hot and many people were feeling sick. . . . After a long wait, the fishermen told us that we couldn't continue the trip because the sea was very rough and there were a large number of coast guard [boats]. . . . We had to go back to Mauritania, and this time the trip took three days as the sea was very rough. . . . We could not wait another day to try again because the conditions in the boat were awful. It was crowded, there were no proper toilets, and many people were feeling sick. . . . At that point everyone wanted to leave the boat and give it all up. . . . Personally, I didn't get seasick because my *marabout* gave me some herbal medicine to avoid it.

Once back in Mauritania, I called my *marabout* and told him what the situation was. He told me that he couldn't see a clear route ahead and told me to go back home. So together with a few friends I traveled back to Senegal by road the next day. The fishermen gave us some money for the journey home but did not return the money we paid for the crossing. . . . They said we could wait another day to try again, and that was when we decided to give up.

Hundreds of thousands of young men like Abdoulaye risk everything in the hope of finding work and prosperity in Europe. Their quest is not merely for survival but also about dignity, because *liggey* (work) makes one a respected person, capable of taking care of oneself as well as others. Young unemployed people in Senegal, Tunisia, Mozambique, and South Africa are fighting for subsistence and dignity by crossing borders with merchandise for sale, hawking goods in the streets of major cities, scavenging garbage dumps, and boarding crowded boats in dangerous journeys to Europe. They struggle for a better life, a life of work and prosperity that they imagine is possible and is visible to them on television screens, in newspapers and magazines, and through the Internet. They are aware of their material deprivation, and they want to share in the "good life" and gain access to modern consumer goods.

Waithood Subcultures or Urban Tribes?[17]

Young people in waithood create independent spaces, or "youthscapes" (Maira and Soep 2005), outside hegemonic power structures. With their own modus vivendi and modus operandi, they constitute what scholars in North America and Europe in the late 1960s and 1970s described as youth subcultures. Although the experience of waithood in Africa is quite different, an examination of subcultural theory sheds light on the survival spaces that youth create on the margins of mainstream society.

Subcultures are defined as groups of people whose beliefs and interests are distinct from the dominant. The study of youth subcultures began among sociologists at the University of Chicago, who sought to understand young people's social life in the city (Downes and Rock 1982). They were the first to suggest that deviance was a product of social problems such as unemployment and poverty (Bennett 2000, 2001). This sociological critique was picked up by British subcultural studies, which began in the 1970s at the Centre for Contemporary Cultural Studies (CCCS) at the University of Birmingham. At the heart of CCCS theory was the notion that subcultures are sites of counter-hegemonic resistance to dominant ideologies (Hall and Jefferson 1976; Kahn-Harris 2007) born out of working-class experiences of subordination. Youth subculture studies emphasized young people's capacity for resistance, rebellion, and opposition to authority (Amit-Talai and Wulff 1995; Pilkington 2004; Ross and Rose 1994; Skelton and Valentine 1998). Subculture studies soon became the dominant theoretical framework for analyzing the lives of marginalized youth in the West. Above all, it challenged the notion that working-class youth were deviant, criminal, and a threat to society (Hebdige 1979, 1981; Griffin 1993). In the Marxist perspective that characterized some CCCS work, subcultures were seen as "a collective critical vanguard to challenge bourgeois order and celebrate creative resistance to authority" (Blackman 2005, 16).

The survival spaces created by young Africans in waithood can arguably be seen as representing interests distinct from those of mainstream society and as counter-hegemonic sites of resistance and rebellion. Although organized around particular forms of livelihood rather than lifestyle preferences or ideological motivations, these groups of disfranchised young people have their own distinct beliefs and practices. Young people are acutely aware of their marginal structural position, and they despise and rebel against the abuse and corruption that they observe as the elites get richer and they become poorer. These youth spaces resemble subcultures because they bring together those who share a common predicament and feel neglected by society.

Here struggling youths in waithood subvert authority, bypass the encumbrances created by the formal system, and fashion new ways of functioning and maneuvering on their own. They may also develop a sense of shared identity. These youth spaces foster opportunities and possibilities for *desenrasque* and *débrouillage*—for "getting by" through improvisation. Young people in waithood pursuing similar livelihoods create their own rules; these norms are understood, shared, and obeyed by others who are part of the scene. Young people living in the streets have their own codes and ways of leading their daily lives. The young *mukheristas* in Mozambique and the cross-border traders and smugglers in Tunisia live on the border between entrepreneurship and illegality, but they draw lines between their own activities and criminal enterprises such as drug smuggling.[18]

Unlike the youth subcultures that existed in Europe during the 1970s, these groupings are not permanent. They are free form, even inchoate, and they appear and dissolve as often as most urban gatherings do. They resemble Michell Maffesoli's idea of "urban tribes" or "neo-tribes," understood as urban micro-groups that share common interests but whose association is largely informal and marked by greater "fluidity, occasional gatherings and dispersal" (1996, 98). In contrast to clearly defined youth subcultures, neo-tribes encompass temporary groups whose composition fluctuates (Bennett 1999; Bennett and Khan-Harris 2004; Vinken 2005; Huq 2006). I found these theories helpful in interpreting the flexibility of young people's associations within waithood.

Those in power often view their ways of operating as distasteful, dangerous, and even criminal. People in the neighborhood fear and recoil from the young men living on the garbage dump, condemn the behavior of *chapa* drivers and pushy street vendors, reproach the smugglers and illegal immigrants. Sociologist Stanley Cohen (1972) examined the media portrayals of the conflict between two British youth subcultures of the 1960s, the Mods and the Rockers, who were distinguished by their choice of motorcycles, their style of dress, and their taste in music, and who fought constantly. The media propagated anxiety and fear, representing these working-class youths as a threat to society and condemning their subcultures as deviant. Scrutinizing this sensational coverage, Cohen developed the concept of "moral panic," which interprets a disturbing phenomenon as a sign of widespread social pathology (Cohen 1972, 27). In Africa, Mamadou Diouf pointed to past and present moral panics surrounding youth. "Not only are young people losing the prestigious status that nationalism gave them in its ascending phase, but they no longer represent the national priority. . . . Excluded from the arenas of power, work, education, and leisure, young Africans construct places of socialization and new sociabilities whose function is to show their difference, either on the margins of society or at its heart, simultaneously as victims and active agents" (2003, 5).

In these new spaces of survival and sociability, young people struggle to get by. The expressions they used, *desenrascar a vida* and *se débrouiller*, highlight the precariousness of the livelihoods that young people scrape together as they cope with the constraints they face in waithood. Apart from some cross-border traders who have become successful and the few migrants who have been fortunate enough to make their way abroad and find work there, most of the young people saw these activities as temporary improvisations.

Anthropologist Henrik Vigh finds a very similar notion in the word *dubriagem* used by young soldiers in Guinea-Bissau. "In a Guinean context *dubriagem* designates the act of making the most of a situation and making things work to one's advantage" (2009, 150). The notions of *desenrascar* and *se débrouiller* situate the waithood experience in the realm of ad-lib, or "making it up as you go along." Vigh elucidated *dubriagem* as simultaneously a way of examining possibilities and of actualizing those possibilities in praxis (2009, 150). In this sense, *desenrascar a vida* implies a conscious effort on the part of young people to assess the challenges and possibilities of their position and to plot scenarios by which they might achieve their goals. *Desenrascar* and *débrouillage* have a dual temporal framework; they help youths cope with immediate circumstances and to envisage possible exits from their situation.

A life of *desenrasque* implies sporadic engagement in *biscatos* (odd jobs), which is very insecure and can be hazardous. Young people in waithood are not passively waiting for their lives to change. They know that existing socioeconomic systems have no place for them, and they are actively engaged in finding solutions to their problems by seizing any possible openings and trying to make something of their lives. We know very little about the spaces of survival that emerge among people in waithood. While they might appear to be just temporary livelihood-driven associations, in some cases they may become important sites for development of solidarity and of a collective counter-hegemonic consciousness that may lead to contestation of power. Later, we discuss politically engaged youth groupings making citizenship claims and driving social change.

The next chapter explores the social and intimate dimensions of wait-hood, especially issues of sexuality, intimacy, and social relationships, and considers young people's limited ability to marry and form families. In the most personal aspects of their lives, as in their pursuit of livelihoods, young people arc improvising new ways of living.

Chapter 5

Intimacy

Waithood has transformed young adults' intimate ties and sexual relationships; their economic situation prevents many from marrying and forming families and generates new social and emotional challenges. In a context of chronic unemployment, precarious livelihoods, and reduced marriage rates, the interconnections among political economy, intimacy, and sexuality become critical for understanding the coping strategies adopted by young people in waithood (Hunter 2010). Sexuality, courtship, and marriage have undergone profound changes that are inextricably linked to dynamic social, economic, and cultural conditions. Amid the current crisis in the transition to adulthood, conventional relationships and identities are being altered as young people engage in practices that are shaped by their socioeconomic conditions. Sexuality and intimacy appear to play a more material role in everyday life and have become fertile grounds for constructing and refashioning personal and collective identities (Bhana et al. 2007).

This chapter makes three main arguments. First, in a context of unemployment and resource scarcity, intimacy and sexuality become more commoditized livelihood assets (Chant and Evans 2010) as young women and men engage in relationships with older, more affluent men and women known as "sugar daddies" and "sugar mamas" who function as providers. These relationships are not simple commercial exchanges, as they involve continuing and reciprocal obligations between partners that include gifts, support, and services, and may involve personal affection. Second, through these new forms of sexual relationships, young men and women are redefining male and female sexuality and challenging existing notions of masculinity and femininity in their societies. Third, waithood is drastically reducing marriage rates and significantly raising the age at first marriage because of the costs associated with betrothal and marriage rituals, as well as with raising a family. Delayed marriage puts a substantial burden on parents and relatives on whom young people continue to depend financially. At the same time, remaining unmarried for an extended period offers men and women unprecedented freedom to experience intimacy and negotiate sexual relationships that would not be possible in the context of marriage. Most young people I interviewed, however, still believe in the importance of marriage as an institution that legitimizes sexual relationships and childbearing and confers adult social status.

Young people in waithood live in an environment that is being transformed by capital-led globalization, and they appear to be affected by it more deeply than their elders. New information and communication technologies connect them more closely to the rest of the world and, at the same time, make them acutely aware of the disparities and inequalities that exist between Africa and developed countries. Globalization is simultaneously bringing people together and widening the divisions between them. Young people are involved in an intricate struggle between constraints and limitations, on the one hand, and freedoms and opportunities, on the other. Many of those I spoke with in Mozambique, Senegal, South Africa, and Tunisia dream of obtaining modern consumer goods and enjoying the "good life" rather than existing in deprivation and uncertainty. The fashionable blue jeans, sneakers, hair extensions, and cell phones they see paraded in hip-hop music videos, soap operas, movies, and magazines that come from the West become objects of desire. Young people use all the means available to them, including their sexuality, to gain access to consumer goods. At the same time, struggling to cope with an independence they cannot sustain financially, they long for protection, emotional support, and affection.

According to Thandeka, a twenty-three-year-old South African woman, "There is a lot of peer pressure and girls want to look modern. . . . It is all about getting fashion, hair, and bling [jewelry]. . . . Girls hook up with older men with money who provide all that and sometimes more. . . . Some girls can get cell phones, televisions, or even cars. . . . It depends on how rich and powerful the man is."

Marta, a twenty-year-old woman who lives in Maputo, explained: "You may have a relationship with your boyfriend, but he is like you and has no money . . . and you want a nice pair of jeans and *mechas* [hair extensions]. . . . [So] you have to find another guy with enough money to offer you the things you want."

Relationships in which young women engage in sex with older, financially stable partners, often called sugar daddies, in exchange for gifts and money are common across Africa (Hunter 2002; Longfield 2004; Hawkins et al. 2009; Chant and Evans 2010; Masvawure 2010). These relationships have become more prevalent because so many young men cannot afford to marry their romantic partners. Young people's difficulties in finding employment and forming families put considerable strain on their intimate and sexual lives.

The sugar daddy is an important factor driving young women's sexual relationships and brings to the fore what Mark Hunter (2002) calls the "materiality of everyday sex," underscoring the role that gifts play in relations between men and women. Hunter (2010) distinguishes between romantic love and provider love, which are often interconnected. Sugar-daddy relationships constitute a form of transactional sex or provider love because they are based on the exchange of sex for gifts. While there are some similarities between these relationships and commercial sex work, not all forms of transactional non-marital sexual relations should be seen as prostitution, as they may involve continuing ties and a set of reciprocal obligations that goes beyond the predetermined payment (Standing 1992; Castle and Konaté 1999; Kaufman and Stavrou 2004; Leclerc-Madlala 2003; Hunter 2002; Cole 2004; Thomas and Cole 2009).

Unlike commercial sex work, sugar-daddy relationships appear to take place within the context of a relationship, however transient. The exchanges of money or gifts do not automatically follow the sex act but are embedded in a system of reciprocal exchanges between partners. While sugar-daddy relationships can sometimes be perceived as empowering young women, commercial sex work is seen as socially unacceptable and a last resort for women in desperate circumstances (Hawkins et al. 2009). Nancy Luke (2005) distinguishes between two types of transactional sex, one that includes gift exchanges and another that involves commodity exchanges. Gift exchanges take place in the context of personal relationships and may include services such as cooking and job advice. They also involve some sort of reciprocity. In commodity exchanges such as prostitution, sexual activity takes place in the market and is traded for its monetary equivalent. But sugar-daddy relationships remain ambiguous, as some may be perceived as commodity exchanges more closely akin to prostitution.

While commercial sex work and sex trafficking also affect young women, this chapter focuses on relationships with sugar daddies and sugar mamas and probes the ways in which these relationships contribute to changing patterns of identity and gender relations among young men and women in waithood.

Young Women, Sugar Daddies, and Boyfriends

In her study of sugar-daddy relationships in Zimbabwe, Tsitsi Masvawure (2010) takes issue with the fact that most of the literature on transactional sex in Africa sees it almost exclusively as a means of economic survival (Chatterji et al. 2004; Luke and Kurz 2002; Machel 2001). She points out that not all women involved in transactional sexual relationships are victims. Some seek these relationships in order to attain an otherwise elusive modern lifestyle; others prefer to avoid the burdens of emotional commitment and sexual exclusivity attached to standard boyfriend-girlfriend or marital relationships (Masvawure 2010). Indeed, there is great diversity and complexity in the exchanges and obligations of partners.

At the age of twenty, Mariana is enrolled in the 11th grade at a secondary school in Maputo. She comes from a family with very modest means. She grew up in Boane, a small town located a little less than twenty miles south of Maputo; her mother works on the family *machamba* (small plot of land), and her father died when she was fourteen. Mariana moved to Maputo to pursue a high school education, staying during the week at a relative's house on the outskirts of the city. Although her elder brother helped with her school fees, she always struggled to find money for transport, food, clothing, and toiletries. Occasionally she braided hair to earn some cash. Then she realized that other girls from backgrounds similar to hers were able to afford a much better lifestyle and buy things that she could not. They had fashionable clothes, wore makeup, and visited hairdressing salons. Mariana wanted to be like them. So she started seeing an older man whom she called a *patrocinador* (sponsor). They would meet for sex two or three times a week, and he would offer her money and gifts. Mariana justified her actions, saying, "I am a poor girl, but I have ambitions. . . . I want to buy nice school supplies, I want nice clothes, and I want to have fun like the other girls. . . . If I don't look for it myself, nobody is going to do it for me. . . . I have to survive and live as best as I can." Mariana also mentioned the affection that developed from her regular encounters with her *patrocinador*.

Christian Groes-Green's study of sexuality and notions of femininity in Maputo showcases a similar story. Maria, now eighteen, had arrived in the capital at the age of fifteen:

> At first she had lived with a cousin who took care of her while she attended secondary school. But her situation changed when she met an older Dutch man in a nightclub who soon became her lover. He decided to give her a monthly contribution so she could rent an apartment where they would be able to meet in privacy when he was in the country to do business. . . . Besides her lover, she also had casual sexual relations with other men she met in the city's nightlife, mostly older men who catered for her and bought her gifts.

She did not want to be completely dependent on the Dutch lover and preferred to keep her options open in case "he turned abusive or . . . decided no longer to support her" (Groes-Green 2011, 299).

Some young women acknowledged having multiple partners, each of whom provides something she needs. As Nolwazi, a thirty-year-old woman from Johannesburg, explained: "Often girls have several partners: they have a boyfriend, someone they really love and enjoy sex with; they have a sugar daddy who has money and can provide them with beautiful stuff . . . cell phones and air time [minutes of credit on phone cards] and also cash. . . . They might also have a sexual relationship with a teacher to make sure they get good grades and pass the class, or with a government official to access subsidies, grants, etc." Indeed, young women are strategically engineering sexual relationships to achieve their goals and maximize their gains. Rosa, a twenty-eight-year-old graduate student from Maputo, was sexually involved with three men:

> One partner is for business; I go out with him and he showers me with money and other things. . . . Another partner is for affection, because I love him and I enjoy making love to him. . . . Another one means friendship; I like spending time and having sex with him, but I don't love him. . . . I end up being with A, B, and C, because A has a lot of money but he doesn't satisfy me sexually . . . I am in love with B, but he is married and has to go back to his family . . . and C is a lot of fun, he is outgoing and we hit the clubs and dance all night.

In his study of sexuality among female university students in Dakar, Tshikala Biaya highlights two types of multiple-partner relationships: the *ménage à trois*, where a girl combines her regular boyfriend with a *thiof*,[1] the local metaphor for sugar daddy, who provides money and gifts in exchange for sexual favors, which the girl uses for herself, her boyfriend, and her family; and the *ménage à quatre*, which is slightly more complicated as it also includes a teacher or administrator from the university who assists with class work and administrative matters in exchange for occasional sexual favors (Biaya 2001; Nyamnjoh 2005).

In South Africa, too, young women in waithood engage in sexual relationships with multiple partners. When Mark Hunter asked Mrs. Buthelezi of Kwazulu Natal whether these young women saw themselves as prostitutes, she responded: "It's different. . . . Here, at the township, the level of unemployment is high. The girl comes from Nongoma [in northern Kwazulu Natal] looking for work, she can't find work and she gets a boyfriend who will pay her rent, another to buy her food, another one who is going to give her money, and the other will help her with transport." "The situation forces her," Mrs. Buthelezi concluded (2010, 180–81).

Mobile phones and text messaging facilitate young women's management of multiple relationships (Bruijn et al. 2009). Some have a mobile phone for each partner, often provided by the man himself, which they use to arrange meetings, as well as to avoid mixups in their communications with different partners. In a clever marketing move, cell phone service providers offer free "please call me," which allows the young women to communicate with their partners even when they have no airtime.

Sugar daddies are not a homogeneous group. "Super" sugar daddies can afford the most extravagant gifts; these are mainly members of cabinet, parliamentarians, diplomats, top businessmen, and wealthy foreigners. "Regular" sugar daddies are middle-class men with some resources to spare; they are mainly civil servants, businessmen, university lecturers, teachers, and the like. Most are married and have families. Their financial power, rather than their looks or sexual performance, guarantees their success with young women. The types of relationships that develop are also diverse, ranging from occasional sexual encounters with little affection to more regular companionship. Some "super" sugar daddies install their mistresses in a small apartment where they can meet regularly. Sharing a common space changes the dynamic of the relationship and the young woman's obligations toward her sugar daddy. Other relationships are less bound, offering young women more room to maneuver.

Sugar-daddy relationships are not exclusive. Many girls in sugar-daddy relationships also have a steady boyfriend, generally a young man their own age who is unable to provide the resources offered by older, more affluent men. The story of Samir, a young man I met in Tunis, illustrates some of the dilemmas that young men face. At twenty-eight, he was sad about losing his girlfriend of three years. The relationship started to deteriorate a year before when his girlfriend turned twenty-six and began mentioning that she wanted to get married; warning him that she was not getting any younger, she urged him to try harder to find a job. While Samir was aware of the difficulties of their situation, all he could get were temporary freelance jobs. Thanks to his diploma in audiovisual arts and computers, he did find occasional short-term computer programming and audiovisual montage jobs. One day a couple of friends told him that they had seen his girlfriend with another man. When he confronted her, she admitted that she had been seeing this man and told him she was leaving him. "I later found out that her new lover was a forty-year-old man, married with two children, who had a good position in a private company. . . . He had a very nice car and showered her with expensive gifts. . . . How could I compete with that?" Samir concluded despondently.

In this case the couple broke up, but in a surprising number of instances the boyfriend remains in the relationship. In the absence of viable economic alternatives, an intergenerational sexual relationship complements the romantic relationship between two young people. The older man provides the young woman with the economic resources she needs, and she shares them with her boyfriend. In this way, as Mark Hunter points out, a sugar daddy is seen as a secondary lover, because there is little expectation that the relationship will lead to marriage (2011, 191).

While some young women may try to hide their sugar-daddy relationships from their boyfriends, many are open about it; after all, it is hard to keep these relationships secret. As Coumba, a twenty-nine-year-old Senegalese woman, put it: "How can you hide the relationship? Your boyfriend will wonder where the money and the nice stuff is coming from, and you need to be able to explain." Boyfriends often resign themselves to the fact that they cannot compete with rich older men and end up accepting the situation and, indeed, benefiting from it.

Sugar Mamas,[2] Beach Boys, and *Toubabs*

"It is not just girls who go out with older rich people. . . . Boys too, they have older women with whom they have sex and receive money, gifts, and other favors from. . . . Some hook up with older *toubab* [European] women," said Fatou, a twenty-five-year-old Senegalese woman.

While it appears that young women more frequently engage in transactional sex, some young men are no less preoccupied with the financial security, fashion, and other gifts and protections that transactional sex may offer. This dynamic is clear in the story of Abdoul, a twenty-eight-year-old man who lives in Tunis. When I interviewed Abdoul, he told me that he owed about 2,500TND (US$1,750) in university fees and had only one week to pay; otherwise he would not be allowed to continue the course. So, he said, "I have to go and see a couple of old ladies that I sleep with from time to time when I need money. . . . One of them wants me to become her regular lover, but I don't want it, I prefer to visit her from time to time when I feel like it . . . or, better, when I need money." Both of these women were in their forties and held well-paid, full-time jobs. One was married; the other, the one who wanted a more regular sexual relationship, was single.

Pap, a twenty-three-year-old Senegalese student, had an ongoing sexual relationship with an older woman he met a few times a week just for sex. He also had a *copine* (girlfriend). According to Pap, sex with the older woman was good, but it was just sex; the person he was really in love with was his girlfriend. Older women who engage in sexual relationships with young men are known in Senegal as *diriyanke* (Nyamnjoh 2005). *Diriyankes* are normally single or divorced women who have been successful in business and are in a position to reward younger men financially. They dress exquisitely in traditional *boubous* (local wide-sleeved robes) and wear lots of expensive jewelry. In general, *diriyankes* are sexually mature and reputed to be expert in the art of seduction (Nyamnjoh 2005). With the income from his sexual transactions with his *diriyanke*, Pap was able to alleviate his financial pressures and afford occasional gifts for his girlfriend as well as take her out to *patisseries* from time to time.

Abdoul's and Pap's sugar mamas were both affluent local women, but Sulemane's sugar mamas are mainly *toubab* women, mostly European tourists. Sulemane, a twenty-seven-year-old Senegalese, was born in Rufiske on the outskirts of Dakar as the fourth in a family of six children. His parents are poor; his father is a tailor and his mother a housewife. He dropped out of school at the age of sixteen and worked as a street vendor until he discovered bodybuilding. He and his friends often do gymnastics on the beach in front of the *corniche*, the famous ocean drive in Dakar. With his virile physique, Sulemane had no trouble attracting the attention of foreign women who visit Senegal for what many youths call the "three Ss: sun, sea, and sex." Sulemane started engaging in transactional sex with older, white European women and became what locals call a *côtéman* (beach boy).[3] *Côtéman* generally hang around hotels and beaches and offer sex to tourists, primarily women but also men, in exchange for money and gifts. A few lucky ones may be able to secure a plane ticket and a visa to visit their sugar mamas in Europe. It is easy to spot a beach boy, I was told, as they are well built with extremely athletic physiques; they normally have long dreadlocks, which they tie back with bandanas in colorful Rastafarian tones. Many wear baggy patchwork trousers of printed African cloth; jewelry made from beads and shells adorns their neck and wrists. This rather stereotypical description of beach boys as presented by the Senegalese I spoke with coincides with Emilie Venables's (2009) account of beach boys in Casamance, on the southern coast of Senegal.

The development and flourishing of sex tourism for Europeans in Senegal and neighboring Gambia has been well documented (Nyanzi et al. 2005; De Jong 2007; Venables 2009; Chant and Evans 2010). Although beach boys are often seen in a negative light and connected with sexual promiscuity and trickery, some scholars argue that this is merely an unconventional way to earn a livelihood. Beach boys seem proud of what they do and see themselves as providing tourists with a commodity they are looking for (Venables

2009). Indeed, while they might be seen as simply selling sex, many beach boys develop skills that enable them to operate in the tourist environment. Many become knowledgeable guides, sell artifacts and African jewelry, or learn how to play drums (*djembes*) and improvise music sessions for their customers. Registered guides formally employed in the tourism industry tend to dislike beach boys and see them as competitors (Venables 2009).

Moussa, a thirty-one-year-old dreadlocked drum player, said that "the women come here alone. They hit on you, and you go with it. . . . They like men with *rastas* [Rastafarian-style dreadlocks] who play the *djembes*. It's part of the ambiance." Being a beach boy is "a question of survival. Life is hard. If I didn't have these women, I'd be struggling."[4] Moussa said that he has received countless gifts from European women visiting Senegal, including CDs, USB drives, a guitar, an MP3 player, and a DVD player. "I don't ask for money. . . . We go out. They pay for everything. We have sex. Before they leave, they give me a bit of cash to help me out." Both Sulemane and Moussa hope that one day they will be lucky enough to meet a woman who will take them to Europe. Moussa says longingly, "I haven't met her yet . . . the woman who will get me a visa and a plane ticket out of here."

Lucas, a thirty-two-year-old Mozambican, traveled to Sweden with his sugar mama and lived there for about a year before returning home. They met in Mozambique when the Swedish woman, twenty-five years his senior, was working there for an international company. What started with occasional sexual encounters turned into a more stable relationship. Lucas moved into her apartment, and six months later they moved to Stockholm. "Life in that country was very hard for me because I didn't speak the language and culturally it was very different. . . . It was very, very cold in the winter. . . . She loved me and treated me well, but I completely depended on her for everything. . . . In the end it wasn't working for me. . . . Deep down I was not really in love with her, and I missed my country. . . . One day I got the courage to tell her that I wanted to come back home." While these relationships may occasionally offer the possibility of moving to Europe, they are not seen as a strategy for international migration.

Transactional sex between young Senegalese women and *toubab* men also occurs in Dakar. Senegalese girls openly display affection toward older, gray-haired, white men in expensive restaurants, luxury hotels, and trendy nightclubs. Some newspapers and magazines carry personals ads that typically state: "Beautiful young Senegalese female looks for white European man for romantic relationship." These relationships vary from prostitution to the sugar-daddy type, depending on the reciprocal obligations involved.

Through transactional sex, young men and women are able to alleviate the financial burdens on their families. They no longer have to draw on family resources; some may even contribute to the family budget and bring home gifts. Many young people I spoke with mentioned that parents are aware of these relationships and welcome the resources they bring to the household. While parents find these relationships morally wrong, they tend to turn a blind eye because it helps alleviate the financial strains they face in everyday life. "Some parents support these sex relationships with older people or with foreigners because they help bring money home. . . . Some even encourage their daughters to seek out rich men who can provide. . . . It is sad but that's what poverty and economic hardship are doing to people in our townships. . . . Those who have money are the ones that people value today," said Thandu, a twenty-four-year-old woman in Soweto.

While these relationships are an important strategy for coping with the difficult conditions young people face, there are risks associated with them, including exposure to HIV and other sexually transmitted infections (STIs). In sub-Saharan Africa rates of HIV infection are increasing faster among young women than among young men.[5] Women constitute more than 75 percent of those living with HIV (UNAIDS 2006), and heterosexual sex is the main form of transmission (Njue et al. 2011). Some scientists have called attention to the fact that women are more susceptible than men to contracting the HIV virus because the female genital tract has a greater exposed surface area than the male genital tract (Pettifor et al. 2007; Hunter 2010). In addition, the most widely promoted form of protection against STIs has been the male condom, whose effectiveness depends entirely on men's willingness to use it. While some young women are able to negotiate safe sex in their relationships, not all of them are able to do so; the youngest and most impoverished are most vulnerable. Prostitution may limit women's ability to demand the use of a condom, as their agency is severely constrained (Leclerc-Madlala 2001; Luke 2009; Njue et al. 2011). Gender-related power differences are critical to understanding the high prevalence of HIV infection among young women.

Virginity, Hymenoplasty, and Marriage

Some young women in Africa struggle with long-established social and religious mores requiring brides to be virgins. Samir, whose girlfriend left him for a sugar daddy, pointed out some of the issues related to premarital intercourse. He was very much in love with his girlfriend, but "during the three years we were together I never touched her [made love to her]. . . . I respected her because I wanted to marry her." Although he believed that women should have the freedom to control their own bodies, he did not want his girlfriend to be humiliated by others. He wanted to preserve her dignity and the honor of her family by making sure she was virgin at the time of their marriage. He believed that was the greatest expression of his love for her. Women's virginity is still a major issue in Tunisia, and there is overwhelming social pressure against premarital sexual intercourse. Despite all the appearances of modernity, female virginity at marriage is a prerequisite for many families across varied social strata.

Today, however, the average age of women's first sexual experience is declining, and the proportion of females engaging in premarital intercourse is increasing (Foster 2002). As in most times of rapid social change, there is a disturbing dissonance between sexual realities and societal expectations. Due to the economic crisis and lack of employment opportunities for youth, the average age at first marriage for Tunisian women is now twenty-eight. Young unemployed men are unable to acquire the resources to marry and establish families of their own. The tensions between socioeconomic reality and social and religious mores place significant pressure on many young women—both those who choose to abstain from sexual activity and those who engage in it. Zeinab, a twenty-six-year-old Tunisian woman, stated clearly that this was a major problem for women, because "our partners want to have sex and we have to say no, and sometimes a girl may lose a boyfriend because of that, as he will look for a girl who gives him sex." Other young women said that men want to have sex but then don't want to marry a girl who is not virgin and criticized the men's hypocrisy. Abdelijelil, a twenty-eight-year-old man, emphasized that young men want to have sexual experiences with their girlfriends before marriage, especially because they have to wait so long to marry. At the same time, if the girls are not virgins, the men often refuse to marry them, mainly because of family, religion, and other social pressures.

> It is a contradiction experienced by Tunisian young men. . . . True, there are girls to marry and girls to play with . . . but at the end of the day every woman is somebody's daughter and somebody's sister. . . . Also you want to share that experience with your girlfriend . . . and the girls also want to have that experience too. . . . It is becoming more difficult for young women to abstain from sex until they get married. . . . We want to enjoy our youth and our freedom.

Pressure to preserve their virginity affects young women from all social strata. For example, young women who leave their hometown for the big cities to pursue a university education are often cast under suspicion. Many are asked by the groom's family to obtain a certificate of virginity issued by a doctor. Even when the potential in-laws do not demand a certificate, the young woman's own family might offer to provide one in order to dispel any possible doubts. Many young women try to find a compromise between their desire to be sexually active and societal pressure to remain virgin. Some opt to refrain from sexual acts that can rupture the hymen. As twenty-four-year-old Aicha explained, "We have to try and be intimate with our partners in ways that preserve our virginity. . . . The positive side of that is that we have to be creative and explore other forms of sexual intimacy and pleasure without vaginal penetration." But some young women I spoke with said that they still felt curious and somewhat unsatisfied because they had not fully experienced sex. As Zeinab stated: "The forbidden fruit is always the more desirable. . . . No matter how pleasurable are the other things you do, you always wonder how it would feel like to do it like everybody else does. . . . After all, vaginal penetration is how most people have sex, so why should we be different?"

Despite their efforts to abstain, more and more young women do not keep their virginity until marriage. "The majority of the girls that I know have already had sexual intercourse," asserted Jamila, a twenty-two-year-old Tunisian woman. As Aicha pointed out: "Our society is full of inconsistencies. . . . Women have rights, they can smoke, they can wear tight jeans, short skirts, and show their bellies. . . . But they can't lose their virginity before marriage."

One of the consequences of the increase in premarital sex is the escalation in requests for virginity certificates and the demand for hymen-repair surgery. In Tunisia, according to Angel Foster, a growing number of gynecologists provide hymen restoration in private clinics, even though the procedure is officially banned. One physician stated: "Though I think it is a form of deception, I reconstruct women's hymens. I don't believe that a girl's life should be ruined because of an adventure. Tunisian mores are conservative and there is a double standard, so I don't feel any guilt about my work" (Foster 2002, 104–5). According to Jamila: "the surgical operations are very popular. . . . Everybody knows about the clinics but nobody says anything. . . . It's like, do it but don't discuss it openly." Young women have recourse to surgery to avoid shame and embarrassment for their families. Having sugar daddies who can cover the costs makes them free to enjoy sexual experiences with both their sugar daddies and their boyfriends. Hymenoplasty is considered a relatively minor surgical procedure, so it has become a convenient solution for many women who can afford it.

A 2010 documentary entitled *National Hymen: The Malaise in Islam"*by Belgian-Tunisian director Jamel Mokni has generated considerable debate. The film showcases interviews with various groups of people in Tunisia about women's virginity and premarital sex. Unlike previous documentaries on sensitive issues, the director and the interviewees agreed not to have their faces blurred. The hour-long film explores how Tunisian mores have changed over time and discusses the rise in the average age at marriage as well as the growth in the demand for hymen surgery. The film highlights society's double standard. Women are rarely forgiven for losing their virginity and are held responsible for upholding their family's honor, while the men to whom they lost their virginity are never responsible for ruining a family's reputation. The documentary was banned from the Carthage Film Festival in October 2010 on the grounds of being offensive to Muslims. Clandestine screenings in the country, however, increased awareness and stimulated discussion. In a television interview Mokni mentioned that even in Belgium and France the film faced strong opposition from Muslim communities. This topic is a delicate one for Muslims, especially men. As Mokni pointed out, the virginity of women instills a sense of masculinity and power in men that they are afraid of losing.[6]

In Senegal widely held Muslim mores require young women to preserve their virginity for marriage, but people appear more tolerant of premarital sex, or at least turn a blind eye. Young people I met in Dakar believe that the majority of girls engage in sex before marriage. "Although the norm is still there nobody really respects it. . . . And nobody talks about it either. . . . We all pretend that everything is okay, even on the wedding night," said Bobo, a twenty-one-year-old woman from Kaolack. According to Anouka van Eerdewijk, who studied premarital sexuality in Dakar, on the wedding night families still claim the virginity of the bride to keep their dignity, even though nobody has any illusions about most brides. False shows of blood have been used for many years; everyone knows, but no one talks about it. The ritual of the wedding night, known as the *jéballe*, in which a woman has to prove that she is a virgin, is still practiced. However, one almost never hears of a wedding being called off because the girl was not a virgin. Following the ritual tradition, the next morning the aunts of the bride visit the couple's room and come out singing that all is in order; the marriage was consummated according to tradition. Indeed, people do not dissociate themselves openly from this practice because "the bride and groom as well as the bride's relatives have a vested interested in claiming virginity" (van Eerdewijk 2009, 13).

In Senegal, as in Tunisia, there is a discrepancy between traditional and religious mores regarding young women's premarital sexuality and the freedom they enjoy today, especially in urban centers. Abdoulaye Diop emphasizes that in Senegal "people make reference to symbols that pretend to refer to the same meanings as before. But they are either trickery and deception, like the nuptial sheet, or purely formal, like the *prix de la virginité* [price of virginity]. They do not carry any real meaning any more apart from expressing an effort to appear to respect a past that, in fact, in many ways substantially differs from the present" (1985, 123). The young women whom I interviewed in Dakar never discussed their particular situations but addressed the issue in general terms, saying that "today girls in Senegal have more control over their sexuality." While they continue to publicly acknowledge the social norm requiring female virginity, they are critical of the ritual of the wedding night, which their families insist on maintaining. Young people's desire for sexual autonomy and their engagement in transactional sex have become part of local constructions of masculinity and femininity in a context of widespread unemployment and scarcity.

Refashioning Masculinity and Femininity

These new geographies of sex among young people are challenging hegemonic notions of masculinity and femininity. African masculinities based on men's position as providers are being undermined by rising unemployment, as men are no longer able to fulfill conventional social expectations (Arnfred 2004). Although today many men in their twenties are unable to get a stable job, build or rent a home, marry, and establish a family, many remain deeply influenced by society's ideal of men as breadwinners. Indeed, the young men I spoke with often felt inadequate and described their predicament as "not being man enough" or being "a worthless man." This sentiment was related to the way society regarded them, as well as to their families' and girlfriends' complaints that they do not provide financial support (Groes-Green 2009). The power that impoverished, unemployed young men have over women is fragile and unstable. In the absence of work, status, and money, "male identity and self-esteem become increasingly linked to sexuality and sexual manifestations" (Silberschmidt 2004, 234). Young men reassert their masculinity through power that derives from the body (Groes-Green 2009), constructing their masculinity on the basis of sexual conquests and sexual performance (Arnfred 2004).

Indeed, unemployed young men in waithood lack the economic advantage over women that employed men have. Sexual power is the only tool left to them. Young men improve their physique and bodily performance to attract older women and foreign tourists; boyfriends try to maintain their relationships with their girlfriends by being better in bed than sugar daddies. Young men's preoccupation with their bodies and with satisfying their female partners illustrate a search for power and authority over women in the sexual arena (Groes-Green 2009). Similarly, some men resort to violence and coercion to express their power and assert control over their girlfriends or other women. Young men feel diminished by their inability to provide help financially and to offer gifts to the women they are intimate with, seeing their poverty as an insult to their manhood (Groes-Green 2009). While not all violence against women can be attributed to the disempowerment of men, many observers have pointed out links between male violence against women and men's marginalization (Bourgois 1995; Silberschmidt 1999; Morrell 2003; Barker 2005; Dunkle et al. 2007). In South Africa, for example, massive male unemployment and the high incidence of rape can be seen as evidence for the socioeconomic basis of violence against women. Mark Hunter points out that the increase in gang rape (called jackrolling) in South Africa appears to be consistent with an unmooring of gender norms at a time when many men are unable to find work and marry (2010, 173).[7]

Femininity has been constructed through passivity and subordination to men. Some researchers emphasize the emergence of notions of female agency and power, including ideas of respectability and female independence (Haram 2005; Spronk 2007). Men have often been depicted as taking the initiative in sexual matters, inviting a woman to have sex or to become his partner, while women are supposed to be passive (Loforte 2000; Bagnol and Chamo 2004). Scholars have contested these views about women's complete powerlessness in sexual matters, however (Groes-Green 2011). The stories of young women engaged in multiple relationships with sugar daddies and boyfriends suggest that women actively initiate and control these sexual relationships. Some appear to have the upper hand over their sexual partners as they navigate among men, put their boyfriends in a position of either accepting the sugar daddy or leaving, and carve their sexual and financial independence by avoiding being controlled by any one man. Maria's refusal to become solely dependent on her Dutch lover and her decision to take on other sugar daddies illustrate the point. Women also make sure that they find sexual satisfaction; a boyfriend's desire to continue the relationship ensures that he pays attention to the woman's pleasure.

Women are increasingly becoming agents in their own sexual lives in places across the global South. Jennifer Gregg's work with young women in Recife, Brazil, demonstrates that women try to guarantee their relative independence by ensuring that the material benefit of sexual engagements do not come from a single man who could exercise control over them, but from a changing and flexible network of men, none of whom is able to wield power over them (Gregg 2003). The agency of young women in these instances is often perceived in negative terms, described as "milking," "sucking," or "putting men in the bottle"[8] (Hawkins et al. 2009). As Christian Groes-Green (2011) asserts, these expressions position young women as powerful agents who extract value and money from men. Men, on the other hand, are seen as victims who are easily manipulated.

These young women do not conceive of themselves as passive or coerced victims in their relationships with men. Rather, they are involved in a continuing process of defining their social and sexual identities and making choices about the activities they engage in and the risks they run. Transactional sex is seen as a strategy by which they are able to reverse the existing balance of gender and power relations and gain access to the material goods and lifestyle that symbolize modernity and success (Hawkins et al. 2009).

Young women's relationships with sugar daddies can be understood as part of a process through which new ideals of female agency and independence are being constructed across Africa, especially in urban settings (Cole 2004; Haram 2005; Silberschmidt and Rasch 2001). Young women's drive to control their sexuality, become independent, and achieve relative economic stability challenges conventional notions of ideal womanhood centering on female virginity, arranged marriage, and obligations to the extended family (Tersbøl 2005; Mills and Ssewakiryanga 2005; Spronk 2007; Groes-Green 2011). These shifts demonstrate the contingent and fluid nature of masculinity and femininity in dynamic social, economic, and cultural settings.

Marriage: A Costly but Desirable Affair

The consequences of unemployment for young people go well beyond seeing their girlfriends or boyfriends become involved with wealthier, older people or having to put up with a triangular relationship that includes a sugar daddy or sugar mama. In the long run poverty makes it impossible for young adults to pay the costs of a marriage, set up a home of their own, and raise children together. Across the continent marriage has been delayed, and the proportion of adults who are married has declined sharply. Most people in their parents' generation had married by their mid-twenties, but today a large proportion of people aged twenty-five to twenty-nine are not married. This delay is mostly involuntary and reflects the economic challenges they face in an environment of high unemployment and low wages (Dhillon and Yousef 2007, 2009). Marriage not only costs more than they can afford but is based on assumptions about providing for a family that they are unable to fulfill.

In most African societies marriage is still considered a critical marker of adulthood and family remains the cornerstone of society. Young people continue to aspire to achieve adult social status through this rite of passage. Moreover, sexual relationships and childbearing only gain legitimacy within the institution of marriage. Today, however, waithood allows young people, especially young women, to enjoy new life experiences and redefine their priorities. Young women are staying in school longer and marrying later, or not at all. Those who previously took for granted the ideal of marriage as the route to social adulthood have now been forced to question it. Even those who affirm the value of the institution cannot avoid facing the fact that it is becoming unattainable.

The high cost of getting married is a serious problem. Many young people I interviewed spoke of the substantial expenditures associated with marriage rituals. Although they vary among societies and cultures, ceremonies can be very complex, last for several days, and involve large amounts of money, especially on the part the groom and his family. In Egypt, Diane Singerman (2007) found, the average cost of a wedding is equivalent to about four years of the entire earnings of both the groom and his father.

In Mozambique young people may choose a civil marriage, a religious marriage, or a traditional marriage. Some people celebrate all three forms, while others settle for one or two. In rural areas the traditional and religious forms are more popular, while in urban settings people generally opt for civil and religious marriages. All these types of marriage are preceded by ceremonies that mark the end of courtship and the intention to marry. *Noivado* is a modern engagement ceremony in which the families of the prospective bride and groom meet for a meal at the bride's home and the groom offers his bride a ring. The traditional betrothal ceremony is called *ku buta*, a Ronga verb meaning to ask for the girl's hand in marriage. The groom has to offer gifts to his bride, mainly clothes and jewelry. While the *ku buta* is followed by the *lobolo*, the traditional ceremony, the *noivado* is followed by civil or religious ceremonies. Even before the wedding the groom and his family have to pay the expenses involved.

Civil marriages are officiated over by the representatives of the state and are legally binding. In a Western-style marriage the bride wears a long white wedding gown and the groom a formal suit. The ceremony is generally held in the Palacio dos Casamentos, a public building designated for weddings, and is followed by a reception at a hotel, restaurant, or family compound. The costs involved in a civil union are extremely high, as people have to pay for clothing, the reception, a rental car, the photographer, and a DJ or a band. Young people estimated that the average cost for a civil wedding today in Maputo ranges between 15 and 20 million MT (US$4,000–6,000). Few young men can afford the expense, even if they have employment, because they also have to build or rent and furnish a house. Among middle-class families the bride's and groom's families may share the costs of the reception, but the groom's side generally contributes a larger amount. Religious marriages take place in a church or mosque and are officiated over by a priest, minister, or imam. Couples frequently have civil and religious marriages on the same day, which minimizes the cost.

Lobolo in Mozambique (known as *lobola* in South Africa) is the traditional marriage ceremony. It involves the presentation of money and gifts by the groom's family to the bride's family. In the past this payment was merely symbolic, but recently it has become a source of revenue. Some families demand hundreds of thousands of meticals for giving their daughters in marriage. They also ask for gifts, such as jewelry for the bride, including a ring; clothes for the bride, her father, mother, and grandmother; and five liters of wine for the family to share with the ancestors and other relatives. The *lobolo* ceremony establishes the union of the two families as well as the union of the couple (Loforte 2000; Granjo 2005; Bagnol 2008). While in the past *lobolo* was enough to legitimize the union and the groom could take his wife home, today people tend to combine the *lobolo* with a civil and/or religious ceremony.

Not only is the cost of *lobolo* unaffordable for the majority of young men, but many of the young women I spoke with in Maputo do not favor the idea of the groom paying a large sum of money to marry them. "It feels like we are being sold. . . . Some families see this as a compensation for their daughter's education; the more educated she is the more money they ask for. . . . It is wrong, I don't agree with it," said twenty-one-year-old Rita. On the other hand, twenty-eight-year-old Nilza said:

> I don't have a problem with *lobolo*; I think it is important because it brings us back to our roots. . . . When I got married last year my family had a *lobolo* ceremony alongside the civil and religious ceremonies. But my *lobolo* was symbolic, not based on an economic transaction, but on bringing together both our families and remembering our ancestors. . . . The gifts that my husband's family brought were mainly traditional gifts like *mukumi ni vemba* [pieces of fabric for women]. . . . They also brought a ring for me and wine to offer the ancestors. The money was symbolic, just 2,500 MT [about US$9].

Making gifts symbolic is one way of perpetuating traditional marriage, but that depends on the families' willingness to forgo conspicuous displays of wealth and the couple's ability to start its own household without such gifts.

In the cities we can witness the recuperation of "tradition," especially among middle-class people who seek to affirm their cultural identity. They incorporate traditional marriage rituals alongside civil and/or religious marriages. In Nilza's case the engagement ceremony was conflated with *lobolo*, as she received her engagement ring alongside the traditional gifts and offerings to the ancestors.

Black South Africans' traditional marriage practices are very similar to those in Mozambique. But some modern elements have been added to *lobola*. In 2007 a South African company decided to offer model agreements to families entering into a traditional marriage. The new *lobola* contract became a legally binding document that confirms that a couple has entered into a marriage and holds the same weight as a community property agreement signed at the Department of Home Affairs or a prenuptial agreement drawn up by an attorney. It offers legal protection to the new generation of Africans who opt to take this traditional route to marriage.[9]

In Senegal and Tunisia, Muslim marriage ceremonies last for almost a week, and the groom has to pay most of the cost. In Tunisia the ritual starts with the ceremony of *mahr* (the bride price), which the groom has to offer the bride's family (Esposito and DeLong-Bas 2001; Fournier 2010). Then come the bride's *henna* ceremonies, which may last up to three days and include a series of *hammam* (traditional steam bath) treatments and *henna* (red dye from a plant) decorations of the body (especially hands and feet) for the bride and her friends. This is followed by a day of rest for the bride and the beginning of the *henna* ceremonies on the groom's side. The wedding ceremony, *nikah*, marks the climax of the celebration. It may take place at home or in a hotel or restaurant and is officiated over by the *mufti* (an official of religious law), who approves the marriage contract, the *Aqd-Nikah*. The ceremony is followed by a reception with a band and plenty of food and drink. The middle classes generally celebrate the final ceremony in a Western style, with the bride wearing a white wedding gown and the groom a formal suit. However, couples who choose a more traditional wedding wear traditional clothing, a *melia* for the bride and a *jebba* for the groom.

Today, *mahr* remains an integral component of a legal Tunisian marriage. Without paying the bride price promptly, the groom cannot legitimately consummate the marriage. Today, however, it has become a symbolic payment of just 20TND (US$10). In the past the bride's family claimed higher compensation to show that their daughter was used to a life of affluence and required her husband to maintain their standards. The groom's family wanted to show that they were financially secure and their son was able to offer his bride a comfortable life. Changes to this tradition came with Habib Bourguiba, the first president of independent Tunisia, who was an advocate of women's rights. On the occasion of his own marriage in 1962, Bourguiba broke with tradition by paying his wife's family a symbolic token of one Tunisian dinar as *mahr* instead of a substantial amount, even though he could have afforded it. He did so precisely to make the point that it was not necessary to pay a lot of money to marry a woman (Fournier 2010). In

Tunisia, unlike Mozambique and South Africa, *mahr* is purely symbolic. Nevertheless, it does not ease the situation for young men, who still have to pay the other costs associated with marriage celebrations.

More and more young people are unable to save the money they need to be able to marry. "I have a job as a gym teacher, but my fiancé doesn't have employment and relies on occasional jobs," said Henda, a twenty-seven-year-old woman in Bizerte. "We would like to get married but cannot afford it. . . . I would be happy to just live together and use the little money we have to start our life together rather than spending it on celebrations. . . . But my family is not happy with the idea; they say I have to leave home properly."

Indeed, some young people I met were willing to skip marriage rituals and find a way of living with their partner and building a life together. They felt that they were getting old and the prospects for the future were depressingly gloomy. The situation was even more difficult for unemployed youths who are still dependent on their parents. Even those with irregular jobs may not be in a position to make such a commitment given the precariousness of their financial situation. Young women, who are more educated and waiting much longer to marry, are weighing their options and considering whether marriage is right for them.

The institution does establish the legitimacy of the couple's relationship and the children they have together. Fathering a child symbolizes a man's virility and raises his social status. While biological fathering is readily achievable, the fulfillment of the social role of fatherhood is much more challenging. Consider Ntembisa, the thirty-one-year-old in Soweto who has three children with his girlfriend and impregnated another girl. Ntembisa lives at his grandmother's house and struggles to provide regular support for his children, who live with their mother in her parents' home. He has been unable to pay the *lobola* fine (a lesser compensatory amount) to the family of the other girl he got pregnant. He is not reliably present in his children's lives and cannot make claims over them because of his inability to provide. His virility is clear, but he lacks the status of a provider and a family man.

Delayed marriages are imposing new costs on society as young people end up being dependent on their parents for longer and children end up being taken care of by their grandparents. This situation places an enormous financial burden on families. The consequences for children who grow up without two co-resident parents are serious and may last for life. The societal effects of the delay and decline in marriage need further study. Some religious groups try to assist young people by helping with the bride-price payments and sponsoring mass weddings to reduce the cost of the ceremony (Salehi-Isfahani and Dhillon 2008). But these forms of assistance are unusual, and most couples prefer personalized ceremonies.

Changing Intimate Relations

Sugar-daddy relationships are found in developed countries as well as in the global South. In the United States, in part as a result of the deepening economic crisis, sugar daddies are becoming attractive to young women struggling with college tuition or inadequate employment. A number of websites link wealthy men with young women for transactional sex. A *New York Times* article mentions that people using the sites are "not searching for longtime soul mates; they want no-strings-attached 'arrangements' that trade in society's most valued currencies: wealth, youth and beauty."[10] A *Huffington Post* article describes young women who resort to sugar daddies to make money and establish contacts with well-placed men who can help their careers. They may be paid US$1,000–3,000 a month, in addition to expensive gifts and travel. Some sugar-daddy websites target needy students, paying to have their ads pop up whenever someone types in "student loan," "tuition help," or "college support."[11] Parties where affluent men pay to meet attractive younger women are held in the United States and the UK.[12] In a time of economic recession young people come to regard their bodies as livelihood assets (Chant and Evans 2010).

In Africa widespread unemployment and underemployment, poverty, and socioeconomic crises induce boyfriends and girlfriends to accept the presence of third parties in their relationship, changing the nature of intimacy. What happens to the emotional dimension of romantic relationships when one party is subsidized by a sugar daddy or sugar mama? How do young men and women adjust to these complex sexual and financial exchanges? Traditional courtship was based on exclusivity, with men feeling possessive of their girlfriends and with lots of jealousy between partners. How are those feelings negotiated and managed in these intricate, multiple-partner relationships? We must also wonder whether young married couples with meager resources engage in transactional sex in order to lead a more comfortable life.

At the same time it is important to recognize that young people are exercising their agency within these complex sexual relationships rather than simply being victimized by the exchange. Investing in their physique and sexual prowess, beach boys in Senegal create an image of exotic Africa that features not only sun, sea, and palm trees but also sculpted black bodies with dreadlocked hair, wearing colorful fabrics and beads, playing drums, and sipping coconut drinks. The young men create and purvey this vision of the exotic "other" that many female European tourists desire. Similarly, young women exercise control in their relationships with sugar daddies. By engaging in relationships with multiple partners, they avoid being dominated by or fully dependent on any one partner. Despite their money and social status, sugar daddies can be manipulated. The delay in marriage offers young women a vast array of options and freedoms that they would not have if they were married.

It is important to remember that these sexual relationships can be lethal. Sugar daddies are often reluctant to use condoms, and young women may find it difficult or impossible to demand that they do so. Although some young women claim that they insist that their sexual partners use condoms, UNAIDS statistics indicate that the risk of HIV transmission remains high; in Mozambique, for example, young women account for 60 percent of all new infections (UNAIDS 2006). The Mozambican Ministry of Health estimated in 2010 that young females were the most vulnerable group to HIV infection, with a prevalence rate of 23 percent in Maputo. HIV/AIDS awareness organizations often fail to appeal to youth. For example, the LoveLife AIDS intervention program for youth in South Africa became caught up in ABC advocacy (**A**bstinence, **B**eing faithful, and **C**ondom use) and was unable to address the complexity of young people's sexual experiences and desires.

As the lack of jobs, inability to find housing, and high cost of marriage rituals, coupled with not finding a suitable spouse or a preference for remaining single, lead people to postpone marriage, sometimes indefinitely, young people are creating new approaches to sexuality and intimate relationships (Singerman 2007). In the process they are fashioning new forms of masculinity and femininity and challenging existing notions of female and male sexuality in their societies. While marriage rates are declining sharply in all four countries, many of the young people I spoke with still aspire to marry and establish their own families. They see their financial inability to do so as a particularly bitter aspect of their situation in waithood.

The next chapter discusses young people's participatory citizenship, looking at the ways they understand the political and socioeconomic situations in which they live and the efforts they are making to contribute to positive change.

Chapter 6

Citizenship

Feeling rejected by their elders who provide no space for youth voices, the waithood generation is rejecting formal party politics and the corruption the young people associate with it. The absence of political role models and spaces for critical youth involvement further distances them from dominant political structures. But young people in waithood are not apathetic. They are politically engaged in different ways, moving away from hegemonic ideologies and structures and creating new spaces for intervention. Young people engage mainly in civil society associations that they create for themselves outside mainstream structures, using music (especially hip hop) and popular culture as ways of contesting the status quo and leading protests against corrupt governments and politicians.

Young people in Africa face serious economic, social, and emotional challenges in their everyday lives. This African waithood generation was hit harder and earlier by the failures of neoliberalism, and thus its response came first. But globalization has spread new technologies and a global message; as the economic crisis expands, young people in Europe and the United States face the same crisis of joblessness and restricted futures. And in each country youth are responding, in what is becoming a global response. Are we in the presence of the new "1968 generation"?

Not socially recognized as adults, young people in waithood are nevertheless taking on their roles as active citizens and are driving change in their societies. To better understand this, it is useful to look back at debates about citizenship and the way they have often conflated two distinct conceptions of citizenship: *state citizenship*, a legal status of full membership in a particular community; and *participatory citizenship*, "a desirable activity where the extent and quality of one's citizenship is a function of one's participation in that community" (Kymlicka and Norman 1994, 356). In participatory citizenship, citizens become "political actors constituting political spaces" (Stewart 1992). Young Africans—and now young people in the North—see themselves excluded from state citizenship, and thus the new waithood generation is creating its own space through participatory citizenship.

Corrupt Politics and Bad Governance

"Good governance" is frequently used by international organizations and aid agencies, civil society groups, and governments at all levels to refer to the activities of government institutions and their relationship with citizens.[1] One of the cornerstones of good governance is effective participation by civil society groups. Young Africans constitute the majority of the population in their countries but feel politically disfranchised. They are disenchanted with politicians and government institutions that fail to respond to their aspirations and acknowledge their basic needs. Some youths refrain from taking part in the mainstream political process but engage in their own alternative forms of activism, while others feel completely marginalized.

Young people in Mozambique, Senegal, South Africa, and Tunisia feel deeply disconnected from the elites that control the government and national politics. Young people in waithood assert that their governments lack clear vision and political will to deal with the crises affecting youth. All they observe are ad hoc and uncoordinated actions that fail to address their problems effectively. Dino, a thirty-five-year-old who lives in Maputo, pointed out that "there has been a breakdown in communication between my generation and the older generation. . . . The politicians do not understand the youth and don't make the effort to understand us. . . . That hinders the passing of the political torch."

Many Mozambican youths criticize politicians as motivated primarily by self-interest and are alienated by the political corruption they perceive. Sadique, a twenty-two-year-old Mozambican man, stated that young people "lack positive political role models. . . . That's why politics is not attractive to most youths. There is a lot of corruption; many politicians only think of enriching themselves rather than the best interests of the people." Young people I spoke with cited corruption, nepotism, and favoritism as major reasons for their lack of involvement in politics. Eva, a twenty-seven-year-old woman who lives in Maputo, said that in Mozambique "there is an illusion of freedom of expression. [But] deep down there is a culture of obedience and a 'yes man' attitude. . . . People may not be jailed for criticizing the government, but they will certainly be ostracized. Opportunities will be closed to them." Young people are convinced that political connections are essential in order to obtain a job. "You are not able to make it if you are not well connected. You need to know someone important or have a *padrinho* [godfather]. . . . If you have the *vermelho*[2] [Frelimo party membership card], that will open many doors for you. The *vermelho* operates like a credit card," asserted twenty-nine-year-old Bento from Inhambane, a coastal city northeast of Maputo. Young people I spoke with believe that politicians are demagogues; in order to appeal to voters during electoral campaigns, they make promises that they know they will not be able to keep. Once elected, "they forget the voters and behave as if the country were their own private backyard," declared Abel, a twenty-eight-year-old resident of Maputo. With such a dim view of politicians, it is not surprising that some young people in Mozambique do not exercise their right to vote.

I met some young people who belong to youth organizations affiliated with political parties and who try to persuade their peers to vote. In Mozambique those who belong to the opposition parties' youth leagues were very critical of Frelimo's governance. "Frelimo is mixing party politics with the state," said Rogerio, a twenty-four-year-old who lives in the capital. "There are Frelimo party cells in every state institution. To be able to be get a job or be promoted, a person has to be a member of Frelimo. . . . That's not a democracy. The party cells in the state administration offices should be eliminated." The Mozambican Youth Organisation (OJM) was first established as a national umbrella for all Mozambican youth. With the advent of multiparty democracy, however, the OJM became the youth branch of Frelimo. The young men and women from OJM protested that some of the criticism lodged against the party is not fair because the country has made great progress since winning independence in 1975. Marisa explained: "It takes time to build a nation and a democracy. Even in this short time we have done a lot; nobody goes to jail for criticizing the president or the government; we have freedom of the press. That doesn't happen in many countries on our continent." Even OJM members, however, acknowledge that the situation is extremely difficult for young people. The soaring unemployment rate, lack of access to credit, and inefficiency of government institutions are among the main problems they pointed out. But they trust their party's leadership to address these problems and improve prospects for young Mozambicans. Ramos, a twenty-six-year-old man who lives in Maputo, explained that OJM and other party youth groups are unappealing to most young people because "we cannot critically discuss issues of corruption and abuses of power in party youth organizations."

Young people I spoke with complained about the poor quality of political leadership and the impossibility of youth participation and intervention. In the revolutionary period Frelimo had a space for *crítica e autocrítica* (criticism and self-criticism), but young people feel that the party no longer accepts critical views. To thrive in the party you have to be a "yes-man." These perceptions weigh heavily in the cynical view that young people have of politics and politicians in the country today. Anthropologist Adriano Biza called the state a "stepfather" to highlight the sense of neglect felt by youth, as a father would be expected to provide for his children and prepare them for an independent life (Biza 2004). The social contract between the state and its citizens has been broken.

The young South Africans whom I met expressed similar concerns about politics and governance in their country, especially after the retirement of the legendary Nelson Mandela. They pointed to widespread corruption and nepotism at all levels. Young people witness politicians and public officials becoming very rich almost overnight. Siniswa, a twenty-two-year-old woman who lives in Alexandra township in Johannesburg, declared that "top politicians are corrupt and so are the ones at the community level. Everyone tries to survive in whatever way they can." Her remarks were seconded by thirty-year-old Tebogo, who lives in Soweto. He pointed out that numerous politicians have been indicted for corruption. "Zuma himself [the current president] has been accused of corruption alongside his former financial adviser and they went to court. . . . But as everyone knows, high-profile people are immune to the law," Tebogo concluded.

In focus groups young South Africans declared that government institutions were failing to serve their interests. "Our politicians preach support for the poor but they live a life of capitalist luxury," said Kevin, a twenty-four-year-old who lives in Troyeville. They mentioned the abuses perpetrated by a corrupt police force that turns a blind eye to criminals in exchange for bribes. But as Monica, a twenty-three-year-old who lives in Soweto, affirmed: "The police are not well paid and that is part of the problem. The other side of it is that there is a lot of greed in our society. . . . People want to be rich very quickly. The examples come from the leadership of the country."

Young people in South Africa are also concerned with racism and xenophobia,[3] and they think that public officials are not addressing these problems with the seriousness they deserve. Vuyo, a twenty-nine-year-old who lives in Hillbrow, an inner-city neighborhood in Johannesburg that used to be a "whites only" area but has become a decaying, albeit vibrant, urban slum, said that "some white people still look down on black people. . . . These days racism is a bit more subtle, but it is there. Also some black people have issues against white people. . . . If a black person befriends white people, the black people call you a coconut"—white inside and black outside. Thaba, a thirty-three-year-old man who lives in the township of Tembissa, agreed: "Apartheid ended seventeen years ago, but there are still fewer opportunities for black people. Today's discrimination is based on geography. If you live in a township you are less likely to succeed because you can't attend good schools, get a good job, and move out of the township. It is still racism because the townships are where the majority of black people live." Affirmative action policies and the Black Economic Empowerment (BEE) program do not serve everyone; instead, as many young people pointed out, they only benefit a select group of well-connected individuals and families.

With regard to xenophobia, Dumisani, a twenty-eight-year-old man who lives in Alexandra, an impoverished township adjacent to the wealthy, predominantly white suburb of Sandton, explained that "these problems arise because the black population in South Africa, particularly in the townships, is struggling with lack of jobs and the cost of living. The lack of government attention to people's suffering makes them turn against their brothers and sisters from other African countries who are also struggling to survive. Poverty turns the poor against each other."

That is what happened in 2008, when violent mobs of xenophobic South Africans attacked foreign immigrants, known in the townships as *makwer-ekwere*, from countries such as Zimbabwe, Mozambique, and Malawi. Some were illegal immigrants trying to earn a livelihood in South Africa, but others were in the country legally and contributing to the South African economy (Kirshner 2011). Billy, a twenty-one-year-old from Kensington, said that the xenophobic attacks "were like a revolution but a revolution in the wrong direction because it should have been directed [against] the government . . . like they did in North Africa."

Julius Malema, the outspoken thirty-year-old president of the ANC Youth League, has sparked controversy by taking radical positions advocating the empowerment of the masses. Malema garnered attention in 2007 for rallying behind Jacob Zuma, helping him become the head of the ANC and then president of South Africa. Malema has spoken out against big business and in favor of the redistribution of resources. He has sided with the poor and the black population, often to the point of opposing some ANC and government policies. But not all young people support him. Sindhi, a twenty-year-old woman who lives on the southwest side of Johannesburg in Ormonde, said: "I don't agree with him. He got up there too quickly, and is very vocal. . . . He believes that he can say just anything to anybody because he supported President Zuma." Although most of the young South Africans I spoke with agreed with Malema's pro-poor positions, they worried that his radical pronouncements can be divisive. As twenty-two-year-old Sibusisiwe asserted, "In the new South Africa we are a very diverse group of people, and we have to find a common ground and live well together."

In August 2011 some media outlets reported that Julius Malema had been reprimanded by the ANC leadership for bringing the party into disrepute with a series of inflammatory outbursts, undermining President Zuma's mediation efforts in Zimbabwe by openly supporting Robert Mugabe. He was also criticized for ignoring a party instruction to stop singing the song "Shoot the Boer."[4] More recently, Malema called for the nationalization of state assets. Some have also accused Malema of bigotry, alleging that his family trust benefits directly from the multimillion–rand tenders it helps to award, an accusation he vehemently denies. Whatever the case, it is true that the ANC Youth League has been one of the loud voices opposing some of the regime's policies. Workers in the trade union organization, COSATU, are also contesting the privatization of state assets undertaken by the government. COSATU members have organized several strikes protesting the high cost of living and low wages. As Zwelinzima Vavi, COSATU's secretary-general, pointed out, "Privatization has never worked in favor of the working class." The organization has joined the ANC Youth League in its call for the nationalization of state assets.[5] COSATU's leader criticized the ANC by saying that individualism and greed were eroding the ANC principle of selflessness; the leaders are not addressing "the real challenges and that is why [one day] they will wake up in Tunisia." They are "making no difference in the lives of ordinary people," Vavi concluded.[6]

In Senegal, too, young people are cynical about politicians. This dissatisfaction was expressed in the late 1990s when youth played a role in turning out the Socialist Party (PS), which had ruled the country for forty years. In 2000 the Senegalese Democratic Party (PDS) won the elections, and Abdoulaye Wade finally replaced Abdou Diouf as president. Today, however, the very same concerns that young people had about the PS are being expressed about the PDS government. Young Senegalese I met were unanimous in saying that the PDS is losing popular support and legitimacy because of its corrupt and *clientéliste* politics and its inability to tackle the economic crisis. Malick, a twenty-seven-year-old from Rufisque, a port city near Dakar, pointed out that "there is a crisis of social and moral values in Senegal. Politics here are very dysfunctional, because the core value of politics for Senegalese politicians is money, just money." Young people said they feel marginalized from formal political life; there are no institutional channels for them to be heard or contribute. Like South African and Mozambican youths, they feel that politicians use them to get elected and then forget about them. "Youth were behind Abdoulaye Wade, but he has done nothing for young people. We have no jobs, we have no credit to start small businesses, nothing! We don't want to be rich; we just need a job." Disillusionment with the current regime and politicians is widespread. Sow, a twenty-five-year-old from Grand Dakar, a neighborhood in the capital, criticized the president for corruption and nepotism. "Wade [and his cronies] built the *corniche* [highway along the beach] and the huge monument in the Mamelles just to get money for themselves.[7] We don't eat monuments;

that money could have been used to create jobs for the youth. . . . Wade is now trying to make his son president of Senegal. . . . This country doesn't belong to his family," Sow concluded angrily.

Many young people I met were not willing to get involved with political parties but wanted their voices to be heard at the polls. President Wade will stand for reelection in 2012, but many young people want to drive him out of power at the ballot box. They declared that they would not be bound by *ndigel*,[8] a voting directive issued by Muslim religious leaders. Twenty-four-year-old Ibrahima from Parcelles Assenies vowed, "I will vote according to my own conscience."

In Tunisia, even after having successfully carried out the first youth-led revolution of the twenty-first century, young people continue to be reluctant to enter the formal political arena. This resistance stems from their experience of politics during the old regime. Like their counterparts in Mozambique, South Africa, and Senegal, many young Tunisians despise politicians and associate them with corruption and abuses of power. They see their own political engagement during the revolution as different from the party politics going on today. "The majority of young people in Tunisia are not interested in politics," said twenty-two-year-old Mahmoud of Metline. "The revolution? Many of us don't see that as politics, but as a fight for our freedom and for better life opportunities, like jobs, liberty of expression on the Internet, etc." In the same vein, Raouf, a twenty-nine-year-old man who lives in Kasserine, vowed: "We don't want to create political parties. We don't want to 'do politics'. . . . We want to create associations to help young people, especially unemployed young people."

Young people have long been excluded from political processes in Tunisia. Cultural and recreational associations for music, sports, and theater were reserved for young people. Ben Ali's regime successfully compartmentalized Tunisian society to such an extent that many young people, especially in the more remote areas, do not even consider their protests during the revolution as a form of political activity. The exclusion of the young from politics has continued into the political transition, though perhaps to a lesser degree (Collins 2011). Many young people I spoke with, especially in the more impoverished regions, think that the democratic transition is becoming a closed, elite-led process centered in the capital. The institutions involved are widely seen as lacking in transparency and excluding youth and citizens from the remote areas. Abidi, a thirty-seven-year-old man who lives in Regueb, a town in Sidi Bouzid, shared his views: "We don't know what is going on in Tunis. These people are now playing politics and political parties. But here we need jobs, not 'politiquing.'" Similarly, Zarai, a twenty-six-year-old woman from Sidi Bouzid, was skeptical about the political transition: "I don't believe in the politicians. Some are the same ones from the time of Ben Ali. Here in Sidi Bouzid we started the protests, but politicians stay in Tunis and don't come here to talk to us to know what we need. Like before, all is done and decided in Tunis."

Despite young Tunisians' limited political experience and their cynicism about politics, the revolution—the protests and sit-ins, and the organizing and networking it required—was a laboratory of participatory citizenship and social engagement. Many told me that, although they do not want to join political parties, they are active in their own youth associations. They are attentive to what is happening in the country; they know what they fought for, and they will not allow the older generation to hijack their revolution.

Civic Engagement, Hip Hop, and Political Protest

Young people's perception is that politics offers them no space for real participation. The state and party politics do not allow for dissenting voices or alternative interventions. The young people I interviewed during this research were deeply disillusioned and skeptical about any positive future prospects for youth. In consequence, disaffected youths tend to withdraw and find space to operate outside mainstream social and political processes. Formal politics is not the only arena where young people can contribute their talents and energies to social improvement. Today youth tend to act through their student councils, independent youth organizations, and a variety of civil society groups in the arts and popular culture, as well as in social movements. The linkages among civic activism, popular culture (especially hip-hop music), and open political protests underscore contemporary forms of contestation by youth. There is no doubt that we are witnessing a new brand of political action outside party politics, even though some youths themselves do not want to call it political, understandably so, as their experiences of political activity have been negative, corrupt, and abusive. Nevertheless, they do not see themselves as apolitical either.

In this section I explore the interconnections between youth civil society actions, hip-hop music and street protests against government policies and authoritarianism. I start by discussing the case of the Y'en a Marre movement, Kuer Gui rap group, and street protests in Senegal,[9] then move on to discuss similar cases in Tunisia, Mozambique, and South Africa. Across the four countries I have selected some youth-established and youth-led civil society associations to showcase the magnitude and diversity of their social engagement. While many youths participate in religious organizations, they appear to be followers in already established religious groups. Although religion plays an important part in their lives, and recent studies point to the rising influence of youth in religious organizations (van Dijk 2008), during my research young people spoke primarily about their involvement in secular associations created by themselves, perhaps because such movements were more conducive to more creative and independent youth action.

Keur Gui, Y'en a Marre, and Street Protests in Senegal

The group Kuer Gui constitutes a critical element of the Senegalese hip-hop movement and was among the main precursors of the Y'en a Marre movement. Established in 1998 in Kaolack, in the south of the country, the group started with three members, Thiat, Kilifeu, and Mollah Morgun. From the beginning they had trouble with the authorities. Their music was censored, and they were severely beaten and arrested on various occasions. Their first album came out in 2001; their second, *Liy Ram* [if we don't watch out], was launched in 2004. *Liy Ram* denounces the fusion of religion and politics, corruption among religious leaders, and competition among Muslim religious brotherhoods in Senegal. In 2008 the group released an album called *Nos Connes Doléances* [our shitty sorrows]. The lyrics of their song "Coup 2 Guelle [let's act on our words]" focus on inequality, corruption, and bad governance.

> I don't even feel Senegalese anymore
> This lustful regime wasted all our money
> It's torturing me
> Who can help me migrate to Europe?
> We can't stop lamenting with this deadly hunger
> We fish with rusty hooks and cultivate potatoes with old
>   tools
> We are the victims of the crisis and real discrimination
> I am fed up with this corrupt justice system.
> Old man, your seven-year presidential reign has been
>   expensive
> We are drowning in hunger and unemployment.

The group toured in Africa and Europe. During the group's last tour Mollah Morgun decided to stay in Europe and Thiat and Kilifeu revamped the group, making it even more radical. Keur Gui's music is regarded as a form of political intervention. The group's legitimacy enhances the self-confidence of youth and empowers them to participate in their society as full-fledged citizens. This stance is especially significant in a culture where *ndaw top mag* is still asserted, that is, young people must obey adults (Niang 2006). Keur

Gui has extended its activism beyond the boundaries of hip-hop music. It has been at the core of the Y'en a Marre movement, which is challenging politicians and fighting for good governance in Senegal. Thiat and Kilifeu are both in the leadership of the movement.

The Y'en a Marre movement in Senegal was formed in January 2011 by Keur Gui and other Senegalese rappers. Y'en a Marre arose out of young people's frustration with the high rates of youth unemployment and underemployment and the lack of prospects for the future. The movement hails from the Dakar suburbs and is led by several local rappers, including Thiat and Kalifeu from Keur Gui, Fou Malad, Matador, and others, such as journalist Cheikh Fadel Barro. Since early March 2011 the Y'en a Marre movement has become the main symbol of popular protests against the government of Abdoulaye Wade. Although the movement initially protested the recurring electricity cuts that paralyze Dakar, it quickly grew into a broader social and political movement aimed at mobilizing young people and giving them a voice in the run-up to the 2012 presidential elections. As its Facebook page states: "The time has passed for moaning in your living rooms. . . . We refuse to accept the systematic rationing . . . to supply electricity. We're sick and tired of it. ENOUGH IS ENOUGH!"

The movement has been able to harness the discontent of young people not only in the capital but also in other regions of the country. It is becoming a strong mobilizing force for youth to claim their rights and protest unemployment, police brutality, and corruption. Y'en a Marre declares that it is not a political movement but rather a "guardian of democracy" that advocates respect for civil rights. As Thiat, a leader of the movement, explained in an interview with Marc-Andre Boisver, "We are on the side of neither the President nor the opposition; we are on the side of the people and we are creating a movement which guards and upholds respect for democracy and the institutions of Senegal."[10]

The first public event hosted by the movement was a protest rally that took place in the Place de l'Obélisque (Obelisk Square) in Dakar on 19 March 2011. The organizers distributed hundreds of black t-shirts to the crowd with the words Y'en a Marre in big white letters. Various rappers performed, touching upon young people's grievances and calling on the government for change. "Between what President Wade has promised, and what he has delivered, it is like night and day," said rapper Thiat.[11]

In preparation for the 2012 elections the movement launched a national campaign called Daas Fanaanal (to protect oneself) aimed at encouraging young people to vote freely. They created a youth slogan for the elections, Ma Carte d'Electeur, Mon Arme (my voting card, my weapon). This declaration signifies a radical shift from the tradition of *ndigel* in Senegal, which Muslim religious leaders use to influence their followers' votes. The movement keeps in touch with its followers through Twitter, Facebook, text messaging, music, and meetings in various neighborhoods. Every week the rappers go out on the streets of Guediaye, Pikine, Parcelles Assenies, and other areas to tell young people about the need to vote and to encourage them to register. Y'en a Marre has been very vocal in criticizing the president, and its members have been harassed by the police. The leaders claim to have been threatened by the authorities. The actions of the Y'en a Marre movement confirm that Senegalese young people believe in the power of the ballot. In the next presidential election Senegal's youth will not be mere spectators. Thiat asserted that its campaign would not end with the 2012 elections. The Y'en a Marre movement plans to lead a public awareness program to create what he calls the "new type of Senegalese," one who refuses to get into "an overcrowded bus, doesn't throw rubbish in the street, refuses to corrupt a police officer, [and] is aware of his rights and duties."[12] The movement was at the forefront of the June 2011 political protests against the government.

The protests started on June 22 when youths from Y'en a Marre movement gathered outside the National Assembly to voice their anger over the constitutional amendments proposed by President Abdoulaye Wade. Thousands of protestors clashed with police during demonstrations as they denounced the eighty-five-year-old president's efforts to run for a third term and protested corruption, high unemployment, and other social ills. Clouds of tear gas enveloped the square as police fought the protestors with gas, rubber bullets, and water cannons. The demonstrations quickly spread from central Dakar into the suburbs and three major towns in the interior as many other citizens joined in. More than one hundred protesters were injured during the two days of rioting.

The trigger for these protests was a set of constitutional amendments proposed by Abdoulaye Wade to drop the threshold for a first-round victory from 50 percent to just 25 percent of votes. He also sought to create the post of vice president, so whomever he appointed would take over automatically in the event he died or resigned. These amendments were seen as a strategy by which Wade could ensure his own victory in the 2012 elections and pave the way for his son, Karim Wade, to succeed him.

Following the massive popular protests, on June 23 President Wade agreed to withdraw the proposed constitutional amendments. These protests posed the greatest challenge to Wade's eleven-year rule and threatened to destabilize Senegal, which had been known as one of the most stable countries in the region. The protest signaled an important victory for youth and all those who joined them, proving that political opposition was still possible. A mass movement arose, the 23 June Movement, uniting the various opposition parties and civil society organizations that were involved in the protests. Young people, some of them associated with Y'en a Marre, were determined to protect the institutions of the Republic. In July 2011, a new wave of protests began after police arrested the pro-democracy activist and Y'en a Marre leader Thiat, also a member of the hip-hop group Keur Gui. He was detained after calling President Wade "old" and a "liar"; he was released after spending a night in prison.[13]

Senegalese youth have a long history of political engagement and protests against the establishment. In 1988 young people protested against the reelection of President Diouf of the Parti Socialiste (Diouf 1996; Havard 2001). In 1989 they started a cleanup campaign in neighborhoods of Dakar and its suburbs that became known as the Set-Setal (make it clean again) movement. The movement quickly took a political stance, rejecting the politics of the PS regime (Diouf 1996; Mbow 2008). In the late 1990s a more aggressive political movement called Bul Faale (don't worry or never mind), which was based on rap music and *lutte traditionelle* (a traditional form of wrestling), captured young people's imaginations (Biaya 2000). According to Elin Seboe, the Bul Faale movement was instrumental in the opposition to the PS regime, which it saw as responsible for the economic crisis (Selboe 2010). The political activism of young people in Senegal has been captured in a documentary film, *Africa Underground: Democracy in Dakar,* directed by Ben Herson, Magee McIlvaine, and Chris Moore, which showcases the role of musical activism in the Senegalese political process. Using hip-hop music as the primary storytelling device, the film chronicles youths' experiences on the streets of Dakar before and after the controversial 2007 presidential elections.

El General and Radio Sada Chaanbi in Tunisia

Hip hop was banned in Tunisia during the regime of President Ben Ali. Hip-hop musicians were not on government-approved play lists for state-controlled television or radio; they did not have permission to perform in public and were barred from recording CDs. In this repressive environment, in November 2010 a young Tunisian rapper from the city of Sfax, Hamada Ben Amor, who called himself El General, posted a song on his Facebook page and on YouTube. At age twenty-two he faced the same problems as many young Tunisians who didn't have reliable work and still lived with their parents. As El General explained in an interview, he had to record his songs underground: "I had two friends, one filmed my songs on a small video camera, and the other edited the videos and put them up on YouTube."[14] His song "Mr. President, Your People Are Dying," blamed Ben Ali for the poverty, unemployment, and social injustice in Tunisia. In the video El General tried to hide his face because at that time it was dangerous to go public. The song was an instant sensation, registering hundreds of thousands of views on YouTube and Facebook. El General's video broke through the climate of fear in which almost no one dared to criticize the president openly. The song captured Tunisians' widespread resentment against the government.

> Mr. President, you told me to speak without fear
> But I know that eventually I will take slaps
> I see too much injustice and so I decided to send this
> message
> even though the people told me that my end is death.
>
> It is a direct robbery by force
> without naming names, everybody already knows who
> they are.
> Much money was pledged for projects and infrastructure,
> schools, hospitals, buildings, houses
> But the sons of bitches have already fattened
> They stole, robbed, kidnapped.

As anti-government protests gained momentum in December 2010, the rapper wrote "Tunisia, Our Country" condemning the abuses of Ben Ali's regime. The government found this threatening, and security forces arrested El General on 6 January 2011, just a week before the fall of the regime. According to El General's brother, "Some thirty plainclothes policemen came to our house and took him away without ever telling us where to. . . . When we asked why they were arresting him, they said, 'he knows why.'"[15] He was jailed in Tunis and repeatedly interrogated about possible political connections. His imprisonment coincided with that of several cyber-activists who were accused of hacking official government websites. Demonstrators in the streets of cities and small towns across the country began demanding their release as well as the president's resignation. The hip-hop artist was freed a few days later. El General became one of the symbols of the youth-led Tunisian revolution, which will be discussed in detail in the next chapter.

Two weeks after Ben Ali's departure, the rapper performed in public for the first time. Now free to make his music without government interference, El General has become a star across the Arab world. He recently launched "Ode to Arab Revolution" calling for uprisings across the region. "Egypt,

Algeria, Libya, Morocco, all must be liberated/Long live free Tunisia," the lyrics proclaim.

Galvanized by the success of the revolution and fall of Ben Ali's dictatorship, three young men in the west central Tunisian town of Kasserine, thirty-one-year-old Ali, twenty-nine-year-old Walid, and thirty-year-old Foued, created an online radio station for young Kasserinians, taking advantage of the fact that the region has more than 100,000 active Internet users. Teaming up with AVDN Flavius, another group of young people already working in the audiovisual field, they founded Radio Sada Chaanbi, which means "the echo of Mount Chaanbi." It refers to Jebel ech Chaanbi, the highest mountain in the country, which stands over Kasserine at 5,066 feet. The regional commission for culture in Kasserine provided them with studio space and basic equipment, and they were authorized to operate by the governorate of Kasserine.

The main objective of the radio station is to create a platform that focuses on issues of interest to young people in Kasserine. It provides a forum for Kasserinians to communicate among themselves and develop their ideas for making the region more prosperous. Walid explained: "We decided to focus on Kasserine because our region has been forgotten by the Ben Ali regime, and there isn't much information in the national media about what is happening here. That has not yet changed, so we decided to do it ourselves." The programs presented by Radio Sada Chaanbi address social, economic, political, historical, and cultural issues of interest to Kasserinians, as well as music and sports. The radio aims to provide young people with reliable information and facilitate their participation in the socioeconomic, historical, and cultural life of Kasserine, as well as in the political transition and the October elections. Ali explained that this was a vital task because "there are a lot of rumors circulating and people are misinformed. Rumors often create trouble because this is a moment of a lot of uncertainty.... We want to give young people accurate information about politics and what is going on in Tunisia at the moment," the thirty-one year old concluded.

The head of political programs at Radio Sada Chaanbi is a very dynamic woman, thirty-four-year-old Hafsia, who studied law and holds a diploma in audiovisual communication. "My program invites lawyers, politicians, and other well informed people to come and explain things to young people. We also carry out debates and young people come to express their views about various issues.... We have a lot to learn. Tunisians were cut off from politics during previous regimes, especially young people. We need to learn quickly to be able to make informed choices during the elections." The radio organizes discussions where young people can share their experiences of the revolution. Another program, also coordinated by Hafsia, deals with the psychological impact of the revolution on residents of Kasserine. Some of the most violent confrontations between demonstrators and the police took place here, and many people were injured or killed. Hafsia and her colleagues believe that the people of Kasserine need healing. They need to "tell their stories, and share their pain with others. . . . We work with psychologists in this program," she remarked.

During the afternoon I spent with the team at Radio Sada Chaanbi, we had interesting discussions and I watched them record their programs. I also gave them a brief interview about my project and my visit to Tunisia, and to Kasserine in particular. The team aspires to start broadcasting on FM as well, but it lacks the resources to do so. Unlike the capital, Kasserine is struggling to attract funding from international organizations and philanthropic institutions. Young people can only rely on themselves and the occasional and limited support from the regional governorate. The success of the radio is already felt in the region, and the young people behind it hope to have a positive impact on the political education of the young electorate in the region.

Azagaia, Sociedade Aberta, and Riots in Mozambique

Edson da Luz, popularly known as Azagaia, is one of the most famous hip-hop artists in Mozambique. This twenty-seven-year-old university graduate was born in Maputo. The rapper's songs contain incendiary lyrics criticizing the government and the status quo, which have angered many in the political elite. His most popular songs—"The Lies of the Truth," "People's Power," "Soldiers of Fortune," "Arrriii," and "My Generation"—have given rise to controversy and even landed him in prison. "The Lies of the Truth" says "the opposition and the government are no different. . . . They both eat from the same plate."

> Not everything they say is true—it's true
> Not everything they don't say is untrue—it's true
> They make you think you know—but you don't know
> Beware of the lies of the truth—that's the truth.

"People's Power" is a panegyric to the riots of February 2008 in Maputo, discussed in the next section. Azagaia's song resonated with the crowds. Expressing skepticism about corrupt officials, he urged youths to keep fighting:

> We're not falling for the old story any more
> We're going out to fight against the scum

The thieves, the corrupt
Shout with me for these people to get out.

We're barricading the streets
We're stopping these buses.
If the police are violent
We respond with violence.

Following the release of this song, Azagaia was summoned and interrogated by the authorities.[16] Journalists and public intellectuals were shocked by government censorship of Mozambican music. Azagaia was grilled about whether he had written the song himself and whether the lyrics would incite people to violence.[17] He was eventually released and has continued to be a critical voice, not just with regard to Mozambican politics but also across the continent, as this 2009 song "Soldiers of Fortune" clearly shows:

This one goes to all African leaders
Those who promised us a better Africa
But all they did was to make it worse
Bunch of sons of bitches.

The first WikiLeaks cables from the U.S. Embassy in Maputo revived the debate about narcotics smuggling in Mozambique that had occurred in mid-2010. The memos denounced the involvement of powerful Mozambican businessman Mohamed Bachir Suleman in the international narcotics traffic.[18] For many years Suleman has been one of the main financial contributors to Frelimo, the ruling party. Following these revelations, voicing the suspicions that many Mozambicans already had, Azagaia came out with "Arrriii," which denounces the links between the government and the narco-traffic. He rapped that the country "runs on cocaine" and that if people at the top are corrupt, then "the little ones will also start getting involved."

Azagaia's voice troubled the government, which tried to keep his songs off public television and radio, and even some privately owned media with close ties to the ruling party.[19] The Mozambican authorities kept a very close eye on Azagaia, and on 30 July 2011 he was arrested for allegedly being in possession of 1.5 grams of marijuana, which is illegal in the country. The arrest occurred the very day the rapper was supposed to launch his new album, titled *Aza-Leaks* (as in WikiLeaks), with a major concert in Maputo. His new work includes the song "Minha Geração" (my generation), which inspires youth to take action and refuse to be silenced. The lyrics assert that his is a generation that "discusses ideas, a generation of competence and not obedience, and a generation of engaged actors and not convenient followers."[20]

Many young Mozambicans regarded this coincidence as evidence that the government sought to repress his new album. The online branch of the youth-led newspaper *A Verdade* (the truth) had posted numerous *netizens* commenting on the incident. "This for me was a failed attempt to tarnish the young man's image . . . orchestrated by a handful of people who feel affected by the lyrics of the musician of the people," said one of the commentators. Others wondered whether his arrest could mean the end of freedom of expression in Mozambique.[21] Similarly another hip-hop group, the Gpro Fam, produced a strong critique to the government in its song "O pais da Marrabenta" (the country of marrabenta—a local music genre).[22] Azagaia's activism goes beyond his lyrics. On 6 May 2011, he announced in his blog the beginning of a non-violent protest movement aimed at rallying young people to fight for their rights and protest government abuses, particularly low-quality education, unemployment, and poverty, as well as corruption, nepotism, and police brutality.[23] Young people in Mozambique have been involved in civic and political activism.

The Sociedade Aberta is a nonprofit association founded in 2004 by young Mozambican professionals Felizberto and Hermenegildo Muhlovo (twin brothers), Herminio Nhaguiombe, and José Dias.[24] They come from the same neighborhood in Matola, a town located about nine miles outside Maputo and have been friends since primary school. They also started their activism by creating a hip-hop group, Nhanda, and writing rap music and poetry. They were very active in the campaign to elect a young man, Carlos Tembe, as mayor of Matola. They also revamped their school's student newspaper. They created a provincial network to combat drug use and organized a large citywide march called "the train against HIV/AIDS." These young men went to university to study social sciences and specialized in rural development, public administration, and sociology. They were involved in a research project on the incidence of HIV/AIDS in Maputo prisons and produced a report that was widely used by various nongovernmental organizations. In 2004, after graduating, they established the Sociedade Aberta to facilitate the engagement of students and young professionals in community service, to contribute to community development and poverty reduction, and to promote social and economic justice.[25] They envisioned working with people from government, the private sector, and other nonprofit organizations.

In one of my visits to Maputo I met Hermenegildo Muhlovo, known as Gil, to discuss this interesting initiative. Now twenty-seven years old, Gil works for the Netherlands Institute for Democracy in Maputo. One of the first research projects undertaken by the Sociedade Aberta was for the Annual National Report on Poverty. Then the association prepared its own report on poverty indicators in the province of Maputo, launched with a seminar open to the communities it studied and to development agencies and government institutions. Gil recalls that "the report was nicely put together, but we noticed that the people from those communities did not recognize themselves in those indicators and statistics. That's when we realized that we needed to change our approach. The point was not to do it for them, but to reach out and do it with them." So the association started working more closely with rural populations on the ground, positioning the community as the principal agent in the partnership. After looking at various proposals, they concluded that "the model of the millennium villages proposed by Jeffrey Sachs from Columbia University is still a top-down approach, with the communities as the implementing party rather than the main agent in the process. So we did not adopt that model. . . . We prepared an alternative model in conjunction with the communities. The millennium goals must be determined by the communities themselves, not the other way around." The Sociedade Aberta promotes dialogue between people and their government and is keen to promote interchange between policies and realities, both locally and globally.

The association has conducted a three-year project to strength civil society participation in decentralized development processes in three districts of Maputo, including community participation in decision making, better provision of services, and accountability. The beneficiaries are community-based organizations, local governmental authorities, and organizations of women and youth. The association has conducted training workshops on participation and decentralized development, new techniques of agricultural production and the construction of greenhouses, and the empowerment of communities with income-generating initiatives. The Sociedade Aberta is one of the most successful civil society associations working on rural development in Mozambique. Gil pointed out that it has received several offers of outside funding, but "our dilemma is how to grow in an organic way without compromising our performance and our independence through funding that often comes with strings attached and might divert us from our core objectives." This is a group of young people who are indeed engaged with society and making a difference in people's lives. While they do not consider themselves a political association, the choices they make—focusing on bottom-up rather than top-down approaches to community development—certainly represent a clear political stance.

On 5 February 2008 Maputo was the scene of violent popular demonstrations as thousands of people took to the streets to protest against the

50 percent rise in the cost of fares for *chapas*, the private minibuses. The majority were young men. Protesters erected barricades and burned tires to cut the main access routes to the city center. Soon the protests degenerated into looting. Angry unemployed young men took control of the streets, vandalized shops and cars, and paralyzed the city, expressing their frustration with the country's dismal economic situation. The police responded by shooting into the air in an attempt to disperse the crowds, but the protesters responded by throwing stones. One person died, and several others were injured.

Just over two and a half years later, on 1 September 2010, protests again erupted in Maputo, halting normal activities in the city for over two days. Thousands of Mozambican youths protested the rise in the prices of staples such as bread, water, and fuel. Aggrieved youths blocked access to the city center, where the middle class lives. All regular services were paralyzed; people had no access to food; and shops, restaurants, and pharmacies were shut down. Then protesters started moving from the periphery toward the center of town. They organized themselves through text messaging, as many youth own cell phones. The police initially used tear gas and rubber bullets but then resorted to real bullets as the confrontation intensified. The protesters faced off against the heavily armed police. According to official estimates, there were more than ten deaths and numerous injuries. I was visiting Maputo during the September riots, and I remember the general sense of uncertainty and vulnerability as the situation escalated.

In 2010, as in 2008, the youth took it upon themselves to confront the government and demand the reversal of the price hikes. After initially dismissing the protests as isolated disturbances by marginal and disorderly youths, the government complied with popular demands and overturned its decision. At the same time, however, it imposed tight controls on cell phones and text messaging, demanding all mobile phone users to register and provide their identification details and residential address. According to MISA-Mozambique (Southern Africa Institute for Social Communication, Mozambique Branch) and the Mozambican Centre for Public Integrity (CIP), the coverage of the protests in the national media was highly restricted. In the first few hours of the morning media outlets began reporting on the popular uprisings, but coverage faded as the day progressed. While people were dying and being injured in the streets of the capital, some television stations were showing soap operas. News coverage of sensitive events is still subject to heavy government control, depriving the public of information. Both MISA and CIP have been very critical of government's interference with freedom of the press.[26]

Commenting on the government's reversal of its price increases, Carlos Serra, a sociologist from University Eduardo Mondlane, declared that the problem was not just bread and other material needs. "We must also consider phenomena such as uncertainty, the search for identity, respect, decency, freedom, the right to speak, freedom to be . . . to envisage a future and so on. Our youth . . . aspire to have a decent life . . . and well-being is something that goes far beyond the stomach."[27] In the same vein, sociologist João Colaço affirmed that these riots "reflect the breakdown of the social contract between state and society. We are facing a phenomenon that is now repeated for the second time . . . with similar motivations and grievances. . . . The belt has tightened and the frustrations are already touching the middle class."[28]

Indeed, the government's failure to take the events of 2008 seriously led to this second wave of riots. Economist João Mosca asserted that "corruption is one of the most serious problems of this country. . . . There are strong ties between government, business and governance." The state's capacity to manage, regulate, and monitor the economy is weak; the state functions as an instrument to further the interests of particular individuals and groups rather than the interests of the people.[29] Although the price increases were reversed, fundamental issues have not been addressed, and poverty, unemployment, corruption, and bad governance continue to affect the lives of Mozambicans, especially youth. That is why Azagaia and other activists continue to rally the youth to fight for their rights.

Umuzi Photo Club and Kwaito Music in South Africa

South Africa's Umuzi Photo Club is a nonprofit organization established in August 2009 by a group of young people. *Umuzi* is a Zulu word that means "village"; these young people in urban Johannesburg sought to create a community among themselves. The Umuzi Photo Club aims to provide young people with photographic skills and empower them through artistic self-expression and critical reflection on society. Through photography, Umuzi Photo Club works to place young people, especially those growing up in impoverished townships, at the center of conversations on important issues, cutting through socioeconomic, political, and generational boundaries.

The club was initiated by a young American photographer who was living in Johannesburg and a group young South Africans who articulated the concept and raised the funds to purchase equipment. The Umuzi Photo Club conducts a series of five- to ten-week workshops for high school students. The sessions include training in photographic techniques as well as discussions of social issues. I was in Johannesburg when the club opened its photo exhibition on teenage pregnancy at the Bernato Park High School in Hillbrow. I was impressed by the quality of the photographs taken by people between sixteen and twenty years of age and by the narratives that accompanied the powerful images. At the exhibition I spoke with Maisare, a seventeen-year-old girl from Brixton, who took part in the project. "We learned about visual communication, how to operate the camera, how to take pictures, how to make captions. We also talked about our lives and our communities and what we wanted the world to know about our communities." Each workshop centers on a theme chosen by the participants; as Maisare put it, they focus on "what they want the world to know about them." This group picked teenage pregnancy. Each participant got a camera to take home and had the task of photographing a pregnant teenager, her boyfriend or the father of her child, and her family. At the opening of the exhibition the photographers organized a presentation in which they shared their experiences and explained what they learned about the people they met and their communities. Maisare said that she became more aware of the world around her and the problems affecting teenage girls. This experience changed her goals as well: "I wanted to be a dermatologist, but now I want to be a writer and photographer."

Similar workshops have been offered in more than ten schools in Johannesburg and Cape Town, and the club is expanding rapidly. The young people who participate in one workshop are then involved in training others, and a few have been hired to photograph public events. For the celebrations of Mandela Day on 18 July 2011, Umuzi Photo Club decided to pay tribute to the ninety-three-year-old former president by launching a multi-platform media campaign called Messages for Madiba.[30] The campaign recorded and relayed heartfelt messages from people of Alexandra Township to the South African icon. Through Umuzi Photo Club young people develop visual literacy and critical thinking skills in interactive workshops and become advocates for change through their visual testimony. The raw, honest images they create are exhibited in communities, schools, and other public spaces to encourage youth-centered dialogues. In this way the club is becoming an important platform for marginalized young people to tell their own stories.[31]

Kwaito is a very popular music genre among South African youths that emerged in the 1990s in Soweto. It shares many characteristics of hip-hop music, with catchy melodies, deep bass lines, and vocals, but it is distinctive in the manner in which the lyrics are sung, rapped, and shouted. Some analysts believe that kwaito is not a variant form of American hip-hop but a local South African phenomenon featuring the use of African sounds that branched out of house music[32] (Mhlambi 2004; Steingo 2005; Swartz

2008; Marco 2009). The word *kwaito* originates from the Afrikaans *kwaai*, which traditionally means "strict or angry," although nowadays it is used to mean "cool." Kwaito music has been responsible for leading a post-apartheid township youth subculture into the mainstream. This form of self-expression features its own dance style, fashion, and way of speaking. Kwaito, some specialists assert, has become a means for creating identity and establishing new societal norms (Swartz 2008). Indeed, kwaito represents the township youth culture in South Africa in much the same way that hip hop mirrors young African American ghetto culture (Swink 2003). Boom Shaka and TKZee are the most influential kwaito groups in South Africa today.

Kwaito lyrics appear to be apolitical. Kwaito artists seem to refuse to engage with contemporary politics and refrain from making statements that denounce the status quo. It is often thought of as escapist and seen as heavily commercialized and mass produced, consisting of sexually driven lyrics and dances and promoting a culture of consumerism. Nevertheless, some kwaito songs do touch upon social issues such as violence, sexuality, drugs, alcohol, and HIV/AIDS. Others reflect on what it means to be South African today. Some kwaito songs express political views through verses, rhymes, and chants. Political critique is not as pervasive in kwaito as it is in hip hop elsewhere on the continent. Simone Swink (2003) points out that kwaito is part and parcel of South Africa's political history, so it is impossible to talk about kwaito music as apolitical; black South African artists could not get signed in the music business during apartheid, and that alone is a political statement. Gavin Steingo finds kwaito overtly political, even though the lyrics have no explicit political content. The political statement here is the desire of young South Africans to leave behind the long years of oppression and the political protests of the apartheid era. Kwaito music may represent an escape from politics, the music "after the struggle" (Steingo 2005).

It is important to note, however, that kwaito represents only part of the South African hip-hop scene. Cape Town hip hop appears to generate a more political style that is influenced by the anti-apartheid ideology of political contestation (Marco 2009). Today it reflects a search for identity and affirmation of black consciousness in a context where racial stratification of whites, coloreds, Indians, and black Africans still divides communities (Marco 2009). According to the Cape Town–based, all-women hip-hop group Godessa: "We were excluded from *kwaito* because we cannot understand it. To us, music is not just about dancing, it is a vehicle for us to speak to the masses" (in Steingo 2005, 342). Godessa often makes use of "gamtaal,"[33] South African colored people's Afrikaans language, to establish a close rapport with the audience. In the same way, kwaito artists routinely rap in the vernacular, such as Xhosa, Sotho, Tswana, and Zulu, in "a conscious attempt to address the social, political, and economic issues that impact marginalized communities in ways that hold particular meaning for them" (Magubane 2006, 215). While there is political engagement in South African hip hop, it does not appear to be in direct open confrontation with the establishment, as in Senegal, Tunisia, and Mozambique.

Indeed, each country is different as various youth cohorts in this waithood generation are defined and shaped by their particular national and local circumstances. However, there is no doubt that the similarities across the countries are striking; the problems experienced by the younger generation are the same, and their responses are analogous. Across the continent the waithood generation is finding its own ways to deal with its particular situations and to confront hegemonic powers that have broken the social contract by failing to create jobs and respect civil liberties. The younger generation is rejecting party politics, which its members see as monopolized by their elders and offering no space for them.

Globalization and Youth Culture

In an era of globalization and new technologies of information and communication, the interconnections and exchanges that exist among members of this generation are unparalleled. Interventions in popular culture, such as theater, art, and music, have long been a privileged domain of youth as they rework old fashions and invent new ones. Processes of globalization have facilitated the spread of hip hop from its origins in New York City and Los Angeles to other parts of the globe, generating the emergence of a global youth culture with its particular music styles, fashions, language, and other forms of expression and behavior (Marco 2009). However, rather than being a mimicry of North American ghetto youth culture, African hip hop has developed an identity of its own by incorporating local elements and domesticating global forms (Niang 2006). Hip-hop music has been an important vehicle for social and political critique in many African countries and there is an extensive body of literature on this topic (Ssewakiryanga 1999; Lock 2005; Niang 2006; Saavedra-Casco 2006; Suriano 2006; Abdullah 2009; Ntarangwi 2009; Shepler 2010; Guadeloupe and Geschiere 2008). Hip hop has developed a global youth subculture that challenges dominant musical styles and fashions as it negotiates the experience of marginalization, brutality, and truncated opportunities within the cultural imperatives of mainstream society (Rose 1994). The literature distinguishes between more commercial forms of hip hop such as gangsta rap (Haupt 2001), which glamorizes consumerism, sex, and drugs and is part of the MTV/ Hollywood media hype that glorifies an imperialistic American culture, and socially and politically conscious hip hop, which serves as a platform for confrontational ideas.

Hip-hop groups and individual rappers compose songs that speak to the daily realities of their lives and confront not only their parents but also the establishment for not enabling them to lead the lives they believe they deserve. A progressive musical genre that publicly critiques hegemonic voices, messages, and spaces, it has become a form of expression for disfranchised youths. Abdoulaye Niang points out that in Senegal hip-hop artists have been creative with their lyrics, for example, refashioning the word *politicien* (politician) into *politichien*, *politi* + *chien* (dog) to drive home the sentiment that politicians are unfit to govern (Niang 2006, 181). As rapper Jay-Z explains in his book *Decoded*, hip-hop music constitutes an "art form . . . about the most human experiences: joy, pain, fear, desire, uncertainty, hope, anger, love" (2010, 307). The rappers' words try to make sense of the world in which they live; they are "witty and blunt, abstract and linear, sober and fucked up. And when we . . . really listen to them with our minds and hearts open we can understand their world better. And ours, too. It's the same world," writes Jay-Z (308).

Thus, hip-hop music is not only a musical genre but also a powerful form of contestation against hegemonic culture, media, and politics (Mhlambi 2004; Steingo 2005; Niang 2006; Swartz 2008; Haupt 2001; Marco 2009). For youth, hip hop represents a space "that is uncontrollable by the institutions and powers that otherwise structure social discourse and identity within the confines of the nation-state" (Ntarangwi 2009, 17). Rapper Azagaia asserted, "I see hip-hop as nonviolent means by which we can mobilize the fight for fair and free democracy."[34]

There are clear links among youth's civic engagement, hip hop, and political protest. Young people are combining these arenas in their efforts to change their situation and contribute to greater social good. The street protests in Mozambique in 2008 and 2010 and in Senegal in 2011 have been instrumental in forcing governments to reverse unpopular economic and political decisions. Yet these uprisings did not lead to regime change, unlike the protests in January 2011 in Tunisia when youths toppled the dictatorial regime of Ben Ali. Nonetheless this waithood generation is building new forms of social activism that are politically informed but are not party ideologically constructed, because, as Raouf, a twenty-nine-year-old man from the town of Kasserine in central western Tunisia, expressed, "We don't want old style politics." The members of the waithood generation are claiming new forms of citizenship.

New Geographies of Citizenship

It is clear that young people in waithood are bringing about new modalities of social engagement and citizen action. Traditional theories understood citizenship as based on the gradual acquisition of civil rights, political rights, and social rights (Marshall 1949). This model presented a passive acceptance of rights (Ignatieff 1989), and some scholars cautioned against converting the citizen into a mere state client (Habermas 1992). More relevant to Africa is the critique against the gradual and sequential acquisition of rights; as Thandika Mkandawire (2007) suggests, human history is not linear, and societies that develop later tend to compress access to all those types of rights. Moreover, Mahmood Mamdani argues that the key citizenship question in post-colonial Africa "is not which rights, but whose rights? Who has the right to rights, the right to be a citizen?" (2007, 5; see also Mamdani 1996). And this is, indeed, a contested terrain in most African societies, where disfranchised minorities make autochthony claims (Geschiere 2005, 2009), and youth and women feel excluded. The narratives clearly demonstrate youths' sense of marginalization and exclusion from mainstream society. Although the constitutions might be beautifully written, in reality they have no political, social, and economic rights. There is an obvious breakdown of the social contract.

A shift in the dominant paradigm from a rights-based discourse to an obligations-based one focuses on citizen participation (Lawson 2001; Lister 1998). The concept of "citizenship as participation" appears in contrast to Marshall's more passive understanding of citizenship (Brannan et al. 2006; Bendix 1964). As the young people's stories reveal, rights are not a given; they have to fight for them. So, an approach to citizenship that encompasses both rights and participation (obligations and contributions to society's greater good) appears to be fitting. Ariadne Vromen's view of political participation broadens it beyond formal and electoral politics to "acts that can occur, either individually or collectively, that are intrinsically concerned with shaping the society that we want to live in" (2003, 82–83). Indeed, the young people I interviewed are engaging their societies using hip-hop culture in radio stations, websites, music lyrics, photographs, as well as public debates and community interventions. They connect with society in the church, the mosque, the streets, their schools, and neighborhoods. They work to improve peasants' agricultural production, protect people from HIV and AIDS, and educate young voters about their right to be heard. They do all this in their own way, not through partisan political engagement. Smaller numbers of young people may participate in formal politics by joining or challenging existing parties, creating their own political parties, and using their ballot to make a difference.

Many governments are losing the ability to control matters that have great significance for the lives of their citizens, which means that politicians are not able to represent the interests of the citizenry (Bauman 2001; Giddens 1992). Public institutions have become unable to translate private sufferings into public issues. Young people's own forms of identification are becoming less fixed as they grapple with the demise of clearly structured pathways to adulthood. The challenges of establishing economic security amid conditions of poverty can inhibit collective political participation because of the primacy of individual struggles for livelihoods and survival (Harris et al. 2010; Harris 2011). At the same time, as demonstrated by the many young people I encountered in these four countries, it can also enhance their commitment to a collective struggle for their rights to employment and decent future prospects.

Young people are often dismissed by their elders and targeted by discourses that construct them as inadequate citizens (Harris 2011) or a "lost generation" (Cruise O'Brien 1996). While they are disengaged from formal social and political processes, the waithood generation is far from being apathetic or apolitical. What may appear to be apathy and depoliticization represents a conscious move away from traditional arenas of party politics toward other forms of political engagement with society and the global world. Its members are coping with waithood by becoming "self-actualizing citizens" (Bennett 2003), "everyday makers" (Bang 2005), or even "makers and breakers" (Honwana and De Boeck 2005), and "troublemakers and peacemakers" (McEvoy-Levy 2006). Indeed, young people I met in Tunisia, Mozambique, South Africa, and Senegal preferred to intervene through their own "youthscapes" (Maira and Soep 2005) in civil society associations, hip-hop music, art, and popular culture as well as other youth-oriented social and political networks.

Sociedade Aberta and Azagaia, Y'en a Marre and Keur Gui, Radio Chaanbi, El General, Umuzi Photo Club, and kwaito are just a few of the many individuals and groups making a difference in their societies. Their voices lead a chorus of many other young people, some of whose voices are barely audible, who contribute to change on a daily basis. HIV/AIDS associations founded and run by youth; theater troupes composed of young people who engage in social critique; university students who organize strikes to demand better living conditions; young women forming rotating credit associations to help them make ends meet; frustrated rural youths who reach the cities and join informal networks; aggravated commuters who rebel against the rising cost of transport—all are making their mark.

Young Africans are exhibiting forms of citizenship that disavow the biases of tradition and challenge the authoritarianism and abuses of political elites (Diouf 2003; De Waal and Argenti 2004; Honwana and De Boeck 2005; Abdullah 2009; Christiansen et al. 2006; Cole and Durham 2007). Through their rejection of existing modalities of political membership, young people are not only redefining the spaces of citizenship but are also questioning the state's authority to define and delimit it (Diouf 2005). As Mamadou Diouf states, "In a way one is witnessing the end of the representation of youth by adults. The prescriptions of the latter have given way to the self-assertion of young people, and the self-realization of their own desires and aspirations. In becoming the producers and writers of their own dramatic narratives, they have opened themselves up to the world" (2005, 231).

Throughout Africa this waithood generation is turning to global hip-hop subculture and other forms of activism to articulate its experience, and voice its position. But this phenomenon goes beyond Africa's borders. A global waithood generation is reshaping and reinterpreting itself politically and is now acting through a range of collective protests across the world. While these youth cohorts are differently fashioned by national cultures and history, globalization has created both the context and the means of communication that allows them to be more widely connected. The waithood generation is no longer circumscribed to its particular localized problems but is also jointly shaped and affected by globalization and failed neoliberal policies that broke the social contract. Worldwide the younger generation is challenging its elders and trying to force through social and political change. Is the waithood generation the twenty-first-century version of the 1968 generation?

The next chapter examines young people's leading role in the first revolution of the twenty-first century, which led to the overthrow of the dictatorship in Tunisia.

Chapter 7

Social Change

Young people have been at the forefront of major social and political change in Africa. Leaders still remember the significant role that the younger generation played in movements for national liberation. In a speech delivered in March 2004, Mozambican president Armando Guebuza affirmed: "It was Mozambican youth who responded to Frelimo's call to join the liberation struggle. . . . Youth were present in the political, military, and diplomatic fronts of our struggle. . . . Youth gave the best they had in terms of creativity and sacrifice. . . . Youth participation in the 25th September generation, the generation of the struggle, was the determining factor in our victory over Portuguese colonialism."[1] Frelimo, Mozambique's national liberation movement, was created and led largely by young people, and its victory provoked a profound social transformation.

Similarly, in 1976 young black South Africans led the Soweto uprising that inspired the final, victorious struggle against the apartheid regime. Students in the all-black township bravely confronted the system by rejecting Afrikaans as the language of instruction in their schools. The protest began peacefully but turned violent when the police opened fire on unarmed students. Unrest quickly spread to other townships around the country. Black youths closed the schools and took to the streets, defiantly occupying city centers. Young black South Africans, both male and female, who had been victimized by segregation and inequality, showed the world they were a force for justice and change. The Soweto uprising was a turning point in the liberation movement. It took another fourteen years before Nelson Mandela was released and democratic elections were held, but the state was never able to restore the stability of the early 1970s as popular resistance grew and the international boycott of the regime strengthened.

Both the liberation struggles against colonialism and the Soweto uprisings against apartheid marked important moments in youth uprising against oppression and discrimination. But they also represented important generational shifts in the way politics and political uprisings were undertaken—and young people were at the forefront of such transformations. As Mamdani observed, the Soweto youth uprising "pioneered an alternative imagination and an alternative mode of struggle." While adult activists still relied on conventional forms of armed struggles waged by trained guerrillas, the young men and women in Soweto transformed the struggle into a popular movement with ordinary people as participants (Mamdani 2011, 200–201).

The Tunisian revolution led by unemployed youth in late 2010 and early 2011 ended twenty-three years of dictatorship and changed the course of history. The first youth-led revolution of the twenty-first century has inspired other young people throughout the African continent and the Arab world. This chapter focuses on young people's involvement in the Tunisian revolution; it is based on interviews I conducted with activists just six months after the overthrow of the government. Young people described their political mobilization, recounted their participation in crucial events, and reflected on the problems they and their country faced in the transition to democracy.

The chapter makes four main arguments: First, the younger generation drew on longstanding and widespread frustration that stemmed from massive unemployment, inequitable distribution of wealth, stifling political repression, and corruption, and it used modern technologies of information and communications such as the Internet to mobilize and communicate with the world. Second, the younger generation is challenging both old and newly established political forces that occupied the void created by Ben Ali's departure in the transition period, not through formal political parties but through civil society organizations and new cyber social networking. The future of the revolution will depend largely on how the existing tensions between the older and younger generations are resolved. Third, the younger generation is no longer bound by hegemonic political discourses and ideologies; young people are creating their own spaces and novel ways of engaging the state and society. The Tunisian revolution constitutes a powerful example of "citizenship from below" that emerged outside traditional political structures. Fourth, the power of generational change lay in the ability of youth to develop a generational consciousness with clear objectives for themselves, as well as in their capacity to mobilize a broad coalition of activists that transcended age, class, gender, ethnic, and regional divides. Tired of living under extremely difficult conditions with no prospects for the future, young people have overcome fear and are boldly challenging incompetent, corrupt, and repressive regimes. Governments can no longer hide behind nationalist and capitalist ideologies and pretenses of democracy; they are under growing pressure to deliver on the socioeconomic expectations of their largely young, globally connected citizens. The younger generation is, indeed, becoming a powerful agent of social change.

The Youth Revolution in Tunisia

Between 18 December 2000 and 14 January 2001, young Tunisians in waithood were at the vanguard of a wave of protests that led to the fall of president Zine El-Abidine Ben Ali. When Ben Ali, his wife, Leila, and a few relatives fled the country into exile in Saudi Arabia, it marked the end of an era in Tunisian history. How did a spontaneous movement led by young people manage to overturn a supposedly stable ruling regime? Who were the protesters? How did the protests spread, broaden their base, and escalate over such a short time? The accounts of the revolution offered by young participants in the movement not only highlight the main events but also articulate the perspectives of those who had been excluded from the political process before they took the situation into their own hands. Their vivid recollections add depth and texture to the headlines and newsflashes that were visible to the rest of the world during this tumultuous time.

The Tunisian revolution started in the center of the country in the small town of Sidi Bouzid where, on 17 December 2010, Mohamed Bouazizi, a twenty-six-year-old fruit vendor, set himself on fire to protest economic conditions and police mistreatment. Bouazizi's father, a construction worker who was employed mainly in Libya, had died when Bouazizi was three, and his mother later remarried his father's brother. Bouazizi did not complete his baccalaureate (high school) degree but left school in his late teens. Unable to find a job, he resorted to selling fruit and vegetables from a cart in his hometown. On 17 December 2010, Fayda Hamdi, a forty-five-year-old female officer of the municipal police, confiscated Bouazizi's wares because he did not have a vendor's permit. Bouazizi was furious and reportedly insulted her. Some people mentioned that he said something like: "What can I do now? Should I weigh my fruits with your two breasts?" Reacting angrily, the officer slapped him in the face in front of everyone. For a Tunisian man, being slapped by a woman in public is a serious insult. As Tunisian journalist Mohamed Kilani pointed out, "Only those who understand the meaning of honor in certain regions in Tunisia . . . may be able to imagine the depth of his humiliation" (2011, 55). Deeply offended, Bouazizi tried to lodge a complaint with municipal authorities. Apparently the governor refused to see him, even after Bouazizi threatened: "If you don't see me, I'll burn myself." True to his word, he acquired a can of paint thinner, doused his left arm, held a lighter in his right hand, and set himself alight while

standing in front of the main government building of Sidi Bouzid. He suc-
cumbed to his wounds at the military hospital in Ben Arous eighteen days
later, on 4 January 2011.

A couple of hours after Bouazizi's self-immolation, several hundred
young people assembled in the same place to express their solidarity with
Bouazizi and protest economic hardship and unemployment as well as police abuses. Clashes between demonstrators and the police erupted as more
people joined in the rallies. Photographs and videos of the protests and of
police brutality against demonstrators surfaced on the Internet through
Facebook. For the moment, however, national media completely ignored
the uprising in Sidi Bouzid.

On December 20, young people in the neighboring towns staged protests
in solidarity with Sidi Bouzid. Over the next few days the demonstrations
spread to new places across the country. Protestors responded to police
violence by throwing stones, burning tires in the middle of the street, and
torching government buildings and cars. The police fired on the demonstrators, killing two eighteen-year-olds and injuring many, but the protestors
did not retreat. More photos and videos were posted on the Internet and
picked up by international media, particularly Al Jazeera and France 24.

On December 25 the regime's development minister announced urgent
measures to deal with youth unemployment in the regions where young
people were demonstrating against the government. The demonstrators were
not placated; protests continued to grow, and participants defied curfews
and police repression. A group of cyber activists organized demonstrations
in the capital, Tunis, in solidarity with those in Sidi Bouzid.

On December 28 President Ben Ali, who had been on vacation in the
Persian Gulf, returned to the country to try to restore order. To appease the
demonstrators, he immediately visited Mohamed Bouazizi at the Burn and
Trauma Centre of the Ben Arous hospital. He then made an impromptu
television address to the nation criticizing the protestors. "A minority of
extremists and agitators in the pay of others, and against the country's interests, resort to violence and street disturbances as means of expression. . . .
The law will be enforced rigorously against these people." Ben Ali's speech
was not well received, and protests continued.

On January 4, 2011, Mohamed Bouazizi died of his burns. After the
announcement of his death, protesters gathered in the streets of towns and
villages across the country. Police responded with a major crackdown. The
funeral of Mohamed Bouazizi took place on January 5 at Garât Benour, a
village located ten miles outside Sidi Bouzid. More than five thousand people
attended the ceremony, which was under police surveillance. As Ali Moncef,
a twenty-six-year-old man from Sidi Bouzid who attended, told me: "Our

quiet presence in the funeral was already a political statement. . . . Many of us did not know Bouazizi or his family personally, but we were there."

On January 6 several cyber activists who played a role in publicizing the events and exposing police brutality nationally and internationally were detained in Tunis. The same day the twenty-two-year-old Tunisian hip-hop artist Hamada Ben Amor, known as El General, was arrested in Sfax. Over the following days police reinforced their crackdown on demonstrators and fired on protesters. More than twenty people were killed (Bettaïeb 2011).

On January 9 the government announced that it would invest US$5 billion in development projects and employ fifty thousand university graduates in the next few months.[2] The next day Ben Ali promised to create 300,000 jobs over the next two years.[3]

On January 11 President Ben Ali fired his minister of the interior, Rafik Haj Kacem, blaming him for authorizing the violent repression of demonstrations. At the same time, he announced the release of everyone who had been arrested for protesting.[4] These measures were aimed at appeasing the young protesters, but "it was too little too late" said thirty-one-year-old Ali from Kasserine. Hafsia, a young woman from Kasserine, remembered that the protesters fought back so hard that they managed to drive the police and the military out of Kasserine. "For us Kasserinians January 11 was like an independence day . . . although we were still a bit afraid of what the regime would do in retaliation." Walid, aged twenty-nine, explained: "The problem we faced after the police and the military left was that there was no order in the city and we risked falling into a chaotic situation, so we quickly decided to establish voluntary neighborhood associations to ensure the security of people and their property."

On January 13 Ben Ali addressed the nation just after the main evening news. He promised to respond positively to the unrest if violence ended right away and declared that he would not seek reelection in 2014. "I have understood you all. . . . I'm speaking to you because the situation needs radical change; yes, a radical change. . . . I understand the unemployed, the needy, the politicians, all those demanding more freedom. I have understood everyone. But what is happening today is not the way Tunisians do things." Ben Ali announced that he had ordered his security forces not to use firearms against the protestors. For the first time in his twenty-three-year presidency, he used colloquial Tunisian rather than Modern Standard Arabic (MSA) in parts of his speech. According to El Mustapha Lahlali, an Arabic scholar, "by switching to dialect, Ben Ali may have been trying to appeal to a wider section of Tunisian society, especially those less educated people who could not easily follow his speech in MSA. He may also have wanted to remind his own people that he is a Tunisian and try to bridge the social gap between himself and the wider Tunisian public. The use of dialect could also be interpreted as an attempt to bypass the middle-class people taking part in the protests" (Lahlali 2011).

Many young people told me that this speech was orchestrated by the regime to gain time, but it did not work; they decided to come out in force against him the next day, January 14. On the night of January 13 the cyber activits jailed on January 6 were released.

"Ben Ali Dégage!" shouted thousands of young Tunisians gathered in front of the Ministry of the Interior in the Avenue Habib Bourguiba in the center of Tunis. On January 14 Tunisians went on strike,[5] and many of them joined the demonstrations in Tunis and other major cities like Sousse and Sfax. Demonstrations were peaceful, and participants shouted "Enough is enough," "We Want Freedom," and "Ben Ali Dégage (Ben Ali go!)."

"But in the afternoon, police started shooting tear gas canisters at the protesters . . . and at around five o'clock the national television announced that Ben Ali would be leaving power in six months," said Yassine, a young man from Tunis. Protestors were not happy; they wanted him to leave right away and shouted even louder: "Ben Ali Dégage!" At around seven p.m. Al Jazeera and France 24 announced that Ben Ali had left the country for exile in Saudi Arabia.

The Jasmine, Facebook, or Tunisian Revolution?

Many names have been given to this youth uprising, including the Jasmine revolution and the Facebook revolution. The Tunisians I spoke with, however, do not agree with these designations, as they see them as appropriations and distortions of their revolution by the West. Zeid, a twenty-one-year-old man from Tunis, explained: "I think the name Jasmine revolution came from Europe and has been picked up by the foreign press. The jasmine flower is the symbol of the Tunisian tourism board, and the Europeans picked up on that; that's what they know when they come as tourists. . . . All they see about us is jasmine, couscous, and camels, the exotic Tunisia. Why not just call it the Tunisian revolution? We say the French revolution and not, hmm, 'the baguette revolution,' for example." Many Tunisians feel that the Jasmine revolution is inadequate to characterize their movement. As Aicha, a twenty-four-year-old from Nabeul, pointed out: "Jasmine is a beautiful flower with a lovely scent and symbolizes beauty and peace. Our struggle was hard; there was a lot of blood; many people lost their lives for liberty and dignity. . . . We Tunisians don't like that expression." The young men and women I interviewed echoed these views and were equally uncomfortable with the Facebook revolution, the dot-com revolution, or the Twitter revolution. While acknowledging the role of the Internet in helping them communicate, they protested that these expressions rob them of agency. Abdel, a twenty-six-year-old from Grombelia, explained: "When people say 'the Internet revolution' it is as if the Internet did it all alone, or it was thanks to Facebook that this revolution happened. No, this revolution happened because of Tunisians; we used Facebook and Twitter . . . only as instruments to fight the regime of Ben Ali. . . . When you wage a war, praise is not for the effective weapons . . . but for those who used them. . . . You don't call it 'the war of Kalashnikovs,' do you?" Concerned that catchy headlines may establish a narrative that diverges from reality, young people suggested that I should call this set of events the Tunisian revolution. Indeed, they were claiming agency and ownership of this process.

Before we analyze how young Tunisians effectively carried out this political uprising, we must take into account the climate of discontent in which the revolution flourished.

Underlying Causes of Discontent

Tensions had been rising steadily within Tunisian society over the past decade. Bouazizi's self-immolation ignited protests that expressed longstanding discontent among various groups and social strata. Frustrations stemmed not only from economic malaise but also from suffocating repression and increasingly visible kleptocracy within the ruling family (Carpenter and Schenker 2011).

Uneven Regional Development and Massive Unemployment

The global economic downturn had especially serious effects on the Tunisian economy between 2007 and 2009. Rates of unemployment and underemployment, which were already high, soared, particularly in the tourism industry. Nearly 30 percent of all Tunisians aged twenty to twenty-four were unemployed, and young university graduates were most seriously affected (World Bank 2008). Popular dissatisfaction was especially acute in the central and western regions of the country, which had been completely neglected by the government. Khaled, a twenty-seven-year-old from Kasserine, pointed to the problem: "Ben Ali's government has not invested in Kasserine at all. We are one of the poorest regions in the country. More than 80 percent of what we consume here comes from Algeria, not from Tunisia. You see those jerry cans of fuel that are being sold in the streets? That is fuel from Algeria, which is much cheaper than Tunisian fuel. Here everything comes from Algeria, food, clothes, furniture, everything. . . . We survive because of Algeria, not because of the Tunisian government."

The neoliberal economic policies of the old regime reinforced a pattern of uneven development that marginalized the south, central, and western regions and concentrated wealth in the northern and eastern coastal regions of the country. This approach also resulted in low wages and job insecurity in the south and failed to generate enough jobs to employ young people entering the workforce. It is not surprising that the revolt against the government began in these impoverished regions, which experienced extremely massive unemployment and poverty rates four times higher than the rest of the country. The government did not make any public investments in these regions; instead, it offered tax breaks and incentives to businesses in the vain hope that private investment would spur local development (Rogers 2011). Few new jobs were created. Unequal regional development was at the heart of young people's discontent and created the conditions for the revolution. In 2008 major revolts occurred in Redeyef, Skhira, and Ben Garden.[6]

State Corruption

The notorious excesses of the authoritarian regime played a major role in exacerbating popular dissatisfaction. Tunisians became more aware of the corruption of Ben Ali and his ruling clique in 2009 through revelations published in international media.[7] It became common knowledge that the president and his wife, Leila Trabelsi, ran a mafia-like network involving relatives and close friends that plundered the country and amassed amazing wealth (Beau and Graciet 2009). They controlled most major businesses, from information and communication technology through banking to manufacturing, retail, transportation, agriculture, and food processing. According to cables sent by the U.S. ambassador to Tunisia, Robert Godec, in July 2009 and published by WikiLeaks in 2010, Ben Ali's son-in-law, twenty-eight-year-old Mohamed Sakher El Materi, owned a shipping and cruise line, concessions for Audi, Volkswagen, Porsche, and Renault, a pharmaceutical manufacturing firm, and several real estate companies. Leila's brother was able to launch a new airline, Karthago, that took over lucrative charter flights previously operated by Tunisair, the state-owned airline, and borrowed Tunisair planes whenever he wanted. As Tunisian sociologist Slaheddine Ben Fredj pointed out, the Ben Ali–Trabelsi clan controlled the economy so tightly that it discouraged direct foreign investment and economic growth. Everything had to go through the family, which would force potential investors into partnerships and joint ventures and threaten those who would not play by their rules (Hibou 2006).

Many Tunisians were familiar with what happened to McDonald's. A WikiLeaks memo published in 2010 describes the situation: "McDonald's undertook lengthy market research, obtained necessary licenses and real estate leases, entered commercial agreements, secured a local partner, and established necessary product supply chains. Their [*sic*] investment, however, was scuttled by a last minute intervention by First Family personalities who reportedly told McDonald's representatives that 'they had chosen the wrong partner.' The implication was clear: either get the 'right' partner or face the consequences. McDonald's chose to pull out completely at great cost." The family also tried to stifle the development of successful national enterprises outside its control by intimidating legitimate businessmen. The Tunisian middle class was gradually excluded in favor of a small, close-knit clique of relatives that included siblings and in-laws as well as distant kin of Ben Ali and Leila Trabelsi (Hibou 2004; Hibou 2006; WikiLeaks 2010). The family threatened small entrepreneurs as well as big businesses, alienating both the middle and the lower classes. I heard several stories of aspiring young entrepreneurs being stifled by the regime and discouraged from undertaking any serious business ventures.

Political Repression and Lack of Freedom

Political repression and the lack of civil liberties was a third important factor that provoked popular discontent. Tunisians were not allowed to voice any criticisms of Ben Ali and his government, and the regime systematically repressed all forms of political dissent. Human rights activists, journalists, and members of the opposition were subjected to constant surveillance, harassment, and imprisonment (Kausch 2009). Legislation used to exert pressure on journalists and editors was amended to tighten restrictions on freedom of expression. The regime developed a sophisticated approach to online censorship and denial of access to the Internet. The authorities blocked access to several Internet sites and engaged in large-scale phishing operations of its citizens' websites and private accounts. Popular criticism of the government and its leaders was systematically repressed. As Nassir from Tozeur put it, "In my thirty-one years of existence the first time I heard someone criticize the president and say things against the government was during this revolution. . . . Nobody dared to voice any criticisms before." In Bizerte, twenty-four-year-old Ayoub told me: "If Ben Ali were still in power you wouldn't be able to speak freely with us about our views regarding our country and our future. . . . You could only do that in the presence of an agent of the regime." Moreover, freedom of association was almost nonexistent. With a few exceptions, such as the Tunisian League for Human Rights, organizations and associations that worked on political issues were denied legal registration (Kausch 2009). Independent groups and opposition parties had a very limited margin for maneuver, since they were not allowed to hold public meetings or engage in any sort of public criticism of the regime (Kausch 2009; Paciello 2011).

The Main Actors of the Revolution

Several factors converged to set off the uprisings that resulted in the fall of Ben Ali's regime. The key actors in this revolution were Mohamed Bouazizi; young cyber activists; young unemployed university graduates; and civil society groups, including the trade union movement, lawyers, and opposition parties that joined as the conflict escalated.

Mohamed Bouazizi: An Accidental Martyr?

The story of Bouazizi and his role in the revolution has been a source of debate. Some present him as a heroic martyr and the father of the Tunisian revolution. He has been credited with galvanizing frustrated youth across the region to stage mass demonstrations and revolt against their government. This view was dominant in the foreign media in late December and early January. Headlines of major foreign newspapers read, for example, "Mohammed Bouazizi: The dutiful son whose death changed Tunisia's fate" (*The Guardian*, London, 23 January 2011) and "How a single match can ignite a revolution" (*The New York Times*, 26 January 2011). The Tunisian-born mayor of Paris, Bertrand Delanoe, announced his decision to name a Parisian square or street after Bouazizi in tribute to the Tunisian revolution (Ben Hammouda 2011, 15).[8] Inside the country some saw Bouazizi as a hero who changed the course of history in Tunisia and influenced events in other North African and Middle Eastern countries.

Many young Tunisians with whom I spoke during my visit to the country in June 2011, however, expressed mixed feelings about the way Mohamed Bouazizi's role in the revolution was portrayed. Aouidet, a twenty-three-year-old actor from Bizerte, contended: "Bouazizi is not *the* hero of this revolution. There have been many other young men who set themselves on fire as a protest against the government before him. For example, in Gafsa in 2008, there were many martyrs who immolated themselves in that revolt. . . . Bouazizi was simply a catalyst." Zeid, a twenty-one-year-old who lives in Tunis, maintained that "Bouazizi was just a trigger, and we should acknowledge him for that, but he shouldn't be seen as the main . . . hero of the revolution. This revolution has many young martyrs, but they are not mentioned in the media, just Bouazizi. . . . We have to end the personality cult; that's what we fought against by overthrowing Ben Ali." Young people's perceptions of Bouazizi and his place in the revolution seem to have shifted following rumors that his family accepted money and favors from Ben Ali. Aouidet explained that "initially many people identified themselves with Bouazizi and his family. But the situation changed a bit when the family started accepting gifts from Ben Ali . . . and from the foreign media and they became like 'stars.' . . . They fell into Ben Ali's trap of trying to silence the revolution with a few bribes."

During my visit to Sidi Bouzid I spoke with many young people who shared these views. They pointed out that the Bouazizi family had moved out of Sidi Bouzid after, supposedly, receiving a large sum of money from Ben Ali and were reported to have visited him at the presidential palace. Haltiti, a nineteen-year-old from Tunis, emphasized that no one person should be treated as a "star" because the revolution was a collective effort and achievement: "In the center of [Sidi Bouzid] they had named a famous square after him [Mohamed Bouazizi], but . . . they changed it and named it the People's Square. It is unfair to place all the importance on Bouazizi." As the young people I met pointed out, youth are the real heroes of this revolution.

Cyber Activism

The Tunisian revolution was fought not only in the streets but also in Internet forums, blogs, Facebook pages, and Twitter feeds. Young bloggers used online social networks to expose government abuses. They distributed information about the situation in Sidi Bouzid and other regions of the country on the web, while the government-controlled print and broadcast media completely ignored the popular uprising. The development of the Internet in Tunisia was rapid; there are publinets (Internet cafés) everywhere in the country. Growing numbers of young people accessed cyberspace to escape the prevailing repression (Ben Hammouda 2012). Tunisia had 2.8 million Internet users by 2009[9] and 3.6 million by March 2011.[10]

The Tunisian regime censored the Internet for many years. Popular video-sharing websites, such as YouTube and Dailymotion, were blocked, and social networking sites, especially Facebook, were shut down periodically. During the revolution, a cyber war raged between the government and Tunisian cyber activists fighting for freedom of expression. Ben Ali's regime selectively targeted and blocked websites and intimidated bloggers who disseminated information against the regime. With cyberspace under siege, Twitter became the activists' bastion.[11] In April 2010 the government blocked more than one hundred blogs, in addition to many websites. The government's approach was invasive and paranoid. As cyber activist Aziz

Amami stressed, "We didn't really have the Internet; what we had was a sort of national Intranet." Anonymous,[12] an "Internet vigilante group," is a loosely knit collective of cyber activists; it drew world attention for supporting the whistle-blowing website WikiLeaks. Anonymous targeted Tunisia after the government censored a Tunisia-based website set up to host the WikiLeaks memos. In collaboration with Anonymous, Tunisian cyber activists managed to put pressure on the regime.[13] As Bullet Skan, a seventeen-year-old cyber activist from Tunis, mentioned, "We asked Anonymous to help us with specific targets." Attacking government websites was dangerous for those living within the country, who risked arrest if they were identified by the authorities. After Anonymous succeeded in disrupting at least eight government websites, including those of the president, the prime minister, the ministry of industry, the ministry of foreign affairs, and the stock exchange, as well as the government Internet agency, several young Tunisian bloggers were arrested in a desperate attempt by Ben Ali's regime to silence online activism. Among them were three young cyber activists whom I interviewed during my stay in Tunisia: Slim Amamou, Aziz Amami, and Bullet Skan.

Slim Amamou, aged thirty-three, is the most widely known Tunisian cyber activist, not just because of his active role in the revolution but also because he became a member of the transitional government after the fall of Ben Ali. Slim had already been targeted by the regime. In May 2010 he and his friend Aziz Amami planned a demonstration in Tunis to protest Internet censorship. The day before they were both arrested and interrogated by Tunisian police and were forced to record and post an online message calling off the protests. Nevertheless, young Tunisians gathered in "flash mobs" wearing white t-shirts to protest Internet censorship.[14] I asked Slim how he became involved in the revolution.

> I am a member of the social network Twitter, and on December 18, 2010, I saw the information about the uprisings in Sidi Bouzid and the Internet postings made by Ali Bouazizi, the cousin of Mohamed Bouazizi. I saw videos of people saying that they wanted to work and they wanted freedom. Because I am an activist for freedom of expression . . . I became interested in the events in Sidi Bouzid. I was already working with a group of activists on issues of freedom of expression and I decided to engage our group in publicizing the events in Sidi Bouzid. I went down to Sidi Bouzid with a few colleagues and we made our own videos of the events in Sidi Bouzid, Kasserine, and other areas. We placed our information on the web, which was immediately picked up by people all over the country and by the international media.

Aziz Amami, a twenty-eight-year-old from Tunis, worked closely with Slim. They went to Sidi Bouzid together to report on the events of December 2010. Amid police repression and brutal attacks against participants in the revolts in Sidi Bouzid and Kasserine, Aziz decided to join the protests. On December 25 and 27, together with Slim and other activists, Aziz helped to organize two large protests in Tunis in solidarity with those in Sidi Bouzid. Aziz was already known for his skill in planning and organizing demonstrations.[15] During the late December protests, which brought hundreds of youths into the streets, Slim Amamou captured the events on his cell phone, which were directly picked up by Al Jazeera and transmitted in real time to the entire world.

Bullet Skan, another cyber activist, started playing with computers as a young child and quickly moved from computer games into hacking people's e-mail. "In my Internet adventures I came across a group of Algerian hackers and befriended them, and they taught me a number of hacking tricks." He then took it upon himself to discover proxy ways of accessing sites the government had blocked and came across the Internet sites of Tunisian dissidents. Takriz, an anonymous network founded in 1998, was one of the most critical cyber voices against the dictatorship of Ben Ali.[16] Through Takriz, Bullet Skan became a cyber activist at the age of fifteen, moving from hacking to helping expose the abuses of the regime. He became involved with other cyber activists in the fight against Internet censorship, including Slim Amamou and Aziz Amami with whom he ended up behind bars when he was just sixteen years old.

Houssem, a twenty-seven-year-old cyber activist in Kasserine, located in the central region twenty-one miles from Sidi Bouzid, took pictures and videos with his cell phone and posted them on his Facebook page. After a few days he started posting them on Al Jazeera's site as well. Houssem said that as the protests intensified in Kasserine, reporters from Al Jazeera, France 24, and other foreign media descended on the city and asked him to assist with information after their departure. But Houssem did not send them anything because he feels that "the foreign media abandoned Tunisia to focus on Egypt."

The work of cyber activists such as Slim, Aziz, Bullet, and Houssem was critical in exposing the brutality of the regime to the Tunisian people and to the world. The regime could no longer say that the protests were simply the actions of isolated young criminal gangs and deny its excessive use of force. Young bloggers and cyber activists were essential in establishing communication among young people through cyberspace. They planned, organized, and shared ideas about their political insurgency through the Internet.

Young Unemployed University Graduates

The majority of the young people who took to the streets were unemployed or underemployed as well as disillusioned with the government. Many have completed university and have valuable technical skills but are still unable to find work. In Tunisia access to higher education is guaranteed to anyone who passes the baccalaureate examination at the end of high school.[17] Largely as a result of this policy the number of Tunisians who graduated from college tripled in a single decade. The Tunisian educational system produced more graduates than the job market was able to absorb.[18] Left with no opportunities for work, young graduates survived in irregular underpaid jobs in the service sector, construction, and foreign call centers. They were also involved in smuggling and cross-border trade. Some migrated to other countries in the region and in Europe. Without any serious support from the state, many unemployed young graduates were forced to seek a livelihood in the informal sector. But these strategies did not offer any job security and made them disillusioned with the government. It is not surprising that they became the main actors of the Tunisian revolution. They were young, knowledgeable, and full of energy, but they had no jobs and no real prospects for the future. They had no stake in society and were prepared to engage in violence out of sheer desperation. During the twenty-nine days of protests, young unemployed graduates came out into the streets in force and skillfully used the Internet to fight the system.

Civil Society Groups

Tunisian lawyers staged large demonstrations in front of the courthouses in Tunis and other cities across the country to protest government abuses and defend human rights. On December 31 the Bar Association called for national demonstrations and staged large protests in Tunis, Sfax, and Djerba. Hundreds of lawyers came out onto the streets dressed in their robes, but they were violently beaten by the police.[19] Civil society groups composed of teachers and journalists joined the lawyers in supporting the demonstrations. As the conflicts escalated, the opposition political parties also became involved (Ben Hammouda 2012). Although the UGTT initially decided to play a mediating role between the government and the demonstrators, it soon changed its position. Local and regional unions decided to join the youth much sooner, forcing the leadership of the UGTT to call for peaceful marches in protest against police repression and in support for young demonstrators on January 11. The participation of the UGTT helped form a broader national coalition against the regime. As Hakim Ben Hammouda points out, at this point the youth revolt was transformed into a revolution as the demands widened from a solution to socioeconomic grievances to regime change (Ben Hammouda 2012). The dissident network Takriz has also been credited with infusing political demands into the movement. But some young people, especially the cyber activists and unemployed graduates, pointed out that they were aware that removing the regime would be necessary in order to effect radical change. As thirty-seven-year-old Hichem put it, "Jobs and food without freedom" would not be enough. "If we went for a minimalist approach we would soon be disappointed and want more. . . . Freedom is paramount."

The Challenges of the Democratic Transition

How do young people view the post–Ben Ali era and the political and social developments that have marked the Tunisian transition? To what extent does the interim coalition government represent the aspirations of the younger generation? What roles do young Tunisians want to play in the process of building a multiparty democracy?

The Transitional Coalition Government

Following the departure of Ben Ali on 14 January 2011, the speaker of parliament, Fouad Mebazaa, immediately became interim president and an interim government was formed on 17 January 2011. The mandate of the provisional government was to manage the first phase of the country's political transition and prepare for the election of the National Constituent Assembly, which would approve a new Tunisian constitution. From the moment it was formed, the new government faced serious challenges. The first and second governments were headed by Interim Prime Minister Mohammed Ghannouchi, who was a cabinet minister under Ben Ali. His first government included members of the ruling party, the RCD (Constitutional Democratic Rally). Young Tunisians rejected this government from its inception, despite the fact that it included cyber activist Slim Amamou. Protesters in Tunis called for the resignation of the interim government. Ten days after its establishment, this government was dissolved and a second, more inclusive government was appointed, still headed by Mohammed Ghannouchi. On February 25 and 26 antigovernment rallies called for Ghannouchi's resignation. Protesters voiced frustration over the slow pace of change and accused Ghannouchi of being too close to Ben Ali's regime.[20] As Hichem asserted: "The revolution has gotten rid of Ben Ali, but his regime is still in power. . . . The RCD is still commanding everything." Other young people made a similar point, saying, "We cut off the head of the beast, but the beast was still very much alive." Indeed, Ghannouchi's government failed to dissolve the RCD and to reform the repressive security apparatus. It was hesitant to break with Ben Ali's regime, making concessions to the revolution without doing away with the old system of power (Paciello 2011).

The interim government did legalize the formation of new political parties and grant amnesty to political prisoners. It issued an international arrest warrant for Ben Ali and his close relatives who had fled abroad, as well as warrants for the arrest of members of his extended family in Tunisia. National committees were established to deal with human rights violations, embezzlement and corruption, and constitutional reform (Paciello 2011). Concerns were raised, however, regarding these committees' ability to carry out their tasks effectively, because they had limited mandates and few resources, and lacked legal authority. Youth took to the streets again, and after days of protest Mohammed Ghannouchi resigned on 27 February 2011. He was replaced by Beji Caid-Essebsi, formerly foreign minister under Habib Bourguiba, who appeared more neutral because he had managed to keep some distance from Ben Ali's regime. Soon after taking up his post, the new interim prime minister announced the dissolution of Ben Ali's political police and security apparatus, which was a critical issue for the young protesters and the opposition parties. The elections, initially scheduled for 24 July 2011, were postponed to October 23.[21] This delay worried many young people because it allowed the old guard to continue its control of the country.

Many young Tunisians I spoke with thought that the interim government was maintaining the status quo while offering a few palliatives to youth and the poor. They were seriously worried about the direction the country was taking and doubted that Caid-Essebsi's government was willing and able to dismantle the power structures of the old regime (Paciello 2011). "They changed Ghannouchi for Caid-Essebsi, but that doesn't solve anything," asserted Ahmed, a twenty-year-old man from Grombelia. "Both of them are part of the same old style of politics of Bourguiba and Ben Ali. . . . They belong to the older generation and they will not bring about the change we need. Youth are not being heard; we are not sufficiently represented in the transitional government." Aicha, a twenty-four-year-old woman from Nabeul, seconded his views, asking: "Where is youth in this transition process? What I see is the absence of the younger generation in the interim government. . . . They put a new young secretary of state for youth as if young people can only deal with youth stuff, which I find quite patronizing."

Young unemployed graduates continued to press the interim government for solutions to their problems. In May 2011 a group of about three hundred took the Kasserine governorate to task by staging a sit-in in Martyrs' Square. "Four months had passed since the fall of Ben Ali, and the governorate had not lifted a finger to help unemployed graduates. After the revolution they made many promises but nothing was happening. . . . They asked us to put together small entrepreneurial projects, and we did. . . . Still, nothing happened. So we decided to do something," explained twenty-nine-year-old Raouf, one of the organizers of the sit-in. The protestors were demanding a response to the proposals they had submitted. When I met Raouf in mid-June, he and his friends were still waiting to hear from the governor.

In an attempt to address the discontent of jobless graduates and appease the young people who were still protesting in the streets at the forefront of the revolution, the transitional government introduced an unemployment subsidy for university graduates actively seeking employment. Young people thought that this monthly grant of 200TND (about US$132) was intended to buy them off; it appeared to be a palliative measure rather than a solution to the country's massive unemployment problem. As twenty-six-year-old Fatma stressed, "Temporary benefits won't solve our main problem; we want stable jobs."

Slim Amamou, the Youth Cabinet Member

Young Tunisians who played a central role in the revolution found themselves on the margins of the transitional process leading to elections and a new government. They have no new outlets for the expression of their political opinions and play no role in the new transitional structures. Thirty-three-year-old Slim Amamou was the only young member of the interim government. He was appointed secretary of state for youth and sport on 17 January 2011 but resigned on 25 May 2011.[22] He accepted the position because he saw it as a "duty and an opportunity to participate in rebuilding the country" and thought it would give him a platform to promote change from within. Some of his fellow cyber activists opposed his entering the government, telling him, "As a dear friend, I ask you @slim404 don't collaborate with those who killed Tunisians, stay clean." He defended his decision as a necessary compromise: "It's a temporary government to set up the elections. I'm here to watch and report and be part of the decisions, not to rule." As a cabinet minister, Amamou was a breath of fresh air. He tweeted from government meetings, even reporting on his clash with the old guard over his refusal to wear a tie to cabinet meetings. He persuaded some ministers to set up Facebook pages to make their agencies more accessible.

I had the opportunity to speak with Slim Amamou about his tenure in the interim government and the reasons for his resignation. He was aware of young people's concerns about the composition of the transitional government.

> From my first day, I was received by demonstrations against the interim government in front of my ministry. . . . My work was to listen to people's demands and try to explain to them that this government's mandate was not to solve problems but to organize the elections. That was the problem, because to properly organize the elections it was not enough to put in place an electoral code and voting booths; it was fundamental to create the proper context for the elections to happen in a suitable climate. That's why it is important to try and resolve their problems. . . . That was the contradiction in the government's mandate.

Amamou's work in the interim government helped produce some positive changes. In addition to helping prepare the electoral code, he was instrumental in pushing for the release of unpublished government data on youth unemployment and for the introduction of "citizen journalism clubs" at youth centers across the country.[23] One of his main concerns while in government was police violence and repression. He wrote on his blog: "I saw very early on the main problem is presented by the Ministry of the Interior, especially the police department. The ministry has been corrupt for years. . . . If there is a ministry that needs to change now it's this one." He soon found, however, that reform "is not simple."[24] As a cabinet member, Slim Amamou sparked some controversy for speaking his mind. For example, he opposed censorship of pornography on the Internet and supported the legalization of marijuana.[25] "The young secretary of state for youth and sport should focus on helping young people deal with unemployment and the difficult economic situation, but instead he is interested in the legalization of drugs and of pornography on the Internet. . . . That's wrong, and against Muslim ways," said Ahmed, a fifty-nine-year-old man from La Marsa. Basti, a twenty-five-year-old man, responded, "Slim didn't say everyone should start smoking cannabis or watch pornography online. . . . He was just advocating for freedom of choice and freedom of the Internet. And he is right, because the government should not decide for adults; the government has to allow people to make their own decisions."

On 27 May 2011 the nation's highest court ordered the Tunisian Internet Agency to block access to all sites with pornographic and adult content following a lawsuit arguing that these sites are contrary to Muslim values and pose a danger to youth. These sites had been available for a short period when censorship was relaxed following the fall of Ben Ali's regime.[26] Since this ruling, the issue has been widely discussed in the Tunisian blogosphere, and many Tunisian youths see the reimposition of censorship as a setback in their fight for freedom of expression. This debate highlights the tensions that exist within Tunisian society today. Young people's more liberal views are in conflict with conservative values in a society that has relied on the state as the arbiter of moral standards. What civil liberties should citizens enjoy? How much freedom is too much? What is the proper role of the state? Who is responsible for morality?[27] These are only some of the questions that young Tunisians are coming to grips with in the post–Ben Ali era.

Slim Amamou became increasingly concerned with the ongoing censorship of the Internet, continued police violence and brutality, and the postponement of the elections. These factors, along with pressure from friends and a sense that he had already done what he could do, were the main reasons for his resignation from the interim government. Amamou's decision was welcomed both in the Tunisian blogosphere and among youth, who felt that the old guard was not allowing any space for young people to make change. When I spoke with Amamou on 15 June 2011, he appeared comfortable with his decision and said that he would be more useful to the revolution by fighting for freedom of expression and civil liberties from outside the government. He planned to work with young people and political parties to provide information about the electoral process so the youth vote cannot be exploited. He wanted to make sure that voters were well informed and that the elections were transparent.

The Emergence of New Political Forces

When Ben Ali's regime was toppled, Tunisia had only eight political parties. Since then the RCD has been abolished, opposition parties have been legalized, and new political forces have been created and authorized to join the electoral register. When elections were held on October 23, eighty-one political parties as well as numerous independent candidates competed for 217 seats in the constituent assembly, which is authorized to appoint a new government and rewrite the constitution.[28]

The proliferation of political parties in Tunisia gives an impression of political pluralism. Some parties align themselves along a left-right axis; others have a religious orientation. Young Tunisians pointed out, however, that they were not involved in the scramble to form political parties. Most have chosen to remain uninvolved in party politics, so their voices are largely absent from those debates. Young Tunisians are keen to participate in the democratic transition, but they are skeptical about the available channels. They expressed concern that individuals, parties, and civil society organizations are attempting to profit from the revolution. Entities with such names as January 14 Front and Council to Protect the Revolution are seen as opportunistic, because they have not earned the right to these titles (Collins 2011). This concern extends to some political actors and groups that had been opposed to Ben Ali's regime but quickly regrouped to stand in the elections without listening to young people. Nizar, a forty-eight-year-old from La Marsa, said, "I see this rush to establish political parties and gain visibility in the political arena as a process of appropriation of the revolution by the adult population, especially the elites."

Few of the new political formations have concrete programs, clear policies, or coherent ideological positions. Parties that were banned under Ben Ali are little known, and those that were coopted by the former regime remain suspect. No single political party appeared to carry, at the time of my visit, widespread legitimacy among youth, and no group was seen as representing the revolution. Young people want a government that is capable of undertaking major reforms in the economy, security, justice, and the media and that represents their interests and those of other impoverished, marginalized people.

Young Tunisians despise party politics, which they associate with corruption and abuse of power. Rather than establishing old-style political parties, they conduct their political intervention through civil society associations and social movements that directly address their problems. Young activists created associations to prepare young people to use their power at the ballot box and the actively participate in the elections.

Sawty Chabeb Tounes (My Voice: The Voice of Tunisian Youth) is a nonprofit, nonpartisan association established by a group of young people after the revolution. Sawty aims to provide objective information about democratic principles and values, political parties and their manifestos, and the role of citizens in democratic transition. Under the slogan, "The future is in our hands!" it operates an informative and interactive website and holds conferences, workshops, interviews, and public debates. In April 2011 Sawty organized a discussion in Tunis about youth employment with leaders of six political parties (the FDTL, PCOT, Republican Party, Ennahda, Social Centre Party, and CPR) so students could hear how these parties planned to address the massive youth unemployment problem. The leaders proposed to include the fundamental right to work in the new constitution, reform employment laws, and create a national center for employment. On a more practical level they advocated encouraging small entrepreneurial projects, supporting young people in their job search, reinforcing professional training and linking it directly to the needs of the job market, and putting an end to corruption and favoritism in the allocation of jobs. While these ideas sounded sensible, many young people I spoke with saw them as empty promises because they were not linked to specific political programs that take into account larger structural problems, such as reform of the educational system, and do not provide the financial resources that their proposals would require. Ultimately, they argued, real reform must change Tunisia's current economic development model, which is heavily focused on tourism and concentrates resources in the northern and eastern coastal regions. The debates and discussions that youth associations organize will contribute to creating a better informed and politically savvy young electorate.

Generations and Social Change

Like the national liberation movement that won Mozambicans independence from Portugal and the Soweto uprisings that accelerated the fall of apartheid in South Africa, the Tunisian revolution constituted a significant process of social change. While recent uprisings against unemployment and the high cost of living led by young people in Mozambique and Senegal did not culminate in revolutions, the grievances that they expressed are very similar, as are the social and economic environments in which young people live. Young people in all these countries agreed that massive unemployment, widespread government corruption, uneven economic development, and unequal distribution of resources, as well as lack of civil liberties, are the major ills affecting their societies. As pointed out before, similar situations are affecting youths worldwide, with recent developments in London, New York, Madrid, and Santiago. All over the world the waithood generation is rising up, mobilizing its consciousness, and fighting corruption, economic greed, and dictatorships in a bottom-up and more innovative process of political citizenship.

Theories about the historical role of generations in processes of social change can be traced back to Greek philosophers. Spanish philosopher José Ortega y Gasset (1929) suggested that culture always sets problems to be resolved by each generation that will bring about a change of collective *vigencias* (the conforming elements of a society). The French Annales school advanced the concept of *mentalités collectives*, shared consciousness (Bloch 1973), to understand the significance of generational change (Esler 1984; Pilcher 1994). In the 1950s and 1960s the study of generations flourished within structural-functionalist sociology as scholars underscored the idea that individuals born at the same time and experiencing major life events together are capable of generating a common consciousness that allows them to engage in social change (Mannheim 1960; Ryder 1965; Bourdieu 1993; Edmunds and Turner 2002).

Karl Mannheim was one of the first theorists to conduct a systematic and comprehensive analysis of generations as a sociological concept. He argued that the notion of generation should be applied to people who belong to a common period of history and whose lives are forged through the same conditions. "Individuals who belong to the same generation . . . are endowed, to that extent, with a common location in the historical dimension of the social process" (1952, 290). Mannheim understood generations as temporal entities defined by experiencing the same dominant social and historical influences, rather than as groupings delineated through chronological life spans. Mannheim's theory of generations was articulated on the basis of three main pillars: "generational location"; "generation actuality"; and "generation unit." Young people have the same "generational location" on the basis of being born in the same time period; experiencing the same concrete social-historical problems makes them part of the same "actual generation"; and "generation units" work up the material of their common experience in specific ways (Simirenko 1966). Thus, rather than mere chronological contemporaneity or the experience of the same history, it is shared generational consciousness that helps to realize a generation's potential as an engine of social change. The critical point that Mannheim's theory addresses is the issue of what makes a generation acquire the social solidarity to forge a collective worldview that can lead to conscious collective action. As June Edmunds and Bryan Turner observed, this distinction is "parallel to the distinction between 'a class in itself' and 'a class for itself,' namely, how classes become historical actors" (2002, 5).

Young Tunisians, Mozambicans, Senegalese, and South Africans were able to go beyond having the same location to sharing the same grievances and generating a common consciousness that led them to fight oppressive regimes and unsound policies. They created their own forms of political expression in cyberspace, hip hop, and the streets. They found new ways of defining their relationship to state politics and new forms of engagement with their society. Young Tunisians resisted Ben Ali's efforts to compensate for the lack of civil and political liberties with palliative policies and token welfare measures (Hibou 2006; Ben Hammouda et al. 2009; Ben Romdhane 2011) by keeping on fighting until the demise of the regime.

Mannheim's theory was also examined in relation to the actions of the generation of 1968 in Europe and North America, when shared consciousness led to a youth movement for social change. As a wave of student protests swept across Europe, the United States, and Japan, university campuses became battlegrounds between the institutional defenders of the status quo and mobilized youth. In 1968, often called the Year of the Barricades, the entire postwar order was challenged by a series of insurrections.[29] While opposition to the Vietnam War and support of civil rights dominated the protests in the United States and opposition to nuclear weapons predominated in the UK, the emergence of the feminist, environmentalist, and gay liberation movements can be traced to this moment. Television played a key role in arousing political opposition by relaying vivid and compelling images and sounds of conflict and injustice. The war in Vietnam was one of the most televised events in history—scenes of devastating bombing; massacres of women, children, and elders; and burning, napalm-covered young people were broadcast nightly into American living rooms.[30] These images came to symbolize the wrongs of the capitalist West and its powerful military-industrial complex. Music was also a powerful influence; the Beatles' "Revolution" and the Rolling Stones' "Street Fighting Man" expressed the revolutionary ethos of that generation.[31]

Technological innovation has also been at the heart of this twenty-first-century revolution. The extensive use of the Internet and social network media such as Facebook, Twitter, and YouTube is critical in enabling the waithood generation to mobilize and communicate with the world. University-educated activists in Tunisia had extensive Internet access and were savvy users of cyberspace. Young cyber activists defended themselves from government censorship and launched serious attacks on official websites. In Mozambique and Senegal, where Internet access is still limited, text messaging played a critical role in mobilizing protestors and communicating with independent media outlets. Similarly, youths camped at Wall Street in New York and St. Paul's Cathedral in London also connected and organized through cyberspace.

Critics of generation studies have remarked that the theory often failed to locate generations and their consciousness within particular political and economic relations and that Mannheim proposed a cyclical process in which each generation was compelled to define itself anew against the older generation (Cohen 1997; White and Wyn 2004). In the Tunisian revolution, rather than entirely breaking away from the older generation, young people mobilized a broad coalition that included unionists, lawyers, journalists, and teachers (Paciello 2011; Alexander 2011; see also Marzouki 2011). Citizens from the forgotten regions joined with elites from the affluent cities of Tunis, Sousse, and Sfax to overthrow Ben Ali. The regime had undermined the relatively large Tunisian middle class and oppressed the poor. Crucially, the military, which Ben Ali had marginalized, sided with the people by refusing to intervene. In contrast to the situation in Egypt, the military had little or no vested interest in the status quo, as it had been overshadowed by the security services (Anderson 2011). In Mozambique and Senegal, while the young people were the main catalysts and the majority, they were able to attract support, even if tacit, from their parents' generation. Although it is still too early to tell, it appears that in both New York and London broader coalitions of citizens against corporate greed are being formed.

Political sociologist Jack Goldstone has asserted that "for a revolution to succeed, a number of factors have to come together. The government must appear so irremediably unjust or inept that it is widely viewed as a threat to the country's future; elites . . . must be alienated from the state and no longer willing to defend it; a broad based section of the population, spanning ethnic and religious groups and socioeconomic classes must mobilize" (Goldstone 2011, 8). In the end, this broad coalition, transcending differences of class, age, ethnicity, religion, and political ideology, turned individual problems into collective grievances and translated immediate socioeconomic demands into a political revolution. While the younger generation in waithood was the main catalyst and took the lead in the Tunisian revolution, its power was enhanced by its capacity to bring others into the fold and foster radical change. In the generational perspective youth can lead such transformations because of their "fresh contact" (Mannheim 1952) with society and their novel outlook as they assimilate, develop, and alter the social and cultural repository they receive. From a vantage point outside dominant ideologies, they can create new forms of association and envision society and the polity anew. This was precisely what happened in the 1976 anti-apartheid uprisings in Soweto, when young people managed to transform significantly the ways in which political struggles were understood and waged.

From Bouazizi's self-immolation to the bloggers and cyber activists who exposed government abuses and the many young people who courageously defied bullets and police brutality shouting "Ben Ali Dégage," there is no doubt that young Tunisians in waithood were the main catalysts of the revolution. However, the transitional period after Ben Ali's departure has presented considerable challenges to youth. Tensions between the older and younger generations continue. The scramble to establish new political parties was an adult-driven process with little participation by youth. Young people who were major players in the revolution appear deeply disgruntled about the course of the democratic transition. They worry that their revolution could be taken over by those still clinging to the old-style politics of the previous regime.

Young people are refusing to take part in "politics as usual" and are not joining or creating political parties. In spite of this, they are not apolitical. They are building new ways of "doing" politics by engaging in more flexible associations and social movements within civil society. Cyber activism and social networking, radio, discussion groups, historical and heritage groups, and popular culture appear to be their preferred spaces for social and political intervention.

Young people in the central and southern regions where the revolution began feel that the world has abandoned them and that their revolution has been stolen. Nevertheless, they are closely watching the political developments in the country and pushing for a transformative agenda. They see themselves, as Arfaoui, a twenty-three-year-old woman from Bizerte living in Tunis, puts it, as "guardians of the revolution" and vow that "the revolution is not over; it has just started." Ultimately, says Ali, a thirty-one-year-old man who lives in Kasserine, "we have done it once," and if need be "we can do it again!"

The members of the waithood generation are indeed uniting and connecting with one another to produce profound political transformations. The links among Tunisian cyber activists with their Egyptian counterparts and with the global online group Anonymous are clear examples of these youth global interconnections and networks. Across Africa and the world, the waithood generation is creating new geographies and forms of participatory citizenship action outside hegemonic models. Youth are refusing to continue living in waithood and demanding the restoration of the social contract. As Frantz Fanon correctly stated, "Each generation must discover its mission, fulfill it or betray it, in relative opacity" (2005, xxxi).

Chapter 8

Global Waithood

Youth are the majority of Africa's population, but they have been pushed to the margins of their societies and live in a limbo between childhood and adulthood. They grapple with deficient educational systems, the lack of stable jobs that pay living wages, and the impossibility of forming their own families. The social processes that formerly enabled youths to make a smooth transition to adulthood have been almost entirely eroded by endemic poverty and chronic unemployment resulting from failed neoliberal economic policies, bad governance, and political crises. The majority are stuck in waithood, an indefinite period beyond childhood in which they cannot expect assistance from parents or the state but do not enjoy the prerogatives of full-fledged adulthood. Increasingly pervasive and prolonged, waithood is becoming the norm, gradually replacing conventional adulthood. The social contract, under which society educated children and integrated them into the economy as productive adults, has been broken. While parents and children carry out their half of the social bargain through schooling, jobs are no longer available, and social adulthood is becoming increasingly elusive.

Young Africans in waithood cope with extremely precarious and taxing conditions in many different ways. Youth in Mozambique, South Africa, Senegal, and Tunisia share many common experiences, but each setting has specific characteristics that shape their predicaments and responses. Yet the young people are not waiting passively for their lives to change, or expecting others to solve their problems. They recognize that they have to fend for themselves in the best way they can. As the actions and words of the young Africans I met so vividly show, they are using their agency by adapting existing practices and fashioning new types of livelihoods and relationships to mitigate their everyday problems.

Aware that existing socioeconomic systems have no place for them and that the state is not upholding the social contract with its citizenry, young people are creatively piecing together independent spaces for sociability, livelihood, and survival outside hegemonic power structures. Flexibility and improvisation characterize all aspects of their lives: their work, their relationships with family and friends, and their engagement with society. But their lives are precarious and offer neither security nor future prospects. They spoke of "desenrascar a vida" (eking out a living), "se debrouiller" (making do), and "just getting by." These expressions imply a conscious effort to assess the possibilities as well as the challenges of their position and to plot scenarios that might enable them to maximize their gains. Also, in a striking reconfiguration of intimacy, they are redefining female and male sexuality and negotiating new meanings for femininity and masculinity, including engaging in sexual relationships with patrons—*patrocinadores* in Portuguese, or sugar daddies and sugar mamas—as part of their livelihood strategies.

We still know very little about these youth spaces or "youthscapes" that they forge in the margins of society, which are often located in the interstices of legal and illegal hustles, weighing the potential profits against the known dangers. Subject to constant harassment by agents of the state, they mistrust government officials and the formal economic system that casts them as marginal and often as dangerous criminals. Youths inhabit these new survival spaces with their own codes of behavior, norms, and values that are commonly understood and collectively, albeit informally, enforced. Not even the garbage dump on the outskirts of Maputo is chaotic; the young men who live there are somewhat organized, balancing cooperation and competition and protecting one another and their common livelihood from outsiders' intervention. Those struggling in waithood manage to subvert authority, bypass the encumbrances created by the system, and find new ways of maneuvering on their own. They are also developing a sense of generational identity.

The young Mozambicans, South Africans, Senegalese, and Tunisians who appear in this book exemplify the multifarious strategies employed by young people across Africa, and around the world, who are coping with waithood, struggling to become socially accepted adults, and remaking society as they make a place for themselves.

But youth in waithood are not simply making do or getting by. Their struggle to cope with their socioeconomic predicament often requires them to engage in processes of contestation that can lead to radical social change. They are remaking their societies—ousting corrupt dictatorships and forcing governments to reverse unpopular decisions. African youth are developing new forms of social activism and participatory citizenship, using hip-hop music to voice popular frustrations and global networking technologies to exchange ideas and experiences and organize. Marginalized young people in waithood are often portrayed as apathetic and a "lost generation," but in reality they are actively engaged with society and the polity outside mainstream institutions and partisan politics. They are mobilizing themselves, and their political protests in the streets have already led to revolutions that toppled corrupt regimes.

Throughout history, young people have been at the forefront of major social and political transformations—a truth that ruling elders and elites tend to forget until they are suddenly awakened by youthful activists who are pulling the rug out from under their feet. Where the energies unleashed by the wave of protests throughout the continent and the revolutions in Tunisia, Egypt, and Libya will take the continent is anyone's guess. Until recently, such revolutionary uprisings seemed unimaginable, and young activists learn by doing as well as by communicating with one another. The grievances that have been articulated by young people in the Arab or African "Spring" are shared by their counterparts not only in Mozambique, Senegal, and South Africa but elsewhere across the continent. This generation is taking upon itself the task of redressing the wrongs of contemporary society and fashioning a better world.

Could this represent the beginning of an era in which young people will no longer allow themselves to be manipulated by the elites into fighting ethnic and religious conflicts but instead choose to fight for their own socioeconomic and political rights? Could this mean that the waithood generation in Africa is shifting the battlefield from identity-based conflict into class inequality and rights-based conflict? The experiences of young Africans in waithood express in particularly acute ways the sharp contradictions of our times. Understanding their responses to their predicament sheds light on what it means to be young globally today.

African youth were the first to experience waithood, but this phenomenon is now emerging among youth elsewhere in the world, as young people in developed societies also experience delayed or blocked transitions to adulthood. North American *adultolescents*, Japanese *freeters*, and Italian *bambuccioni* have attracted attention because they are unable to follow the previously prescribed paths to mature independence. Working-class and impoverished youths, especially members of racial-ethnic minority groups who were already disadvantaged, bear the heaviest burdens brought by economic recession. Their experiences are similar to those of most young Africans, in the same way that the condition of the few privileged young

Africans corresponds to that of their Western counterparts. Waithood is not about geographical divisions but, fundamentally, about class inequalities. The current crisis facing the middle class all over the world is steadily pushing more and more young people into waithood. Unemployment and under-employment and the postponement of marriage make adult independence seem like the unattainable goal of an interminable struggle.

A recent study by the Organization for Economic Cooperation and Development (OECD)[1] revealed a growing divide between rich and poor all across Europe. Social services are being slashed and school budgets and health care services significantly reduced. These austerity measures have fed an increasingly pervasive sense of hopelessness among young people. Even in Germany, whose economy is in relatively good shape, the National Poverty Conference (NAK) warned recently that prospects for young people are deteriorating.[2] Europe has recently experienced a wave of youth uprisings. In Portugal more than thirty thousand people, mostly in their twenties and thirties, filled the streets in March 2011 to vent their frustrations about massive unemployment and the absence of career prospects.[3] In May 2011 young people in Spain who call themselves the *indignados* (indignant) protested soaring unemployment rates.[4] These demonstrations have been more explicitly political than the riots that occurred in England in August 2011. The problem goes beyond Europe. In August 2011 an estimated 100,000 young people in Chile took to the streets of capital to demand a free, quality public education, and they have sustained their protests over several months.[5] In the United States many young Americans struggling to find work and pay for their college education joined the Occupy Wall Street movement to protest "corporations' undue influence and disproportionate clout over government."[6] Even India and China, whose economies are still expanding, have witnessed popular protests against government policies and economic injustice.[7]

Although national and regional contexts differ and grievances are diverse, young people's anger derives from deepening social inequalities; they are affected by the same ills created by globalization and failed neoliberal poli-cies that broke the social contract. As globalized communications raise their expectations, local conditions and public policies push those aspirations out of reach. These developments suggest a much broader crisis in transitions to adulthood. Waithood is a global phenomenon. The protest movements that this waithood generation is leading around the world—from Maputo and Santiago to London, Paris, and New York—are still inchoate, and only time will tell what they will become. Nonetheless, it is clear that, globally as well as in Africa, this is "the time of youth." The waithood generation is actively asserting itself and contesting economic policies that exacerbate poverty, class inequalities, and uneven development, as well as government corruption and repression. They are raising their voices to demand a better future. Will this waithood generation become the next 1968 generation?

Notes

1. Youth

1. The lyrics of Bob Dylan's song are available on the www.azlyrics.com website.

2. Social adults refers to people who are recognized by their culture as able to partake in the social responsibilities of adulthood.

3. These are not real names. I use pseudonyms to identify the young people who participated generously and shared their lives and views with us during this research.

4. See articles in *Time* (2003) and *Newsweek* (2005) magazines.

5. Freeter (*furita*) is a Japanese expression for people between the ages of fifteen and thirty-four who lack full-time employment or are unemployed.

6. In October 2007 Tommaso Padoa-Schioppa, then minister of economy and finance, spoke to a parliamentary committee about the government's plan for tax relief (approximately 500€/year) to people twenty to thirty years old, especially males, who are still living with their family, saying it would help them to move out on their own. He used the ironic or sarcastic term *bamboccioni*. Many Italians found the term offensive because in their opinion the problem is not the youth themselves but rather the system. A substantial number of young Italians live on approximately 1000€ per month and cannot afford to leave their parents' house.

7. See CIA World Factbook, Mozambique, available on the www.cia.gov website. See also INE (Instituto Nacional de Estatistica) 2009, available on the www.ine.gov.mz website.

8. See CIA World Factbook, Mozambique.

9. Ibid. See also the National Population Unit (NPU) Fact Sheet on the Structure of the South African Population.

10. CIA World Factbook, South Africa, available on the www.cia.gov website.

11. Ibid.

12. See CIA World Factbook, Senegal, available on the www.cia.gov website.

13. Ibid.

14. IRIN 2007, available on the www.irinnews.org website.

15. Ibid.

16. See CIA World Factbook, Tunisia, available on the www.cia.gov website.

17. Ibid.

2. Waithood

1. "Youthman" was written and performed by Lansana Sheriff, popularly known as Steady Bongo, an internationally recognized Sierra Leonean musician and producer of Afropop music.

2. In inner-city black neighborhoods the conventional model of adult manhood is not simply unattainable by today's youth but has not been attained by their fathers and uncles. Most black men in the ghetto have a "hustle" in the informal or illegal economy. Those black men who do attain social adulthood by holding a job and parenting their children generally leave the inner city.

3. In September 2011 the Washington DC–based Population Reference Bureau (PRB) released an article stating that an increasing number of young men are delaying marriage and staying in their parents' homes. Since 2007, the proportion of young men living at home has increased sharply, from 14 percent to almost 19 percent, while that of women living with their parents has remained fairly steady at around 10 percent. See Mark Mather, "In U.S., a Sharp Increase in Young Men Living at Home," available on the www.prb.org website.

4. See "Bringing Up Adultolescents" by Peg Tyre in *Newsweek* (25 March 2002); and "Grow Up? Not So Fast" by Lev Grossman in *Time* (16 January 2005). See also Patricia Cohen, "Long Road to Adulthood Is Growing Even Longer," *New York Times* (13 June 2010).

5. See Luke Johnson, "A National Epidemic that Hurts the Young," *Financial Times*, 13 September 2011, available on the www.ft.com website.

6. Chavez Campbell was interviewed by the *Guardian*, and his story appears in Alexandra Topping, "Trouble Isn't Over Yet, Says Teenager Who Predicted Riots" (12 August 2011), available on the www.guardian.co website.

7. Jay Kast's story was reported in "Youth Educator Defends London Rioters: It's Their Pain Speaking," posted 10 August 2011 on the http://observers.france24 .com website.

8. Comment posted 12 August 2011 on the http://observers.france24.com website.

9. Ibid.

3. Aspirations

1. See "Youth Unemployment," *Africa Economic Outlook*, available on the www.africaneconomicoutlook.org website.

2. Interviews by the author with Nabil Mâalel and Zouahir El Khadi in Tunis, June 2011.

3. Bettina Holzhausen, Youth culture in rural Mozambique. Zurich: Swiss Agency, 2007, available on the http://nestcepas.ch website.

4. Model C are well-funded and high-performing public schools. Most of them were "white only" schools during the apartheid era and are located in the most affluent neighborhoods.

5. For more information on COSATU's paper on education reform, see *The Shop Steward* 4(19) (August/September 2010), available on the www.cosatu.org .za website.

6. See Gumisai Matume, "Wanted Jobs for Africa's Youth: Seeking Urgent Solutions for Armies of Young Unemployed" (2006). Available on the www.un.org website.

7. These publications included the UN secretary-general's report, *Global Analysis and Evaluation of National Action Plans on Youth Employment* (2005); the ILO's background paper *Youth Employment: From a National Challenge to a Global Development Goal* (2005); and the World Bank's *Children and Youth: A Framework for Action* (2005).

8. Carlos Nuno Castel-Branco, interview with author, Maputo, March 2011.

9. The 5 February 2008 uprising occurred just one day after the president of the World Bank declared Mozambique an economic success story.

10. See Youth Employment Network and International Youth Foundation, "Private Sector Demand for Youth Labour in Ghana and Senegal" (2009), available on the www.ilo.org website.

11. Mamadou Ndione is quoted in IRIN, "The Missing Middle" (March 2009), available on the www.irinnews.org website.

12. South African National Treasury, "Confronting Youth Unemployment: Policy Options for South Africa" (February 2011), available on the www.treasury .gov.za website.

13. Maura Quatorze, "Mozambique Youth Unemployment Takes the Shine off Economic Growth" (March 2006), available on the www.bizcommunity.com website.

14. *Colored* is a racial designation that was imposed under apartheid, which stratified society along racial lines. People of mixed black-and-white parentage, as well as South Asians, Chinese, and Arabs, were classified as colored.

15. See IRIN, "Senegal: The Missing Middle: Tackling Youth Unemployment" (10 March 2011), available on the www.irinnews.org website.

16. This development grant was established in 2006 and represented 2 percent of the state budget. Although the amount has grown over the years, the program is still known as "7 million."

4. Getting By

1. Kasserine's population is around eighty thousand, and the city serves the surrounding region as a commercial and administrative center.

2. See Naomi Schwarz, "Senegal Temporarily Lifts Street-Selling Ban," in REI (2007), available on the http://developingtimes.blogspot.com website.

3. See Erin Thornton, "Meeting with Street Traders in Dakar," posted on *ONE* in 2010, available on the www.one.org website.

4. "Senegal Offer after Hawkers Riot," BBC (22 November 2007), available on the http://news.bbc.co.uk website.

5. Thornton, "Meeting with Street Traders in Dakar."

6. "When Fashion Met Famine: Benetton's Third World Crusade," *The Independent* (9 March 2008), available on the www.indepedent.co./uk website.

7. Thornton, "Meeting with Street Traders in Dakar."

8. Model C schools are the best government-funded high schools. Generally located in affluent, previously white areas, they have good infrastructure and well-trained teachers. The quality of education is good, with very high matric pass rates.

9. One of the stories explaining the origin of this term is that originally a bus ride cost 100MT. Because the term *chapas* also means roof tiles, another story is that some vehicles were so beat up that they looked like corrugated metal slapped together into makeshift roofs.

10. France's family reunification policy was institutionalized by French President Giscard d'Estaing and Prime Minister Jacques Chirac in the mid-1970s. Decree No. 76-383, approved on 29 April 1976, provided the conditions of entry and residence in France for family members of foreign immigrants.

11. In what is thought to be a response to European pressure, Tunisia passed laws imposing criminal penalties for illegally crossing national borders. Tunisia has signed an agreement with the Italian government for the surveillance of its borders and the readmission of illegal migrants who arrive in Europe through Tunisia, even if they are not Tunisian citizens.

12. See Salah Zeghidi, "Unemployment Could Become an Explosive Time-bomb," available on the http://zawaya.magharebia.com website.

13. See "Tunisian Migrants of Lampedusa: France Is Shivering," *Masr wa Touness* (24 April 2011), available on the http://masrwatouness.wordpress.com website.

14. Algeria, which is even closer to Regueb, does not attract migrants because the Algerian currency is weaker than the Tunisian dinar.

15. More than 94 percent of the Senegalese population is Muslim and belongs to one of four Sufi brotherhoods: the Tidjani, the Mouride, the Khadre, or the

Layenne. Muslim brotherhoods were already well established in Senegal at the time of independence from France in 1960 (Patterson 2010; Cernadas 2008). They have continued to grow in popularity and membership (Ndiaye 2005). The Muslim brotherhoods have played a key role in the country's political and cultural history. The Mouride is the most influential, both politically and economically, and counts Senegalese president Abdoulaye Wade among its followers (Ndiaye 2005).

16. A *marabout* is a personal spiritual leader, often a scholar of the Qur'an. Many make amulets for good luck, preside at ceremonies, and actively guide the lives of their followers (Patterson 2010).

17. Here the term is not used in the sense of tribe in African anthropology, but more as an abstract conceptual notion used in Michel Mafesoli's theory.

18. Youth groups such as the Tsotis in South Africa and the Rastapharians (a bit all over the continent), among others, can also be identified as subcultures.

5. Intimacy

1. *Thiof* is the name of the most prized and expensive fish in Senegal, affordable only by the elites (see Nyamnjoh 2005).

2. Various terms are used to describe these women; I have come across sugar-mommies, sugar-mothers, and sugar-aunties. I use *sugar mamas* because this was the term suggested by a group of young people with whom I discussed the issue.

3. The word *côtéman* is taken from the French word *côté*, meaning "side," because they are always at the side of tourists (De Jong 2007; Venables 2009).

4. Moussa's account is presented in Anne Look, "Senegal Draws Tourists with Sun, Sea and Sex: Female Sex Tourism in Senegal Attracts Women Who Will Pay for Romance," *Global Post* (April 2010), available on the www.globalpost .com website.

5. World Health Organization, *Gender Inequalities and HIV* (Geneva: WHO), available on the www.who.int website.

6. Jemel Mokni was interviewed by TV 5 Monde on 11 March 2011. The interview is available on http://www.youtube.com/watch?v=Gf5fgzplZN4.

7. Mark Hunter also stresses that women's increasing employment and the erosion of the "patriarchal bargain" centered on marriage have made male-female relations more contested, and gang rape is linked to these contestations in complex ways (2010, 173).

8. "Milking" and "sucking" relate to the young women's ability to get whatever they want from these men; "putting men in the bottle" means exercising control over them. These terms often portray the young women as taking advantage of

the men, but at the same time they present an image of these men as being easily manipulated or manipulable by the young women.

9. See "Lobola in a New South Africa" (November 2004), available on the www.southafrica.info website.

10. Ruth Pidawer, "Keeping Up with Being Kept," *New York Times* (10 April 2009), available on the www.nytimes.com website.

11. Amanda Fairbanks, "Seeking Arrangement: College Students Using 'Sugar Daddies' To Pay Off Loan Debt," *Huffington Post* (31 July 2011), available on the www.huffingtonpost.com website.

12. Craig Dawson, "American-style Sugar Daddy Parties Are Coming to the UK," NewsBrat, BBC Radio 1, available on the www.bbc.co.uk website.

6. Citizenship

1. According to the Centre for Civil Society at the London School of Economics, civil society is the arena of non-coercive collective action around shared interests, purposes, and values.

2. *Vermelho*, which means "red," is the color of Frelimo's membership card.

3. In May 2008 xenophobic violence wracked the townships of Johannesburg, Pretoria, Cape Town, and Durban. Mobs of South Africans attacked African migrants, demanding that they leave the country and stop taking their jobs and their women. More than sixty people were killed, and many thousands were left homeless. Thousands of Mozambicans and Malawians fled in fear of being harassed or even killed. See Crush 2008; Neocosmos 2010.

4. See Deon de Lange, "End of Road for Malema Is 'Unlikely'" (8 August 2011), available on the www.iol.co.za website.

5. See "Vavi Joins ANCYL in Calls for Nationalizations," *Mail and Guardian* (6 August 2011), available on the http://mg.co.za website.

6. See Bekezela Phakathi, "Cosatu's Vavi Decries ANC's Careerism," *Business Day* (Johannesburg) (7 August 2011), available on the www.businessday.co.za website.

7. The Mamelles are the hills that rise above Dakar where Wade had the "Monument de la Renaissance Africaine" erected.

8. *Ndigel* is a directive given by a spiritual leader, the marabout, that the followers must comply with. Because of the central role that Muslim brotherhoods play in the country's political life, marabouts are known to influence their followers' votes. Politicians provide financial support to mosques and religious groups, especially during electoral campaigns, in order to gain votes. President Wade belongs to the Mouride brotherhood, the largest and most influential Muslim brotherhood in Senegal.

9. *Y'en a Marre* has been translated as "Enough Is Enough," "We've Had It," and "Fed Up," which are all valid translations. "Enough Is Enough" is used here.

10. Thiat was quoted in Marc-Andre Boisver, "Y'En a Marre," *Public Enemy Africa* (10 June 2011), available on the www.publicenemyafrica.com website.

11. Thiat was quoted in Malick Rokhy Ba, "Fed Up Shakes up Senegalese Politics" (14 July 2011), available on the www.iol.co.za website.

12. Ibid.

13. See "Senegal: To Wade or Not to Wade," *Al Jazeera* (28 July 2011), available on the http://stream.aljazeera.com website.

14. El General was quoted in "The Hip-Hop Rhythm of Arab Revolt," *Hip Hop Diplomacy*, available on the http://hiphopdiplomacy.org website.

15. Ibid.

16. Mediafax, an independent news sheet circulated by fax, reported that the rapper appeared for questioning at the Maputo City attorney general's office on 30 April 2008.

17. Paul Fauvet, journalist of the Agência de Informação de Moçambique (AIM) in Maputo, cited in an article by Freemuse (Freedom of Musical Expression), available on the www.freemuse.org website.

18. The U.S. State Department added Bachir to its list of international drug kingpins, freezing all his U.S.-held assets and preventing Americans from engaging in any business with him.

19. See Azagaia's interview with Freemuse in August 2010, available on the www.freemuse.org website.

20. See lyrics of "Minha Geração" by Azagaia (2011).

21. "Moçambique: Por Detrás da Detenção do Azagaia," *Global Voices* (4 August 2011), available on the http://pt.globalvoicesonline.org website.

22. See lyrics on the www.lyricstime.com website.

23. See www.gestosdaspalavras.blogspot.com.

24. This association has no connections to George Soros's Open Societies Institute.

25. See the Open Society Association website, sociedadeaberta.afrisis.net.

26. See "Manifestações de 5 de Fevereiro confirmam a existência de censura nos media moçambicanos," in Mocambique Para Todos Blog (2 November 2008).

27. Interview with Celso Ricardo, "Manifestações para além do custo do pão," in *O Pais* (Maputo), available on the opais.sapo.mz website.

28. Ibid.

29. Ibid.

30. Madiba, one of the many names by which Mandela is known in South Africa, comes from the name of his clan and refers to an ancestor who was a ruling chief in Transkei during the eighteenth century.

31. See Umuzi's Photo Club's website, www.umuziphotoclub.blogspot.com.

32. House music is a style of electronic dance music that originated among African Americans in Chicago in the 1980s.

33. *Gamtaal* is a derogatory word to describe the language and its "colored" speakers. It highlights an identity that differs from Afrikaner identity, although both groups speak Afrikaans. See Marco, 2009.

34. Statement made in a conversation with the author in August 2010 in Maputo.

7. Social Change

1. Armando Guebuza, "A Geração de 8 de Março: Antes e Depois" (March 2004), available on the www.macua.org website.

2. "Tunisia Unemployment Protests Continue, at Least 14 Dead," *Arab Reform Bulletin* (11 January 2011), available on the www.carnegieendowment.org website.

3. "Tunisie: Ben Ali s'engage à créer 300 000 emplois entre 2011 et 2012," *Le Monde* (10 January 2011), available on the www.lemonde.fr website.

4. See "Tunisie: le régime libère des manifestants mais emprisonne un dirigeant," *Le Monde* (12 January 2011), available on the www.lemonde.fr website.

5. Coincidently, the Tunisian General Labour Union (UGTT) had already planned a day of strike on January 14.

6. The January 2008 protests in Redeyef, Gafsa, constituted one of the first open demonstrations against Ben Ali's regime. The revolt was sparked by the unfair and fraudulent recruitment practices by the region's major employer, the Gafsa Phosphate Company (GPC). Job applicants demanded more employment opportunities and protested favoritism in the recruitment process. The unrest in Redeyef quickly expanded to other mining areas and froze activities in the mining industry for several months (Amnesty International 2009). Unemployed youths also staged protests in Skhira and Ben Gardane in 2008.

7. Nicolas Beau and Catherine Graciet, *La Régente de Carthage: Main Basse sur la Tunisie* (The regent of Carthage: A stranglehold on Tunisia) appeared in France in 2009. Another source was WikiLeaks, which published memos in 2010 that exposed the magnitude of corruption among Ben Ali and his family.

8. See also "Tunisia: Paris to Have either a Rue or Place Mohammad Bouazizi," *Los Angeles Times* (9 February 2011), available on the latimesblogs.latimes.com website.

9. Mohamed Meddah, "Tunisia: Number of Internet Users Reaches 2.8 Million" (2009), available on the http://tn-pla.net website.

10. According to Internet World Stats, Facebook alone had 2.4 million users in March 2011, more than one-fifth of the population. It is estimated that today

84 percent of users access the Internet at home, 76 percent use the Internet at work, and 24 percent use public Internet cafés (www.internetworldstats.com/stats.htm).

11. Because people could access Twitter via clients rather than going through the website, many Tunisians could still communicate online. The web-savvy used proxies to browse censored sites. For more information, see Yasmine Ryan, "Tunisia's Bitter Cyberwar," *Al Jazeera* (6 January 2011), available on the http://english .aljazeera.net website.

12. According to Slim Amamou, the power of Anonymous resides in its universality and its broad representation that goes beyond any existing criteria for distinguishing among human beings. This common identity, or rather non-identity, allows its members to speak and act freely. See Slim Amamou's presentation of Anonymous for TED Carthage, available on the http://tedxcarthage .com/en website.

13. Ryan, "Tunisia's Bitter Cyberwar."

14. Steve Stecklow, "Web's Openness Is Tested in Tunisia," available on the http://online.wsj.com website.

15. Since high school Aziz has been involved in organizing strikes and protest marches, including one during the second Palestinian *intifada*. In 2008 he was expelled from the university for being the main organizer of a protest in solidarity with the revolts in Redeyef in Gafsa.

16. Takriz has been an apolitical and independent network since its inception; its core values are freedom, truth, and anonymity. Takriz is regarded by many youths as a voice of resistance against the establishment, and since 2000 it has been censored by the regime of Ben Ali. Takriz has hundreds of active members online and offline, inside and outside Tunisia. Takriz advocates freedom of speech and human rights in Tunisia. See www.takriz.com.

17. For more information, see "The New Education Reform in Tunisia—An Education Strategy for the Future, 2002–2007, Towards a Society of Knowledge and Skills" (Tunis: Ministry of Education and Training, January 2003).

18. Basic education in Tunisia is divided into two cycles, six years of primary education and three years of preparatory education; it is free and compulsory for all Tunisians. Secondary education lasts four years and is aimed at preparing students for university-level studies or entry into the workforce. Post-secondary education includes three cycles of schooling. After two or three years students are awarded a diploma for the first cycle of university studies (Diplôme d'études universitaires de premier cycle, DEUPC) or a diploma for technological university studies (Diplôme d'études universitaires technologiques, DUT). The second cycle of higher education lasts four or five years and leads to a master's degree or a diploma that allows the graduate to work or continue studying. The third cycle leads to terminal degrees at the doctoral level, the professional diploma of specialized higher studies (Diplôme d'etudes supérieurs spécialisées, DESS).

19. See Lina Ben Mhenni, "Tunisia: Lawyers Assaulted for Their Sidi Bouzid Stand," Global Voices Online (1 January 2011), available on the http:// globalvoicesonline.org website.

20. See Kim Wilshear, "Tunisian Prime Minister Mohamed Ghannouchi Resigns amid Unrest" (27 February 2011), available on the www.guardian.co.uk website. See also "Two Tunisian Ministers Quit Government," BBC Africa (28 January 2011), available on the www.bbc.co.uk website.

21. See Ira Kumaran, "Tunisian Interim Government Delays Constituent Assembly Elections" (29 June 2011), available on the www.wsws.org website.

22. Robert Mackey, "Tunisian Blogger Joins Government," *The Lede-New York Times* (18 January 2011), available on the thelede.blogs.nytimes.com website.

23. Stecklow, "Web's Openness Is Tested in Tunisia."

24. See Slim Amamou's blog, http://nomemoryspace.wordpress.com.

25. See "Tunisie: Slim Amamou, secrétaire d'Etat à tête d'anarchiste" (18 May 2011), available on the www.tekiano.com website.

26. See "Tunisia's Internet Agency Agrees to Block Porn" (15 June 2011), available on the www.i-policy.irg website.

27. Erik Churchill, "Give Me My Porno" (6 July 2011), available on the kefteji.wordpress.com website.

28. For analysis, see Sam Bollier, "Who Are Tunisia's Political Parties" (27 October 2011), available on the http://english.aljazeera.net website.

29. Steven Kreis. *The History Guide: Lectures on Twentieth Century Europe—Lecture 15, The Year of the Barricades* (2000), available on the www .historyguide.org website.

30. Ibid.

31. Ibid.

8. Global Waithood

1. "Growing Income Inequality in OECD Countries: What Drives It and How Can Policy Tackle it?" *Forum* (Paris) (2 May 2011), available on the www.oecd.org website.

2. "Europe's Angry Youth: Flash Points Across the Continent," Spiegel Online (12 August 2011), available on the www.spiegel.de website.

3. "Portuguese Youth Protest Joblessness" (12 March 2011), available on the www.irishexaminer.com website.

4. Syliva Poggoli, "Youth Protests Sweep Spain as Unemployment Soars," National Public Radio (26 May 2011), available on the www.npr.org website.

5. "Chilean Youths Embark in Protests," *AfroEuro* (10 August 2011), available on the afroeuro.org website.

6. "Why Is America's Youth Protesting Wall Street"? Fox News video (6 October 2011), available on the video.foxbusiness.com website.

7. Pankaj Mishra, "The Dead End of Globalisation Looms Before Our Youth" (25 August 2011), available on the www.guardian.co.uk website.

Reference List

Abbink, Jon. 2005. Being young in Africa: The politics of despair and renewal. In *Vanguard or vandals? Youth, politics, and conflict in Africa*, ed. Jon Abbink and Ineke van Kessel, 1–36. Leiden: Brill.

Abbink, Jon, and Ineke van Kessel, eds. 2005. *Vanguard or vandals? Youth, politics, and conflict in Africa*. Leiden: Brill.

Abdullah, Ibrahim. 1998. Bush path to destruction: The origin and character of the Revolutionary United Font/Sierra Leone. *Journal of Modern African Studies* 36(2):203–34.

———. 2009. Popular culture, subaltern agency, and people's power: The 2007 presidential and parliamentary elections and democracy in Sierra Leone. *CODESRIA Bulletin* 1 and 2:14–16.

Abdullah, Ibrahim, and Yussuf Bangura, eds. 1997. Lumpen youth culture and political violence: The Sierra Leone civil war. *Africa Development* (CODESRIA), special issue 23:3–4.

African Development Bank (AfDB). 2011. Tackling youth unemployment in the Maghreb. Tunis: African Development Bank Economic Brief.

African Union. 2006. *Youth charter*. Addis-Ababa: African Union.

Agbu, Osita. 2009. *Children and youth in the labour process in Africa*. Dakar: CODESRIA.

Aguilar, Mario, ed. 1998. *The politics of age and gerontocracy in Africa: Ethnographies of the past and memories of the present*. Trenton, NJ: Africa World Press.

———, ed. 2007. *Rethinking age in Africa: Colonial, postcolonial and contemporary interpretations of cultural representations*. Trenton, NJ: Africa World Press.

Alber, Erdmute, Sjaak van der Geest, and Susan Reynolds Whyte. 2008. *Generations in Africa: Connections and conflicts*. Berlin: Lit Verlag.

Alexander, Christopher. 2011. Tunisia's protest wave: Where it comes from and what it means. *Foreign Policy: The Middle East Channel* (January 3).

Al-Samarrai, Samer, and Paul Bennell. 2007. Where has all the education gone in sub-Saharan Africa? Employment and other outcomes among secondary school and university leavers. *Journal of Development Studies* 43(7):1270–1300.

Amit-Talai, Vered, and Helena Wulff. 1995. *Youth cultures: A cross-cultural perspective*. New York: Routledge.

Amnesty International. 2009. Behind Tunisia's "economic miracle": Inequality and criminalization of protest.

Anderson, Lisa. 2011. Demystifying the Arab Spring: Parsing the differences between Tunisia, Egypt, and Libya. *Foreign Affairs* 90(3):2–7.

Apter, Terri. 2001. *Myth of maturity: What teenagers need from parents to become adults*. New York: W. W. Norton.

Argenti, Nicolas. 2007. *The intestines of the state: Youth, violence, and belated histories in the Cameroon grassfields*. Chicago: University of Chicago Press.

———. 1998. Air youth: Performance, violence and the state in Cameroon. *Journal of the Royal Anthropological Institute* 4(4):753–81.

Arnett, Jeffrey. 1998. Learning to stand alone: The contemporary American transition to adulthood in cultural and historical context. *Human Development* 41:295–315.

———. 2004. *Emerging adulthood: The winding road from the late teens through the twenties*. Oxford: Oxford University Press.

Arnett, Jeffrey, and Susan Taber. 1994. Adolescence terminable and interminable: When does adolescence end? *Journal of Youth and Adolescence* 23:517–37.

Arnfred, Signe. 2004. Re-thinking sexualities in Africa: Introduction. In *Re-thinking sexualities in Africa*, ed. Signe Arnfred, 1–27. Uppsala: Nordic Africa Institute.

Ashford, Lori. 2007. Africa's youthful population: Risk or opportunity? Washington DC: Population Reference Bureau.

Bagnol, Brigitte. 2008. Lovolo e espíritos no Sul de Moçambique. *Análise Social* 43(2):251–72.

Bagnol, Brigitte, and Ernesto Chamo. 2004. Intergenerational relationships in Mozambique. *Sexual Health Exchange* no. 3/4.

Bang, Henrik. 2005. Among everyday makers and expert citizens. In *Remaking governance: Peoples, politics, and the public sphere*, ed. Janet Newman, 81–100. Bristol: Policy Press.

Barbarin, Oscar, and Linda Richter. 2001. *Mandela's children: Growing up in post-Apartheid South Africa*. New York: Routledge.

Barker, Gary. 2005. *Dying to be men: Youth, masculinity, and social exclusion*. London: Routledge.

Barry, Monica. 2005. The inclusive illusion of youth transitions. In *Youth policy and social inclusion: Critical debates with young people*, ed. Monica Barry, 78–95. Abingdon: Routledge.

Bassene, Jeane. 2010. Illegal migration: The Senegalese experience and plans. *Siyahamba* 19.

Bauman, Zygmunt. 2001. *The individualized society*. Cambridge: Polity Press.

Bayat, Asef, and Linda Herrera. 2010. Introduction: Being young and Muslim in neoliberal times. In *Being young and Muslim: New cultural politics in the global South and North*, ed. Linda Herrera and Asef Bayat, 3–24. Oxford: Oxford University Press.

Bayart, Jean-François, Achille Mbembe, and Comi M. Toulabor. 1992. *Le Politique par le bas en Afrique Noire: Contributions à une problematique de la démocracie*. Paris: Karthala.

Bazenguissa-Ganga, Rémy. 1996. Milices politiques et bandes armées à Brazzaville: Enquête sur la violence politique et sociale des jeunes déclassés. *Les Études du CERI* (Centre d'Études et de Recherches Internationales), no. 13.

Beau, Nicolas, and Catherine Graciet. 2009. *La régente de carthage: Main basse sur la Tunisie*. Paris: Editions La Découverte.

Beck, Ulrich. 1992. *Risk society: Towards a new modernity*. London: Sage Publications.

———. 2000. *The brave new world of work*. Cambridge: Cambridge University Press.

Beck, Ulrich, Anthony Giddens, and Scott Lash. 1994. *Reflexive modernization: Politics, tradition, and aesthetics in the modern social order*. Cambridge: Polity Press.

Bendit, Rene, and Hahn-Bleibtreu, eds. 2008. *Youth transitions: Processes of social inclusion and patterns of vulnerability in a globalised world*. Opladen: Barbara Budrich Publishers.

Bendix, Reinhard. 1964. *Nation-building and citizenship: Studies of our changing social order*. New York: John Wiley.

Ben Hammouda, Hakim. 2011. Les anti-héros de la révolution arabe. Vers la fin de l'avant-garde des grands récits de la modernité. Unpublished paper.

———. 2012. *Tunisie: L'économie Politique d'une Révolution*. Bruxelles: De Boeck.

Ben Hammouda, Hakim, Mohamed Bchir, and Mohamed Chemingui. 2009. Ten years after implementing the Barcelona process: What can be learned from the Tunisian experience. *Journal of North African Studies* 14(2):123–44.

Bennett, Andy. 1999. Subcultures or neo-tribes? Rethinking the relationship between youth, style, and musical taste. *Sociology* 33(3):599–617.

———. 2000. *Popular music and youth culture: Music, identity and place*. Basingstoke: Macmillan.

———. 2001. *Cultures of popular music*. Buckingham: Open University Press.

———. 2003. The use of insider knowledge in ethnographic research on contemporary youth music scenes. In *Researching youth*, ed. Andy Bennett, Mark Cieslik, and Stephen Miles, 186–200. New York: Palgrave Macmillan.

Bennett, Andy, and Keith Kahn-Harris. 2004. *After subculture: Critical studies in contemporary youth culture*. New York: Palgrave Macmillan.

Ben Romdhane, Mahmoud. 2011. *Tunisie: Ètat, conomie et Société: Resources politiques, legitimation, regulations sociales*. Tunis: Sud Editions.

Berman, Paul. 1996. *A tale of two utopias: The political journey of the generation of 1968*. London: W. W. Norton.

Bettaïeb, Viviane. 2011. *Dégage: La Révolution Tunisienne: Livre-Temoignages du 17 Décembre 2010 au 14 Janvier 2011*. Tunis: Éditions du Layeur.

Bhana, Deevia, Robert Morrell, Jeff Hearn, and Relebohile Moletsane. 2007. Power and identity: An introduction to sexualities in Southern Africa. *Sexualities* 10(2):131–39.

Bhowmik, Sharit. 2004. Survey of research on street vendors in Asia. Cambridge, MA: Women in Informal Employment: Globalizing and Organizing (WEIGO).

Biaya, Tsikala. 2000. Jeunes et culture de la rue en Afrique urbaine. *Politique Africaine* 80:12–31.

———. 2001. Les plaisirs de la ville: Masculinité, sexualité et féminité à Dakar (1997–2000). *African Studies Review* 44(2):71–85.

Biza, Adriano. 2004. O Estado Face a Juventude: Um pai que virou padrasto. Unpublished paper.

Blackman, Shane. 2005. Youth subcultural theory: A critical engagement with the concept, its origins and politics, from the Chicago school to postmodernism. *Journal of Youth Studies* 8(1):1–20.

Blatterer, Harry. 2007. Contemporary adulthood: Reconceptualizing an uncontested category. *Current Sociology* 55:771–92.

———. 2009. *Coming of age in times of uncertainty*. New York: Berghahn Books.

———. 2010. The changing semantics of youth and adulthood. *Cultural Sociology* 4(1):63–79.

Bloch, Marc. 1973 [1924]. *The royal touch: Monarchy and miracles in France and England* (*Les rois thaumaturges*), trans. J. E. Anderson. London: Routledge and Kegan Paul.

Bonczar, Thomas, and Allen Beck. 1997. Lifetime likelihood of going to state or federal prison. Bureau of Justice Statistics Bulletin, NCJ 1600092. Washington DC: United States Department of Justice.

Bosick, Stacey, and Angela Gover. 2010. Incarceration during the transition to adulthood: A "snapshot" of at-risk males at 25. *American Journal of Criminal Justice* 35(3):93–104.

Boubakri, Hassen. 2004. Transit migration between Tunisia, Libya, and Sub-Saharan Africa: Study based on Greater Tunis. Paper read at Migrants in Transit Countries: Sharing Responsibility for Management and Protection, 30 September –1 October 2004, Istanbul.

Bourdieu, Pierre. 1993. Youth is just a word. In *Sociology in Question*, trans. Richard Nice, 94–102. London: Sage Publications.

———. 1998. Job insecurity is everywhere now. In *Acts of Resistance Against the Tyranny of the Market*, trans. Richard Nice, 82–87. Cambridge: Polity Press.

Bourgois, Philippe. 1995. *In search of respect: Selling crack in El Barrio*. Cambridge: Cambridge University Press.

Bradley, Harriet, and Ranji Devadason. 2008. Fractured transitions: Young adults' pathways into contemporary labour markets. *Sociology* 42(1):119–36.

Brannan, Tessa, Peter John, and Gerry Stoker. 2006. Active citizenship and effective public services and programmes: How can we know what really works? *Urban Studies* 43(5–6):993–1008.

Brannen, Julia, and Ann Nilsen. 2002. Young people's time perspectives: From youth to adulthood. *Sociology* 36(3):513–37.

Bruijn, Mirjam, Francis Nyamnjoh, and Inge Brinkman, eds. 2009. *Mobile phones: The new talking drums of everyday Africa*. Bamenda, Cameroon: Langaa.

Bucholtz, Mary. 2002. Youth and cultural practice. *Annual Review of Anthropology* 31:525–52.

Bundy, Colin. 1987. Street sociology and pavement politics: Aspects of youth and student resistance in Cape Town 1985. *Journal of Southern African Studies* 13:303–30.

Burgess, Thomas. 2005. Introduction to youth and citizenship in East Africa. *Africa Today* 51(3):vii–xxiv.

Bynner, John. 2005. Reconstructing the youth phase of the life course: The case of emerging adulthood. *Journal of Youth Studies* 8:367–84.

Calvès, Anne-Emmanuèle, Jean-François Kobiane, and Edith Martel. 2007. Changing transitions to adulthood in urban Burkina Faso. *Journal of Comparative Family Studies* 38(2):265–83.

Campbell, Catherine, Andrew Gibbs, Sbongile Maimane, Yugi Nair, and Zweni Sibiya. 2009. Youth participation in the fight against AIDS in South Africa: From policy to practice. *Journal of Youth Studies* 12(1):93–109.

Canet, Raphaël, Laurent Pech, and Maura Stewart. 2009. France's burning issue: Understanding the urban riots of November. In *Riot: Resistance and rebellion in Britain and France, 1381 to the present*, ed. Brett Bowden and Michael T. Davis. London: Palgrave Macmillan.

Capelli, Peter. 2003. Career jobs are dead. In *Benefits for the workplace of the future*, ed. Olivia S. Mitchell, David S. Blitzstein, Michael Gordon, and Judith F. Mazo, 203–325. Philadelphia: University of Pennsylvania Press.

Carling, Jorgen. 2007. Unauthorized migration from Africa to Spain. *International Migration* 45(4):3–36.

Carpenter, J. Scott, and David Schenker. 2011. Tunisia on edge. Washington Institute, January 18.

Carton, Benedict. 2000. *Blood from your children: The colonial origins of generational conflict in South Africa*. Charlottesville: University of Virginia Press.

Castel-Branco, Carlos Nuno. 2010. Pobreza, Riqueza e Dependência em Moçambique. Maputo: Instituto de Estudos Sociais e Económicos, Cadernos (IESE), no. 3.

Castle, Sarah, and Mamadou Konaté. 1999. The context and consequences of economic transactions associated with sexual relations among Malian adolescents. Paper presented at Third African Population Conference, December 6–10, Durban, South Africa.

Cernadas, Celia. 2008. *El rol de las autoridades tradicionales en los regímes democráticos africanos*. Barcelona: Institute Barcelona d'Estudis Internacionals.

Chant, Sylvia, and Alice Evans. 2010. Looking for the one(s): Young love and urban poverty in The Gambia. *Environment and Urbanization* 22(2):353–69.

Chatterji, Minky, Nancy Murray, David London, and Philip Anglewicz. 2004. The factors influencing transactional sex among young men and women in 12 sub-Saharan African countries. Washington DC: Policy Project.

Chen, Martha. 2006. Rethinking the informal economy: Linkages with the formal economy and the formal regulatory environment. In *Linking the formal and informal economy: Concepts and policies*, ed. Basudeb Guha-Khasnobis, Ravi Kanbur, and Elinor Ostrom, 75–92. Oxford: Oxford University Press.

Chen, Martha, Joann Vanek, and Marilyn Carr. 2004. *Mainstreaming informal employment and gender in poverty reduction: A handbook for policy-makers and other stakeholders*. London: Commonwealth Secretariat.

Chigunta, Francis. 2007. An investigation into youth livelihoods and entrepreneurship in the urban informal sector in Zambia. D.Phil. thesis, University of Oxford.

Chimanikire, Donald, ed. 2009. *Youth and higher education in Africa: The cases of Cameroon, South Africa, Eritrea, and Zimbabwe*. Dakar: CODESRIA.

Chisholm, Lynne. 1999. From systems to networks: The reconstruction of youth transitions in Europe. In *From education to work: Cross-national perspectives*, ed. Walter R. Heinz, 298–318. Cambridge: Cambridge University Press.

Christiansen, Catrine, Mats Utas, and Henrik Vigh. 2006. Navigating youth, generating adulthood: Social becoming in an African context. *African Affairs* 108(430):137–39.

Cling, Jean-Pierre Gubert, Flore Nordman, J. Christophe, and Anne-Sophie Robilliard. 2007. Youth and labour markets in Africa: A critical review of literature. Document de Travail no. 49. Paris: Agence Française de Développement.

Cohen, Phil. 1997. *Rethinking the youth question*. London: Macmillan.

Cohen, Phil, and Patrick Ainley. 2000. In the country of the blind: Youth studies and cultural studies in Britain. *Journal of Youth Studies* 3(1):79–95.

Cohen, Stanley. 1972. *Folk devils and moral panics: The creation of the Mods and Rockers*. London: MacGibbon and Kee.

Cole, Jennifer. 2004. Fresh contact in Tamatave, Madagascar: Sex, money, and intergenerational transformation. *American Ethnologist* 31(4):573–88.

Cole, Jennifer, and Deborah Durham, eds. 2007. *Generations and globalization: Youth, age, and family in the new world economy.* Bloomington: Indiana University Press.

———. 2008. *Figuring the future: Globalization and the temporalities of children and youth.* Santa Fe, NM: School for Advanced Research Press.

Collignon, René, and Mamadou Diouf, eds. 2001. Les Jeunes, hantise de l'espâce public dans les societes du Sud? Special issue of *Autrepart* 18.

Collins, Nicholas. 2011. Voices of a revolution: Conversations with Tunisia's youth. Washington DC: National Democratic Institute (NDI).

Comaroff, Jean, and John Comaroff. 2005. Reflection on youth. In *Makers and breakers: Children and youth in postcolonial Africa,* ed. Alcinda Honwana and Filip De Boeck, 19–30. Oxford: James Currey Publishers.

Coulter, Chris. 2009. *Bush wives and girl soldiers.* Ithaca, NY: Cornell University Press.

Cross, John. 2000. Street vendors, modernity, and postmodernity: Conflict and compromise in the global economy. *International Journal of Sociology and Social Policy* 20(1/2):29–51.

Cruise O'Brien, Donald. 1996. A lost generation: Youth identity and state decay in West Africa. In *Postcolonial Identities in Africa,* ed. Richard Webner and Terence Ranger, 57–74. London: Zed Books.

Crush, Jonathan. 2008. *The perfect storm: The realities of xenophobia in contemporary South Africa.* Cape Town: Institute for Democracy in Africa, South Africa.

De Boeck, Filip, and Alcinda Honwana. 2005. Children and youth in Africa: Agency, identity and place. In *Makers and breakers: Children and youth in postcolonial Africa,* ed. Alcinda Honwana and Filip De Boeck, 1–18. Oxford: James Currey Publishers.

De Jong, Lou. 2007. *"We plakken als vliegen, maar steken niet als muggen": Ontmoetingen tussen coteman en toeristen in Senegal ("We stick like flies, but do not sting like mosquitoes": Encounters between coteman and tourists in Senegal).* Amsterdam: Aksant.

De Soto, Hernando. 1989. *The other path: The invisible revolution in the Third World.* New York: Harper and Row.

De Waal, Alex, and Nicolas Argenti. 2004. *Young Africa: Realising the rights of children and youth.* Trenton, NJ: Africa World Press.

Dhillon, Navtej, and Tarik Yousef. 2007. Inclusion: Meeting the 100 million youth challenge. Middle East Youth Initiative Report. Washington DC and Dubai: Brookings Wolfensohn Center for Development and Dubai School of Government.

———, eds. 2009. *Generation in waiting: The unfulfilled promise of young people in the Middle East.* Washington DC: Brookings Institution Press.

Diop, Abdoulaye. 1985. *La famille Wolof.* Paris: Karthala.

Diouf, Mamadou. 1996. Urban youth and Senegalese politics: Dakar 1988–1994. *Public Culture* 8(2):225–49.

———. 2003. Engaging postcolonial cultures: African youth and public space. *African Studies Review* 46(2):1–12.

———. 2005. Afterword. In *Makers and breakers: Children and youth in postcolonial Africa,* ed. Alcinda Honwana and Filip De Boeck, 229–34. Oxford: James Currey Publishers.

Downes, Andrew. 1998. An economic analysis of unemployment in Trinidad and Tobago. Paper presented at Labour Market: Between Solidarity and Loyalty, seminar sponsored by the Inter-American Development Bank, May 19–20. Montevideo, Uruguay.

Downes, David, and Paul Rock.1982. *Understanding deviance: A guide to the sociology of crime and rule breaking.* Oxford: Oxford University Press.

Dunkle, Kristin, Rachel Jewkes, Mzikazi Nduna, Jonathan Levin, Yandisa Sikweyiyam, and Mary Koss. 2007. Transactional sex with casual and main partners among young South African men in the rural Eastern Cape: Prevalence, predictors, and associations with gender-based violence. *Social Science and Medicine* 65(6):1235–48.

Durham, Deborah. 2000. Youth and the social imagination in Africa: Introduction to parts 1 and 2. *Anthropological Quarterly* 73(3):113–20.

———. 2002. Love and jealousy in the space of death. *Ethnos* 67(2):155–79.

Dwyer, Peter, and Johanna Wyn. 2001. *Youth, education, and risk: Facing the future.* London: Routledge Falmer.

Eddy, Gail, and Lucy Holborn. 2011. *Fractured families: A crisis for South Africa.* Johannesburg: South African Institute of Race Relations.

Edmunds, June, and Bryan Turner. 2002. *Generations, culture, and society.* Buckingham: Open University Press.

Elder, Glen, Jr. 1974. *Children of the Great Depression: Social change in life experience.* Chicago: University of Chicago Press.

El Kenz, Ali. 1996. Youth and violence. In *Africa now: People, policies, institutions,* ed. Stephen Ellis. The Hague: Directorate-General for International Cooperation; London: James Currey; and Portsmouth: Heinemann.

Ellwood, David, and Christopher Jencks. 2004. The uneven spread of single-parent families: What do we know? Where do we look for answers? In *Social inequality,* ed. Kathryn M. Neckerman, 3–78. New York: Russell Sage Foundation.

Esler, Anthony. 1984. The truest community: Social generations as collective mentalities. *Journal of Political and Military Sociology* 12:99–112.

Esposito, John, and Natana DeLong-Bas. 2001. *Women in Muslim family law.* Syracuse, NY: Syracuse University Press.

Evans-Pritchard, Edward. 1940. *The Nuer: A description of the modes of livelihood and political institutions of a Nilotic people.* Oxford: Clarendon Press.

Fanon, Frantz. 2005 [1963]. *The wretched of the earth*, trans. Richard Philcox. New York: Grove Press.

Fares, Jean, Claudio Montenegro, and Peter Orazem. 2006. How are youth faring in the labor market? Evidence from around the world. Policy Research Working Paper Series 4071. Washington DC: World Bank.

Fargues, Phillipe. 2005. Temporary migration: Matching demand in the EU with supply from the MENA [Middle East and North Africa]. In *Analytic and Synthetic Notes 2005/11:* Demographic and Economic Module. Brussels: European University Institute, Robert Schuman Centre for Advanced Studies (RSCAS).

Fasih, Tazeen. 2008. Linking education policy to labor market outcomes. Working paper. Washington DC: World Bank.

Fiske, Edward, and Helen Ladd. 2004. Elusive equity: Education reform in post-Apartheid South Africa. Washington DC: Brookings Institution Press.

Flahaux, Marie-Louise. 2010. Partir, revenir: Tendances et facteurs desmigrations africaines intra et extra-continentales. *MAFE* Working Paper, no. 7.

Fortes, Meyer. 1945. *The dynamics of clanship among the Tallensi.* Oxford: Oxford University Press.

Foster, Angel. 2002. Young women's sexuality in Tunisia: The health consequences of misinformation among university students. In *Everyday life in the Muslim Middle East*, ed. Donna Lee Bowen and Evelyn A. Early, 98–110. Bloomington: Indiana University Press.

Foucault, Michel. 1976. *Mental illness and psychology*, trans. Alan Sheridan. New York: Harper Colophon.

Fournier, Pascale. 2010. Flirting with God in Western courts: Mahr in the West. *International Journal of Law, Policy, and Family* 24(1):67–94.

France, Alan. 2007. *Understanding youth in late modernity*. Berkshire: Open University Press.

Fraser, Nancy. 2000. Rethinking recognition. *New Left Review* 3 (May/June):107–20.

Freeman, Richard. 1996. Why do so many young American men commit crimes and what might we do about it? *Journal of Economic Perspectives* 10(1):25–42.

Furstenberg, Frank, Jr., Thomas D. Cook, Jacquelynne Eccles, Glen H. Elder Jr., and Arnold Sameroff. 1999. *Managing to make it: Urban families and adolescent success.* Chicago: University of Chicago Press.

Fussell, Elizabeth. 2007. How to define youth? Essay in youth and development. *World Development Report*. Washington DC: World Bank.

Fussell, Elizabeth, and Frank Furstenberg Jr. 2005. The transition to adulthood during the 20th century: Race, nativity, and gender. In *On the frontier of adulthood: Theory, research and public policy*, ed. Richard. A. Settersten Jr., Frank F. Furstenberg Jr., and Rubén G. Rumbaut, 29–75. Chicago: University of Chicago Press.

Galland, Olivier 1991. *Sociologie de la jeunesse: L'entrée dans la vie*. Paris: Armand Colin.

Garland, David. 2001. *The culture of control: Crime and social order in contemporary society*. Chicago: University of Chicago Press.

Geschiere, Peter. 2005. Autochthony and citizenship: New modes in the struggle over belonging and exclusion in Africa. *African Journal of Philosophy* 18: 9–24.

———. 2009. *The perils of belonging: Autochthony, citizenship, and exclusion in Africa and Europe*. Chicago: University of Chicago Press.

Giddens, Anthony. 1992. *The transformation of intimacy: Sexuality, love, and eroticism in modern societies*. Cambridge: Polity Press.

Gladwin, Christina. 1991. *Structural adjustment and African women farmers*. Gainesville: University Press of Florida.

Goldstone, Jack. 2011. Understanding the revolutions of 2011: Weakness and resilience in Middle Eastern autocracies. *Foreign Affairs* (May/June):8–16.

Gondola, Didier. 1999. Dreams and drama: The search for elegance among Congolese youth. *African Studies Review* 42(1):23–48.

Gouliquer, Lynne. 2000. Pandora's box: The paradox of flexibility in today's workplace. *Current Sociology* 48(1):29–38.

Granjo, Paulo. 2005. *Lobolo em Maputo: Um Velho Idioma para Novas Vivências Conjugais*. Porto: Campo das Letras.

Gregg, Jennifer. 2003. *Virtually virgins: Sexual strategies and cervical cancer in Recife, Brazil*. Palo Alto, CA: Stanford University Press.

Griffin, Christine. 1993. *Representations of youth: The study of youth and adolescence in Britain and America*. Oxford: Polity Press.

Groes-Green, Christian. 2009. Hegemonic and subordinated masculinities: Class, violence and sexual performance among young Mozambican men. *Young: Nordic Journal of Youth Research* 18 (4):286–304.

———. 2011. The bling scandal: Transforming young femininities in Mozambique. *Young: Nordic Journal of Youth Research* 19(3):291–312.

Grossman, Lev. 2005. Grow up? Not so fast. *Time Magazine*. January 16.

Guadeloupe, Francis, and Peter Geschiere. 2000. The religion of the urban cool: Kut Marokkanen, sapeurs, and bushfallers. Paper presented at conference "Young People in Africa: From Marginalization to Citizenship," The Hague, November.

Gubbay, Jon. 1994. A critique of conventional justifications for transferable skills. In *Transferable skills in higher education*, ed. D. Bridges. Norwich: University of East Anglia.

Guha-Khasnobis, Basudeb, Ravi Kanbur, and Elinor Ostrom, eds. 2006. *Linking the formal and informal economy: Concepts and policies*. Oxford: Oxford University Press.

Habermas, Jürgen. 1992. Citizenship and national identity: Some reflections on the future of Europe. *Praxis International* 12:1–19.

Hall, Stuart, and Paul Du Gay. 1996. *Questions of cultural identity*. London: Sage.

Hall, Stuart, and Tony Jefferson, eds. 1976. *Resistance through rituals*. London: Hutchinson.

Hanlon, Joseph, and Teresa Smart. 2008. *Do bicycles equal development in Mozambique?* Suffolk: James Currey Publishers.

Haram, Liv. 2005. Eyes have no curtains: The moral economy of secrecy in managing love affairs among adolescents in Northern Tanzania in the time of AIDS. *Africa Today* 51(4):57–73.

Harris, Anita. 2011. Australian youth studies: New research on participation, citizenship and connection. *Society for Research on Adolescence Newsletter* 1(9).

Harris, Anita, Johanna Wyn, and Salem Younes. 2010. Beyond apathetic or activist youth. *Young: Nordic Journal of Youth Research* 18(1):9–32.

Hart, Keith. 1970. Small-scale entrepreneurs in Ghana and development planning. *Journal of Development Studies* 6:104–20.

Havard, Jean-François. 2001. Ethos "bul faale" et nouvelles figures de la réussite au Sénégal. *Politique Africaine* 82:63–77.

Harvey, David. 1989. *The condition of postmodernity: An enquiry into the origins of cultural change*. Oxford: Blackwell.

Haupt, Adam. 2001. Black thing: Hip hop, nationalism, race, and gender in Prophets of da City and Brasse vannie Kaap. In *Coloured by history, shaped by place: New perspectives on coloured identities in Cape Town*, ed. Zimitri Erasmus, 173–91. Cape Town: Kwela Books.

Hawkins, Kirstan, Neil Price, and Fatima Mussá. 2009. Milking the cow: Young women's construction of identity and risk in age-disparate transactional sexual relationships in Maputo, Mozambique. *Global Public Health* 4(2):169–82.

Hebdige, Dick. 1979. *Subculture, the meaning of style*. London: Taylor and Francis.

———. 1981. Skinheads and the search for white working class identity. *New Socialist* 1(1):38–41.

Herrera, Linda, and Asef Bayat, eds. 2010. *Being young and Muslim: New cultural politics in the Global South and North*. Oxford: Oxford University Press.

Hibou, Beatrice. 2004. Fiscal trajectories in Morocco and Tunisia. In *Networks of privilege in the Middle East: The politics of economic reform revisited*, ed. Steven Heydemann, 201–22. New York: Palgrave Macmillan.

———. 2006. *La force de l'obéissance: économie politique de la répression en Tunisie*. Paris: Editions La Découverte.

Hobsbawm, Eric. 1995. *The age of extremes: The short twentieth century, 1914–1991.* London: Michael Joseph.

Holdsworth, Clare, and David Morgan. 2005. *Transitions in context: Leaving home, independence, and adulthood.* London: Open University Press.

Holmes, Len. 2002. Reframing the skills agenda in higher education: Graduate identity and the double warrant. In *The university of crisis*, ed. David Preston, 135–52. Amsterdam: Editions Rodopi BV.

Honwana, Alcinda. 1999. Negotiating post-war identities: Child soldiers in Mozambique and Angola. *CODESRIA Bulletin* 1 and 2:4–13.

———. 2001. Children of war: Local understandings of war and war trauma in Mozambique and Angola. In *Civilians at war*, ed. Simon Chesterman, 123–44. Boulder, CO: Lynne Rienner.

———. 2006. *Child soldiers in Africa.* Philadelphia: University of Pennsylvania Press.

Honwana, Alcinda, and Filip De Boeck, eds. 2005. *Makers and breakers: Children and youth in postcolonial Africa.* Oxford: James Currey Publishers.

Hunter, Mark. 2002. The materiality of everyday sex: Thinking beyond "prostitution." *African Studies* 61(1):99–120.

———. 2007. The changing political economy of sex in South Africa: The significance of unemployment and inequalities to the scale of the AIDS pandemic. *Social Science and Medicine* 64(3):689–700.

———. 2010. *Love in the time of AIDS: Inequality, gender, and rights in South Africa.* Bloomington: Indiana University Press.

Huq, Rupa. 2006. *Beyond subculture: Pop, youth, and identity in a postcolonial world.* London: Routledge.

Ignatieff, Michael. 1989. Citizenship and moral narcissism. *Political Quarterly* 60:63–74.

ILO (International Labour Organization). 1997. Decent work: A common goal of trade unions. Geneva: ILO.

———. 2006. The ILO multilateral framework on labour migration: Non-binding principles and guidelines for a rights-based approach to labour migration. Geneva: ILO.

———. 2007. A global alliance for youth employment: Recommendations of the high-level panel on youth employment. Geneva: ILO.

———. 2010. Global employment trends for youth. Geneva: ILO.

Jay-Z. 2010. *Decoded.* New York: Spiegel and Grau.

Jenkins, Paul. 2008. Youth and the challenges of urbanization in Africa. Paper presented at conference "Young People in Africa: From Marginalization to Citizenship," The Hague, November.

Johnson-Hanks, Jennifer. 2002. On the limits of life stages in ethnography: Toward a theory of vital conjunctures. *American Anthropologist* 104(3):865–80.

Jones, Gill. 2009. *Youth*. Cambridge: Polity Press.

Kahn-Harris, Keith. 2007. *Extreme metal: Music and culture on the edge*. Oxford: Berg.

Kakwenzire, Joan. 1996. Preconditions for demarginalizing women and youth in Ugandan politics. In *Law and the struggle for democracy in East Africa*, ed. J. Oloka-Onyango, K. Kibwana, and C. M. Peters, 293–311. Nairobi: Clairpress.

Kallander, Amy. 2011. Tunisia's post-Ben Ali challenge: A primer. New York: Middle East Research and Information Project.

Kamat, Sangeeta. 2007. Populism repackaged: The World Bank perspective on equity and youth. *Development and Change* 30(6):1209–18.

Kararach, George, Kobena Hanson, and Frannie Léautier. 2011. Regional integration policies to support job creation for Africa's burgeoning youth population. *World Journal of Entrepreneurship, Management and Sustainable Development* 7(2/3/4):177–215.

Kassimir, Ronald, and Constance Flanagan. 2009. Youth civic engagement in the developing world: Challenges and opportunities. In *Handbook of research on civic engagement in youth*, ed. Lonnie R. Sherrod, Judith Torney-Purta, and Constance A. Flanagan, 91–114. Hoboken, NJ: Wiley and Sons.

Kaufman, Carol, and Stravos Stavrou. 2004. "Bus fare please": The economics of sex and gifts among young people in urban South Africa. *Culture, Health and Sexuality* 6(5):377–91.

Kausch, Kristina. 2009. Tunisia: The Life of Others project on freedom of association in the Middle East and North Africa. Working Paper no. 85. Fundación para los Relaciones Internacionales y Diálogo Exterior (Madrid).

Kilani, Mohamed. 2011. *La revolution des braves*. Tunis: Impression Simpact.

Kinyanjui, Mary. 2008. From vulnerability to enterprise: Youth in Jua Kali in Kenya. Paper presented at conference "Young People in Africa: From Marginalization to Citizenship," The Hague, November.

Kirshner, Joshua. 2011. "We are Gauteng people": Challenging the politics of xenophobia in Khutsong, South Africa. In *Politics and Sociology Seminar*. Rhodes University, South Africa.

Kjeldgaard, Dannie, and Søren Askegaard. 2006. The glocalization of youth culture: The global youth segment as structures of common difference. *Journal of Consumer Research, Inc.* 33 (September).

Kmec, Julie, and Frank Furstenberg Jr. 2002. Racial and gender differences in the transition to adulthood: A follow-up study of Philadelphia youth. In *New *perspectives in the life course: Socialization*, vol. 7, ed. Richard A. Settersten and Timothy J. Owens, 435–70. London: Elsevier.

Kohli, Martin. 1986. The world we forgot: A historical review of the life course. In *Later life: The social psychology of ageing*, ed. Victor Marshall, 271–303. Beverly Hills, CA: Sage.

Kosugi, Reiko. 2002. The transition from school to work in recent Japan: The experiences of freeters. *Journal of Educational Sociology* 70:59–74.

———. 2006. Changes in transitions from school to work: Employment behavior and transitions of youth in metropolitan areas. Japan Institute for Labour Policy and Training (JILPT) Research Report, no. 72.

Kurimoto, Eisei, and Simon Simonse. 1998. *Conflict, age and power in North East Africa*. Oxford: James Currey Publishers.

Kymlicka, Will, and Wayne Norman. 1994. Return to the citizen: A survey of recent work on citizenship theory. *Ethics* 104:360–67.

La Fontaine, Jean. 1977. The power of rights. *Man* 12:421–37.

La Hausse, Paul. 1990. The cows of Nongoloza: Youth, crime, and Amalaita gangs in Durban, 1900–1930. *Journal of Southern African Studies* 16(1):79–111.

Lahlali, El Mustapha. 2011. The Arab Spring and the discourse of desperation. *Arab Media and Society* (Summer).

Lam, David, and Jeremy Seekings. 2005. Transitions to adulthood in urban South Africa: Evidence from a panel survey. Centre for Social Science Research, University of Cape Town. Paper prepared for International Union for the Scientific Study of Population (IUSSP) General Conference, July 18–23, Tours, France.

Last, Murray, 1991. Adolescents in a Muslim city: The cultural context of danger and risk. *Kano Studies*. Special issue: *Youth and Health in Kano Today*, 41–70.

Lawson, Helen, 2001. Active citizenship in schools and the community. *Curriculum Journal* 12(2):163–78.

Lee, Nick, 2001. *Childhood and society: Growing up in an age of uncertainty*. Buckingham: Open University Press.

Leaths, Bill, Roger Bonner, P. K. Das, Ripin Kalra, and Nigel Wakeham. 2009. Delivering cost effective and sustainable school infrastructure. Department for International Development /Technology Infrastructure—Urban Planning (TI-UP).

Leclerc-Madlala, Suzanne. 2001. Virginity testing: Managing sexuality in a maturing HIV/AIDS epidemic. *Medical Anthropology Quartely* 15(4):533–52.

———. 2003. Transactional sex and the pursuit of modernity. *Social Dynamics* 29(2):213–33.

Lessault, David, and Chris Beauchemin. 2009. Ni Invasion, Ni Exode. Regards statistiques sur les migrations d'Afrique subsaharienne. *Revue Européenne des Migrations Internationales* 25:163–94.

Lister, Ruth. 1998. Citizen in action: Citizenship and community development in the Northern Ireland context. *Community Development Journal* 33(3):226–35.

Lock, Katrin. 2005. Who is listening? Hip hop in Sierra Leone, Liberia and Senegal. In *Resounding international relations: On music, culture and politics*, ed. Marianne L. Franklin, 141–60. New York: Palgrave MacMillan

Loforte, Ana. 2000. *Gênero e Poder entre os Tsonga de Moçambique*. Maputo: Pro-média.

Longfield, Kim. 2004. Rich fools, spare tyres, and boyfriends: Partner categories, relationship dynamics, and Ivorian women's risk for STIs and HIV. *Culture Health and Sexuality* 6(6):483–500.

Luke, Nancy. 2005. Investigating exchange in sexual relationships in sub-Saharan Africa using survey data. In *Sex without consent: Young people in developing countries*, ed. Shireen J. Jejeebhoy, Iqbal Shah, and Shyam Thapa, 105–24. London: Zed Books.

Luke, Nancy, and Kathleen Kurz. 2002. Cross-generational and transactional sex relations in sub-Saharan Africa: Prevalence of behaviour and implications for negotiating safer sex practices. Washington DC: International Center for Research on Women.

Ly, Boubakar. 1988. The present situation of youth in Africa. In *Perspectives on contemporary youth*, ed. Janusz Kuczynski, S. N. Eisenstadt, Boubakar Ly, and Lotika Sarkar, 153–55. Tokyo: United Nations University.

Maccoby, Eleanor. 1998. *The two sexes: Growing up apart, coming together*. Cambridge, MA: Harvard University Press.

MacDonald, Robert, and Jane Marsh. 2005. *Disconnected youth? Growing up in Britain's poor neighbourhoods*. Basingstoke: Palgrave.

MacDonald, Robert, T. Shildrick, C. Webster, and D. Simpson. 2005. Growing up in poor neighbourhoods: The significance of class and place in the extended transitions of "socially excluded" young adults. *Sociology* 39(5):873–89.

MacGaffey, Janet, and Remy Bazenguissa-Ganga. 2000. *Congo-Paris: Transnational traders on the margins of the law*. Indianapolis: Indiana University Press.

Machel, Josina. 2001. Unsafe sexual behaviour among schoolgirls in Mozambique: A matter of gender and class. *Reproductive Health Matters* 9(17):82–90.

Maffesoli, Michel. 1996. *The time of the tribe: The decline of individualism in mass society*. Translated by Don French. London: Sage Publications.

Magubane, Zine. 2006. Globalization and gangster rap: Hip-hop in the post-Apartheid city. In *The vinyl ain't final: Hip hop and the globalization of black popular culture*, ed. Dipannita Basu and Sidney J. Lemelle, 208–29. London: Pluto Press.

Maira, Sunaina, and Elisabeth Soep, eds. 2005. *Youthscapes: The popular, the national, the global*. Philadelphia: University of Pennsylvania Press.

Mamdani, Mahmood. 1996. *Citizen and subject: Contemporary Africa and the legacy of late colonialism*. Princeton, NJ: Princeton University Press.

———. 2007. Political violence and state formation in post-colonial Africa. Working Paper 1. International Development Centre, Open University.

———. 2011. An African Reflection of Tahrir Square. In *African Awakenings: The Emerging Revolutions*, ed. Firoze Manji and Sokari Ekine, 198–210. Oxford: Pambazuka Press.

Manji, Firoze. 1998. The depoliticization of poverty. In *Development and rights*, ed. D. Eade, 12–33. Oxford: Oxfam.

———. 2011. African awakenings: The courage to invent the future. In *African awakenings: The emerging revolutions*, ed. Firoze Manji and Sokari Ekine, 1–18. Oxford: Pambazuka Press.

Manji, Firoze, A. Free, and C. Mark. 2011. New media in Africa: Tools for liberation, tools for subjugation. In *New Media and Alternative Politics*. Working Paper 2. Cambridge (in press).

Mannheim, Karl. 1952 [1927]. The problem of generations. In *Essays on the sociology of knowledge*, ed. P. Kecskemeti. London: Routledge.

———. 1960. *Ideology and utopia*. London: Routledge.

Manuel, Sandra. 2008. *Love and desire: Concepts, narratives and practices of sex amongst youths in Maputo city*. Dakar: CODESRIA.

Marco, Derilene. 2009. A "coloured" history, a Black future: Contesting the dominant representations in the media through hip-hop beats. Department of Media Studies, University of the Witwatersrand, Johannesburg.

Marks, Monique. 2001. *Young warriors: Youth politics, identity, and violence in South Africa*. Johannesburg: Witwatersrand University Press.

Marshall, Thomas Humphrey. 1949. *Citizenship and social class and other essays*. Cambridge: Cambridge University Press.

Marwick, Arthur. 1999. *The sixties: Cultural revolution in Britain, France, Italy, and the United States, c.1958–c.1974*. Oxford: Oxford University Press.

Marzouki, Nadia. 2011. Tunisia's wall has fallen. *MERIP* (January 19). Available on the www.merip.org website.

Masvawure, Tsitsi. 2010. I just need to be flashy on campus: Female students and transactional sex at a university in Zimbabwe. *Culture, Health, and Sexuality* 12(8):857–70.

Mbembe, Achille. 1985. *Les jeunes et l'ordre politique en Afrique noire.* Paris: Editions L'Harmattan.

Mbow, Penda. 2008. Senegal: The return of personalism. *Journal of Democracy* 19(1):156–69.

McEvoy-Levy, Siobhán. 2006. Troublemakers or peacemakers? Youth and post-accord peacebuilding. Notre Dame, IN: University of Notre Dame Press.

Meillassoux, Claude. 1981. *Maidens, meal, and money: Capitalism and the domestic community.* Cambridge: Cambridge University Press.

Meyer, Birgit. 1995. Delivered from the powers of darkness: Confessions of satanic riches in Christian Ghana. *Africa* 65(2):236–55.

Mhlambi, Thokozani. 2004. "Kwaitofabulous": The study of a South African urban genre. *Journal of the Musical Arts in Africa* 1:116–27.

Mills, David, and Richard Ssewakiryanga. 2005. No romance without finance: Commodities, masculinities, and relationships amongst Kampalan students. In *Readings in Gender in Africa*, ed. Andrea Cornwall, 90–94. Oxford: James Currey Publishers.

Mintz, Sidney. 2008. Reflections on age as a category of historical analysis. *Journal of the History of Childhood and Youth* 1(1):91–94.

Miyamoto, Michiko. 2002. *Wakamono ga Shakaiteki Jyakusha ni Tenraku Suru* (*The emergence of youth as a socially disadvantaged class*). Tokyo: Ysensha.

———. 2004. Shakaiteki haijo to jyakunen mugyō: Igirisu to Suēden no taiō (Social exclusion and youth non-employment: The responses of the UK and Sweden). *Nihon Rōdō Kenkyū Zasshi* 533:17–26.

Mkandawire, Thandika. 2007. Transformative social policy and innovation in developing countries. *European Journal of Development Research* 19(1):13–29.

Molgat, Marc. 2007. Do transitions and social structures matter? How "emerging adults" define themselves as adults. *Journal of Youth Studies* 10(5):495–516.

Momoh, Abubakar. 2000. Youth culture and area boys in Lagos. In *Identity transformation and identity politics under structural adjustment in Nigeria*, ed. Attahiru Jega, 181–203. Stockholm: Nordic Africa Institute.

Moore, Henrietta. 2011. *Still life: Hopes, desires, and satisfaction.* Cambridge: Polity Press.

Morrell, Robert. 2003. Silence, sexuality, and HIV/AIDS in South African schools. *Australian Educational Researcher* 30(1):41–62

Moser, Caroline. 1978. Informal sector or petty commodity production: Dualism or independence in urban development. *World Development* 6:1041–64.

Mwiturubani, Donald, Ayalew Gebre, Margarida Paulo, Rekopantswe Mate, and Antoine Socpa. 2009. *Youth, HIV/AIDS and social transformation in Africa.* Dakar: CODESRIA.

Nayak, Anoop. 2003. *Race, place and globalization: Youth cultures in a changing world*. New York: Berg.

Ndiaye, Babacar. 2005. Confréries Musulmanes au Sénégal. *Revue Défense Nationale* 4 (April):91–98.

Ndjio, Basile. 2008. Overcoming social and economic marginalization: Young confidence tricksters from Cameroon and Nigeria. Paper presented at conference "Young People in Africa: From Marginalization to Citizenship," The Hague, November.

Neocosmos, Michael. 2010. *From "foreign natives" to "native foreigners": Explaining xenophobia in post-Apartheid South Africa*. Dakar: CODESRIA.

Neugarten, Bernice, and Nancy Datan. 1973. Sociological perspectives on the life cycle. In *The meaning of age*, ed. Bernice Neugarten, 96–113. Chicago: University of Chicago Press.

Niang, Abdoulaye. 2006. B-boys: Hip hop culture in Dakar, Senegal. In *Global youth? Hybrid identities, plural worlds*, ed. Pam Nilan and Carles Feixa, 167–85. Abingdon: Routledge.

Njue, Carolyne, Helene Voeten, and Remes Pieter. 2011. Porn video shows, local brew, and transactional sex: HIV risk among youth in Kisumu, Kenya. *BMC Public Health* 11(1):635.

Nowotny, Helga. 1994. *Time: The modern and postmodern experience*. Cambridge: Polity Press.

Ntarangwi, Mwenda. 2009. *East African hip hop: youth culture and globalization*. Urbana: University of Illinois Press.

Nyamnjoh, Francis. 2005. Fishing in troubled waters: Disquettes and thiofs in Dakar. *Africa* 75(3):295–324.

Nyanzi, Stella, Ousman Rosenberg-Jallow, Ousman Bah, and Susan Nyanzi. 2005. Bumsters, big black organs, and old white gold: Embodied racial myths in sexual relationships of Gambian beach boys. *Culture, Health, and Sexuality* 7(6):557–69.

Obadare, Ebenezer. 2010. *Statism, youth, and civic imagination: A critical study of the National Youth Service Corps Programme in Nigeria*. Dakar: CODESRIA.

O'Higgins, Niall. 1997. The challenge of youth unemployment. *International Social Security Review* 50:63–94.

———. 2001. *Youth unemployment and employment policy: A global perspective*. Geneva: International Labour Organization.

Okwany, Auma. 2008. Negotiating tensions in girlhood: Marginalization and agency in Kenya. Paper presented at conference "Young People in Africa: From Marginalization to Citizenship," The Hague, November.

Okojie, Christiana. 2003. Employment creation for youth in Africa: The gender dimension. Paper presented at Expert Group Meeting on Jobs for Youth:

National Strategies for Employment Promotion, 15–16 January 2003, Geneva, Switzerland.

Olonisakin, 'Funmi, and Olawale Ismail. 2008. Marginality as a resource: Gender dimensions of youth's transformation of vulnerability in West Africa. Paper presented at conference "Young People in Africa: From Marginalization to Citizenship," The Hague, November.

Ortega y Gasset, José. 1929. *La Rebelión de las Masas* (*The Revolt of the Masses*). Translated by Anthony Kerrigan. Notre Dame, IN: University of Notre Dame Press.

Paciello, Maria Cristina. 2011. Tunisia: Changes and challenges of political transition. Centre for European Policy Studies. Mediterranean Prospects (MEDPRO) Technical Report no. 3. May.

Patterson, Jennifer. 2010. Eldorado or the great deception: The immigrant experience of Senegalese street vendors from the Mouride and Tidjane brotherhoods in France, Spain, and Italy. Department of International Relations, University of Barcelona.

Pettifor, Audrey, Michael Hudgens, Brooke Levandowski, Helen Rees, and Myron Cohen. 2007. Highly efficient HIV transmission to young women in South Africa. *AIDS* 21(7):861–65.

Pettit, Becky, and Bruce Western. 2004. Mass imprisonment and the life course: Race and class inequality in U.S. incarceration. *American Sociological Review* 69(2):151–69.

Pilcher, Jane. 1994. Mannheim's sociology of generations: An undervalued legacy. *British Journal of Sociology* 45(3):481–95.

Pilcher, Jane, J. Williams, and C. Pole. 2003. Rethinking adulthood: Families, transitions, and social change. *Sociological Research Online* 8(4).

Pilkington, Hilary. 2004. Youth strategies for glocal living: Space, power, and communication in everyday cultural practice. In *After Subculture: Critical studies of contemporary youth culture*, ed. A. Bennett and K. Kahn-Harris, 119–34. New York: Palgrave Macmillan.

Poeze, Miranda. 2010. *In search of greener pastures? Boat-migrants from Senegal to the Canary Islands.* Master's thesis. African Studies Collection no. 27. Leiden: African Studies Centre.

Poku, Nana. 2006. *AIDS in Africa: How the poor are dying.* Cambridge: Polity Press.

Poku, Nana, and Alan Whiteside. 2004. *The political economy of AIDS in Africa.* Burlington: Ashgate.

Pollock, Gary. 2002. Contingent identities: Updating the transitional discourse. *Young: Nordic Journal of Youth Research* 10(1):59–72.

———. 2008. Youth transitions: Debates over the social context of becoming an adult. *Sociology Compass* 2(2):467–84.

Portes, Alejandro, Manuel Castells, and Lauren Benton, eds. 1989. *The informal economy: Studies in advanced and less developed countries*. Baltimore, MD: Johns Hopkins University Press.

Potts, Deborah. 2000. Urban unemployment and migrants in Africa: Evidence from Harare, 1985–1994. *Development and Change* 31:879–910.

Rey, Pierre-Phillipe. 1973. *Les Alliances de Classes*. Paris: Maspero.

Reynolds, Pamela. 2008. On leaving the young out of history. *Journal of the History of Childhood and Youth* 1(1):150–56.

Riccio, Bruno. 2004. Transnational Mouridism and the Afro-Muslim critique of Italy. *Journal of Ethnic and Migration Studies* 30(5):929–44.

———. 2005. Talkin' about migration: Some ethnographic notes on the ambivalent representation of migrants in contemporary Senegal. *Stichproben. Wiener Zeitschrift für kritische Afrikastudien* 8(5):99–118.

Richards, Audrey. 1956. *Chisungu: A girl's initiation ceremony among the Bemba of Northern Rhodesia*. London: Faber.

Richards, Paul. 1996. *Fighting for the rain forest: War, youth, and resources in Sierra Leone*. Oxford: James Currey Publishers.

Riley, Matilda, Anne Foner, and Joan Waring. 1988. Sociology of age. In *Handbook of sociology*, ed. Neil Smesler, 243–88. Thousand Oaks, CA: Sage.

Rogers, William. 2011. Tunisia's economic problems still festering. *Left Labour Report* (April 20).

Rogerson, Christian. 1997. Globalization or informalization? African urban economies in the 1990s. In *The urban challenge in Africa: Growth and management of its large cities*, ed. C. Rakodi, 337–70. Tokyo: United Nations University Press.

Rose, Tricia. 1994. A style nobody can deal with: Politics, style, and the post-industrial city in hip-hop. In *Microphone fiends: Youth music and youth culture*, ed. Andrew Ross and Tricia Rose, 71–88. London: Routledge.

Ross, Andrew, and Tricia Rose, eds. 1994. *Microphone fiends: Youth music and youth culture*. New York: Routledge.

Ryder, Norman. 1965. The cohort as a concept in the study of social change. *American Sociological Review* 30(6):843–61.

Saavedra-Casco, José. 2006. The language of the young people: Rap, urban culture and protest in Tanzania. *Journal of Asian and African Studies* 41(3):229–48.

Salehi-Isfahani, Djavad, and Navtej Dhillon. 2008. Stalled youth transitions in the Middle East: A framework for policy reform. Working paper no. 8 (October). Washington DC: Brookings Wolfensohn Center for Development; Dubai: Dubai School of Government.

Samy, Shahira. 2008. Irregular migration in the South Eastern Mediterranean: Socio-political perspectives. In *CARIM Analytical and Synthetic Notes* 69:1–13, Irregular Migration Series Socio Political Module.

Sarr, Makha. 2000. Youth employment in Africa: The Senegalese experience. In *UN/ILO/World Bank Brainstorming Meeting on Youth Employment*. New York: United Nations.

———. 2004. Poverty reduction strategy and youth employment in Senegal. Paper presented at expert group meeting, "Strategies for creating urban youth employment in Africa." June 25. Nairobi, Kenya.

Schwartz, Seth, James Coté, and Jeffrey Arnett. 2005. Identity and agency in emerging adulthood: Two developmental routes in the individualization process. *Youth and Society* 37(2):201–29.

Seekings, Jeremy, and David Everatt. 1993. *Heroes or villains? Youth politics in the 1980s*. Johannesburg: Ravan Press.

Selboe, Elin. 2010. Youth and social change in Dakar, Senegal: Intergenerational differences and power battles in local mosques. *Forum for Development Studies* 37(3):365–83.

Sennett, Richard. 1998. *The corrosion of character: The personal consequences of work in the new capitalism*. New York: W. W. Norton.

Sethuraman, Salem. 1976. The urban informal sector: Concept, measurement, and policy. *International Labour Review* 114(1):69–81.

———, ed. 1981. *The urban informal sector in developing countries: Employment, poverty and environment*. Geneva: ILO.

Shanahan, Michael. 2000. Pathways to adulthood in changing societies: Variability and mechanisms in life course perspective. *Annual Review of Sociology* 26:667–92.

Shaw, Rosalind. 2007. Displacing violence: Making Pentecostal memory in postwar Sierra Leone. *Cultural Anthropology* 22(1):66–93.

Shepler, Susan. 2005. The rites of the child: Global discourses of youth and reintegrating child soldiers in Sierra Leone. *Journal of Human Rights* 4(2):197–211.

———. 2010. Youth music and politics in post-war Sierra Leone. *Journal of Modern African Studies* 48(4):627–42.

Sika, Nadine. 2009. Irregular migration in North Africa: Libya, Tunisia, and Algeria. Ipswich, MA: Partners in Development.

Silberschmidt, Margrethe. 1999. *Women forget that men are the masters*. Nordic Africa Institute. Stockholm: Almquist and Wiksell International.

———. 2004. Masculinities, sexualities, and socio-economic change in rural and urban East Africa. In *Re-thinking Sexialities in Africa*, ed. Signe Arnfred, 233–50. Uppsala: Nordic Africa Institute.

———. 2005. Poverty, male disempowerment, and male sexuality: Rethinking men and masculinities in rural and urban East Africa. In *African masculinities*, ed. Lahouzine Ouzgane and Robert Morrell, 189–203. New York: Palgrave Macmillan.

Silberschmidt, Margrethe, and Vibeke Rasch. 2001. Adolescent girls, illegal abortions, and "sugar daddies" in Dar es Salaam: Vulnerable victims and active social agents. *Social Science and Medicine* 52(12):1815–26.

Simirenko, Alex. 1966. Mannheim's generational analysis and acculturation. *British Journal of Sociology* 17:292–99.

Singerman, Diane. 2007. The economic imperatives of marriage: Emerging practices and identities among youth in the Middle East. Working Paper 6. Washington DC and Dubai: Wolfensohn Centre for Development and Dubai School of Government.

Skelton, Tracey, and Gill Valentine, eds. 1998. *Cool places: Geographies of youth cultures*. New York: Routledge.

Sommers, Marc. 2012. *Stuck: Rwandan Youth and the Struggle for Adulthood*. Atlanta: University of Georgia Press.

South Africa National Treasury. 2011. Confronting youth unemployment: Policy options for South Africa. Johannesburg: South Africa National Treasury.

Spronk, Rachel. 2007. Beyond pain, towards pleasure in the study of sexuality in Africa. *Sexuality in Africa Magazine* 4(3):3–6.

Ssewakiryanga, Richard. 1999. What has become of our teens? *Popular Culture and the Disciplines. ENRECA Occasional Working Papers* 5:108–20.

Standing, Hilary. 1992. AIDS: Conceptual and methodological issues in researching sexual behaviour in sub-Saharan Africa. *Social Science and Medicine* 34(5):475–83.

Steingo, Gavin. 2005. South African music after apartheid: Kwaito, the "party politic," and the appropriation of gold as a sign of success. *Popular Music and Society* 28(3):333–57.

Stewart, Angus. 1992. Two conceptions of citizenship. *British Journal of Sociology* 46(1):63–78.

Sukarieh, Mayssoun, and Stuart Tannock. 2008. In the best interests of youth or neoliberalism? The World Bank and the New Global Youth Empowerment Project. *Journal of Youth Studies* 11(3):301–12.

Suriano, Maria. 2006. Hip hop and bongo flavour music in contemporary Tanzania: Youths' experiences, agency, aspirations and contradictions. Paper presented at the conference Youth and the Global South: Religion, Politics and the Making of Youth in Africa, Asia and the Middle East, Dakar, 13–15 October 2006.

Swartz, Sharlene. 2008. Is Kwaito South African hip-hop? Why the answer matters and who it matters to. *World of Music* 50(2):15–33.

Swink, Simone. 2003. Kwaito: Much more than music. Available on the www.southafrica.info website.

Taiwo, Olumide, and Nelipher Moyo. 2011. The crisis in Tunisia: Africa's youth unemployment time bomb. Washington DC: Brookings Institution.

Tersbøl, Britt. 2005. At a loss in the land of the brave: A study of sexual relationships in the context of HIV/AIDS and poverty in Namibia. Ph.D. thesis. Institute of Public Health, University of Copenhagen.

Thomas, Lynn M., and Jennifer Cole. 2009. Thinking through love in Africa. In *Love in Africa*, ed. Jennifer Cole and Lynn Thomas, 1–30. Chicago: University of Chicago Press.

Tokman, Victor. 1978. An exploration into the nature of the informal-formal sector relationship. *World Development* 6(9/10):1065–75.

Toulabor, Comi M. 1995. Jeunes, violence et democratization au Togo. *Afrique Contemporaire* 180:106–25.

Toungara, Jeanne Maddox. 1995. Generational tensions in the Parti Démocratique de Côte d'Ivoire. *African Studies Review* 38(2):11–38.

Toynbee, Polly. 2003. *Hard work: Life in low-pay Britain*. London: Bloomsbury.

Turner, Victor. 1969. *The ritual process: Structure and anti-structure*. Chicago: Aldine Publishing Company.

Tyyskä, Vappu. 2005. Conceptualizing and theorizing youth: Global perspectives. In *Contemporary youth research: Local expressions and global connections*, ed. H. Helve and G. Holm, 3–14. Aldershot: Ashgate.

UNAIDS. 2006. *Report on the global AIDS epidemic*. Geneva: UNAIDS.

UNCTAD. 2001. Globalization and the labour markets. Working Paper. Division on Globalization and Development Strategies. November.

UNECA (United Nations Economic Commission for Africa). 2005. Meeting youth unemployment head on. *Economic Report on Africa*. Addis Ababa: UNECA.

UNESCO. 2005. Capacity building of teacher training institutions in sub-Saharan Africa. Paris: UNESCO.

United Nations. 2007. *World youth report 2007: Young people's transition to adulthood: progress and challenges*. New York: United Nations.

USAID. 2006. Urban transportation policy for Greater Maputo. Washington DC: USAID.

Utas, Mats. 2003. *Sweet battlefields: Youth and the Liberian civil war*. Uppsala: Institute for Cultural Anthropology and Ethnology.

van Dijk, Rijk. 2008. Self-framing and self-mobilization: Pentecostal faith, agency and youth ideology in Africa. Paper presented at conference "Young people in Africa: From marginalization to citizenship," The Hague, November.

van Eerdewijk, Anouka. 2009. Silence, pleasure and agency: Sexuality of unmarried girls in Dakar, Senegal. *Contemporary Islam* 3(1):7–24.

van Gennep, Arnold. 1960. *The rites of passage*. Translated by Monika B. Vizedom and Gabrielle L. Caffee. Chicago: University of Chicago Press.

Venables, Emilie. 2009. "If you give me some sexing, I might talk to you": Researching the Senegalese beach-boys at my side. *Anthropology Matters* 11(1):1–11.

Vigh, Henrik. 2006. *Navigating terrains of war: Youth and soldiering in Guinea-Bissau.* Oxford: Berghahn Books.

————. 2009. Youth mobilization as social navigation: Reflections on the concept of *dubriagem*. In *Cadernos de Estudos Africanos* 18/19:140–64, Instituto Universitário de Lisboa (ISCTE).

Vinken, Henk. 2005. Young people's civic engagement: The need for new perspectives. In *Contemporary youth research: Local expressions and global connections,* ed. H. Helve and G. Holm, 147–58. Hampshire, UK: Ashgate.

Vromen, Ariadne. 2003. "People try to put us down": Participatory citizenship for the Generation X. *Australian Journal of Political Science* 38(1):79–99.

Wai, Zubairu. 2008. The role of youths and the Sierra Leone diaspora in democratic awakening. In *The quest for sustainable democracy, development and peace: The 2007 Sierra Leone elections,* ed. Alfred Babatunde Zack-Williams, 37–63. Uppsala: Nordic African Institute.

Walther, Andreas. 2006. Regimes of youth transitions. *Young: Nordic Journal of Youth Research* 14(2):119–39.

Wegner, Lucia. 2008. Investing in Africa's youth. *OECD Development Centre Policy Insights.* OECD Development Centre. Working Paper No. 62.

Weiss, Brad. 2009. *Street dreams and hip hop barbershops: Global fantasy in urban Tanzania.* Bloomington: Indiana University Press.

White, Robert, and Johanna Wyn. 2004. *Youth and society.* Oxford: Oxford University Press.

Whyte, Michael. 2006. Afterword. In *Navigating youth, generating adulthood: Social becoming in an African context,* ed. Catrine Christiansen, Mats Utas, and Henrik Vigh, 255–66. Uppsala: Nordic African Institute.

Williamson, Jeffrey. 1965. Regional inequality and the process of national development: A description of the patterns. *Economic Development and Cultural Change* 13(4):1–84.

Willis, Paul. 1977. *Learning to labor: How working class kids get working class jobs.* New York: Columbia University Press.

Wilson, William Julius. 1996. *When work disappears: The world of the new urban poor.* New York: Alfred A. Knopf.

Woolley, Claire. 2004. Shaping lives: Agency in young adult transitions. MsC thesis, Department of Political, International, and Policy Studies, University of Surrey, Surrey.

World Bank. 2007. *World development report: Development and the next generation.* Washington DC: World Bank.

————. 2008. *For a better integration into the labor market in Tunisia.* Washington DC: World Bank.

Wyn, Johanna, and Robert White. 1997. Rethinking youth. *Children and Society* 11(3):205–6.

Wyn, Johanna, and Dan Woodman. 2006. Generation, youth, and social change in Australia. *Journal of Youth Studies* 9(5):495–514.

Index

Also available from Kumarian Press

Coming of Age in a Globalized World: The Next Generation
J. Michael Adams and Angelo Carfagna

"This thoughtful and lively book offers documentation and analysis to help us understand the proliferation of changes and connections throughout the world. Adams and Carfagna masterfully make clear the imperative of overcoming ignorance of the cultures, histories and languages of other societies. Globalization, they assert, means education!"

—*John Brademas, President Emeritus, New York University,*
Former member of the U.S. House of Representatives (Indiana)

Born of War: Protecting Children of Sexual Violence in Conflict Zones
R. Charli Carpenter

"This book sheds light on a serious human security concern that persists despite the abundance of international legal instruments designed to protect children who by accident of birth happen to be in conflict zones. This excellently edited volume, with its rich case studies and thoughtful recommendations, is a cutting edge work that will attract the interest of academics and policymakers working in the humanitarian field."

—*Dr. W. Andy Knight, Professor, International Relations,*
University of Alberta and Director,
Children and Armed Conflict project

A World Turned Upside Down: Social Ecological Approaches to Children in War Zones
Neil Boothby, Alisaon Strang, and Michael Wessells

"Little is left out of this volume, which encompasses culture and gender economics. It even takes in a longitudinal study by Boothby, who reports on research that has followed children over 16 years in search of what may have facilitated their reintegration and reconciliation after war . . . comprehensive and informative, making it a 'must read' for practitioners."

—*Journal of Refugee Studies*

Visit Kumarian Press at **www.kpbooks.com** or call
toll-free 800.232.0223 for a complete catalog.

Kumarian Press, located in Sterling, Virginia, is a forward-looking, scholarly press that promotes active international engagement and an awareness of global connectedness.